Mastering Gradle

Master the technique of developing, migrating,
and building automation using Gradle

Mainak Mitra

PUBLISHING

BIRMINGHAM - MUMBAI

Mastering Gradle

First published: July 2015

Production reference: 1280715

Published by Packt Publishing Ltd.
Livery Place
35 Livery Street
Birmingham B3 2PB, UK.

ISBN 978-1-78398-136-6

www.packtpub.com

Credits

Author
Mainak Mitra

Reviewers
Alexander Barnes
Scott Battaglia
Michael Putters
Andreas Schmid

Commissioning Editor
Amarabha Banerjee

Acquisition Editor
Nadeem N. Bagban

Content Development Editor
Parita Khedekar

Technical Editor
Namrata Patil

Copy Editors
Mario Cecére
Kausambhi Majumdar
Angad Singh
Laxmi Subramanian

Project Coordinator
Milton Dsouza

Proofreader
Safis Editing

Indexer
Rekha Nair

Graphics
Jason Monteiro

Production Coordinator
Aparna Bhagat

Cover Work
Aparna Bhagat

About the Author

Mainak Mitra is a software developer who has rich experience in enterprise software development and automation frameworks. He is an electrical engineer from Jadavpur University, Kolkata. He is currently working for an online gaming company. Prior to this, he worked for various product development companies, such as Yahoo Inc., CA Technologies. He can be contacted at mitramkm@gmail.com.

First, I would like to thank the Gradle team for creating such a robust build automation tool. This book would not exist without this open source tool.

I would also like to thank the editors at Packt Publishing, who inspired and helped me to write this book. The Packt Publishing team, especially Parita and Namrata, provided insightful feedback to help me.

Before this book reached you, it was reviewed by many people at different stages. Without their comments, feedback, and criticism, this book would not have been possible. I acknowledge the people involved here: Alexander Barnes, Scott Battaglia, Michael Putters, Andreas Schmid.

Special thanks goes to my friend Abhinandan for his contribution to this book and for compromising his weekends for me. He reviewed all the chapters in this book and guided me in writing most of the topics. Without his expertise and support, this book would not have been possible.

About the Reviewers

Alexander Barnes has been a professional software engineer for over 5 years after graduating summa from the Texas A&M class of '09 with a BS in computer engineering and a minor in mathematics. He started his career at Cisco Systems, working with a variety of Java web technologies and tools. At Cisco, he played a leading role in developing the RESTful User Data Services (UDS) for the CallManager product and helped develop and maintain the administration and user portals. He pioneered the transformation of his team's build system from Ant to Gradle for the numerous project tools and utilities maintained by the team and became a subject-matter expert on Git, Gradle, and Linux in particular.

Alex decided to move closer to his family, recently joining Novo Dia Group in Austin as a senior Java developer. He is an avid advocate of best software practices and the usage of the right tools for the job. Some of his favorite tools include Git, Gerrit, Jenkins, Sonar, Gradle, Java, and Linux. He strives to design and develop freely, refactor to consistent design patterns as appropriate, and focus on reducing mutable states. Alex occasionally blogs about technologies and other interests on his website at `http://toastedbits.com/`.

Alex enjoys pursuing other creative hobbies in his spare time; playing his guitar and listening to a lot of rock, metal, and electronic music. He also wishes to pick up piano and music production techniques to create his own electronic tracks in the future. He is also an enthusiast of craft beers and playing board games and poker with friends.

I would like to thank my friends and family for giving me their love and encouragement to achieve my dreams. Also, thanks to the Electronic Frontier Foundation, GNU, and Apache Software Foundation for making our software world a much more respectful community.

Scott Battaglia is a senior software development engineer for Audible Inc. (an Amazon.com, Inc. company), the leading provider of premium digital spoken audio information. He currently leads the shared Android platform team and coaches on a variety of topics, including open source, interviewing, and scrum. Prior to this, he was an identity management architect and senior application developer with Rutgers, the State University of New Jersey.

He has actively contributed to various open source projects, including Apereo Central Authentication Service and Inspektr, and has previously contributed to Spring Security, Apereo OpenRegistry, and Apereo uPortal. He has spoken at a variety of conferences, including Jasig, EDUCAUSE, and Spring Forward on topics such as CAS, Identity Management, Spring Security, and software development practices.

Michael Putters has been working with various technologies for the past 15 years, from low-level assembler projects to Angular websites, his main interests being compiler and graphics development. More recently, he's been involved with the Gradle project as it is the only build system capable of handling any type of project, Java-based applications, native C++ software, mobile applications on iOS and Android, and even JavaScript and TypeScript websites. Currently, he's acting as the CTO at a number of tech companies in Paris, France.

Andreas Schmid was born in 1985 and started working as a technology consultant in Munich in 2009 after an apprenticeship as an IT specialist and business informatics studies. His passion is creating software and solving difficult IT problems.

In his career, he has participated in Java enterprise projects, contributing to database migrations, expediting the automation of various topics, as well as introducing and coaching new software engineering techniques such as agile software development and test-driven development. It's been over 7 years since he started using it and the relies on continuous integration and delivery as much as possible.

Further, he believes in the advantages of open source software and likes to immerse himself into these tools to get the most out of them. This deep understanding also enables him to contribute by providing patches and fixes in his spare time to further improve these tools.

While being a software engineer and doing things right, he also had the pleasure of being a product owner. In this area, the important question he had to answer was, "Do we do the right things?" So, he also gets his teeth into validated learning for shorter product development cycles.

He likes to be where state-of-the-art software engineering practices and reality collide.

www.PacktPub.com

Support files, eBooks, discount offers, and more

For support files and downloads related to your book, please visit www.PacktPub.com.

Did you know that Packt offers eBook versions of every book published, with PDF and ePub files available? You can upgrade to the eBook version at www.PacktPub.com and as a print book customer, you are entitled to a discount on the eBook copy. Get in touch with us at service@packtpub.com for more details.

At www.PacktPub.com, you can also read a collection of free technical articles, sign up for a range of free newsletters and receive exclusive discounts and offers on Packt books and eBooks.

https://www2.packtpub.com/books/subscription/packtlib

Do you need instant solutions to your IT questions? PacktLib is Packt's online digital book library. Here, you can search, access, and read Packt's entire library of books.

Why subscribe?

- Fully searchable across every book published by Packt
- Copy and paste, print, and bookmark content
- On demand and accessible via a web browser

Free access for Packt account holders

If you have an account with Packt at www.PacktPub.com, you can use this to access PacktLib today and view 9 entirely free books. Simply use your login credentials for immediate access.

Table of Contents

Preface

This book is a practical guide to learning enterprise build systems with Gradle. This book helps you to master the core concepts of the tool and to quickly apply the knowledge to real-life projects. Throughout the book, all the chapters are supported by sufficient examples so that the reader can easily follow and absorb the concepts. The book is divided into 10 chapters. The first six chapters are aimed at gaining knowledge about fundamental topics such as Task, Plugins, Dependency Management, various in-built plugins, and a lot more. The next few chapters cover diverse topics such as Continuous Integration, Migration, and Deployment, which enables readers to learn concepts that are very useful for agile software development. The last chapter of the book focuses on the Android build system with Gradle, which will be useful for mobile developers.

What this book covers

Chapter 1, *Getting Started with Gradle*, discusses briefly about the build automation system, its needs, and how Gradle can help developers to automate the build and deployment process. Along with the Gradle installation, configuration, and features, this chapter also talks about some important concepts such as the initialization script, the Gradle GUI interface, and the Gradle command-line options.

Chapter 2, *Groovy Essentials for Gradle*, talks about the fundamental concepts of Groovy programming language. This chapter also discusses the classes, beans, and collection frameworks. This chapter gives the reader a heads up on Groovy, which is required for Gradle.

Chapter 3, *Managing Task*, discusses Tasks in detail, which is the basic unit of action in Gradle. Developers learn about different flavors of Tasks such as in-built tasks and custom tasks. This chapter also discusses task configurations, task ordering, and task dependencies.

Chapter 4, *Plugin Management*, talks about one of the important building blocks of Gradle, plugins. The reader will learn to create simple plugins and custom plugins. Also, the user will be able to configure plugins as per his/her needs. This chapter also discusses one of the most usable plugins, the Java plugin, in detail. The user will learn about different conventions supported and how to customize the standard conventions as per the project's/organization's requirements.

Chapter 5, *Dependency Management*, discusses one of the other important features of Gradle, dependency management, in detail. It discusses the dependency resolution, dependency configuration, and dependency customization. It also discusses repository management. It provides a deep insight of how the user can configure different external repositories, internal repositories, as well as use the local filesystem as a repository.

Chapter 6, *Working with Gradle*, discusses two additional plugins, War and Scala. It also discusses various topics such as property management, multi-project build, and the logging features. The user will learn about different I/O operations, as well as unit testing features using JUnit and TestNG in Gradle.

Chapter 7, *Continuous Integration*, talks about the continuous integration concepts and tools such as Jenkins and TeamCity, and their integration with Gradle. It also discusses different code quality plugin (Checkstyle, PMD, and Sonar) integrations with Gradle.

Chapter 8, *Migration*, fulfills one of the critical requirements of users who are already using other build tools such as Ant or Maven and want to migrate to Gradle. It talks about different migration strategies to convert the existing Ant and Maven scripts to Gradle.

Chapter 9, *Deployment*, explains the deployment aspect of software engineering. How smoothly the user can automate the deployment process, which saves lots of developer as well as operation team time and efforts. It discusses container-based deployment automation processes and tools; Docker. It gives details about Docker installation, useful Docker commands, and how to integrate Docker with continuous integration tools and Gradle to create a build-deploy-test workflow.

Chapter 10, *Building Android Applications with Gradle*, talks about mobile application development and deployment. Gradle is an official build tool for Android. This chapter focuses on sample Android application development and different deployment strategies such as deploying the debug version, the release version, deployment on different configurations, and so on.

What you need for this book

Your system must have the following software before executing the code mentioned in the book:

- Gradle 2.4
- Java 1.7 or above
- Jenkins
- TeamCity
- Ant 1.9.4
- Maven 3.2.2
- Docker 1.5.0
- Android 5.0

Who this book is for

If you are a Java developer with some experience in Gradle and want to become an expert, then this book is for you. Basic knowledge of Gradle is essential.

Conventions

In this book, you will find a number of text styles that distinguish between different kinds of information. Here are some examples of these styles and an explanation of their meaning.

Code words in text, database table names, folder names, filenames, file extensions, pathnames, dummy URLs, user input, and Twitter handles are shown as follows: "Gradle shares the same JVM options set by the environment variable JAVA_OPTS."

A block of code is set as follows:

```
def methodMissing(String name, args) {
  if (name.startsWith("plus") ) {
// write your own implementation
    return "plus method intercepted"
  }
  else {
    println "Method name does not start with plus"
    throw new MissingMethodException(name, this.class, args)
  }
}
```

When we wish to draw your attention to a particular part of a code block, the relevant lines or items are set in bold:

```
apply plugin: 'java'
version=1.0
configurations {
  customDep
}
repositories {
  mavenCentral()
}
```

Any command-line input or output is written as follows:

```
$ gradle -b build_customconf.gradle showCustomDep
```

```
:showCustomDep
```

New terms and **important words** are shown in bold. Words that you see on the screen, for example, in menus or dialog boxes, appear in the text like this: "Click on **OK** to add the repository."

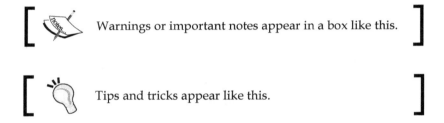

Warnings or important notes appear in a box like this.

Tips and tricks appear like this.

Reader feedback

Feedback from our readers is always welcome. Let us know what you think about this book—what you liked or disliked. Reader feedback is important for us as it helps us develop titles that you will really get the most out of.

To send us general feedback, simply e-mail feedback@packtpub.com, and mention the book's title in the subject of your message.

If there is a topic that you have expertise in and you are interested in either writing or contributing to a book, see our author guide at www.packtpub.com/authors.

Customer support

Now that you are the proud owner of a Packt book, we have a number of things to help you to get the most from your purchase.

Downloading the example code

You can download the example code files from your account at http://www.packtpub.com for all the Packt Publishing books you have purchased. If you purchased this book elsewhere, you can visit http://www.packtpub.com/support and register to have the files e-mailed directly to you.

Errata

Although we have taken every care to ensure the accuracy of our content, mistakes do happen. If you find a mistake in one of our books—maybe a mistake in the text or the code—we would be grateful if you could report this to us. By doing so, you can save other readers from frustration and help us improve subsequent versions of this book. If you find any errata, please report them by visiting http://www.packtpub.com/submit-errata, selecting your book, clicking on the **Errata Submission Form** link, and entering the details of your errata. Once your errata are verified, your submission will be accepted and the errata will be uploaded to our website or added to any list of existing errata under the Errata section of that title.

To view the previously submitted errata, go to https://www.packtpub.com/books/content/support and enter the name of the book in the search field. The required information will appear under the **Errata** section.

Piracy

Piracy of copyrighted material on the Internet is an ongoing problem across all media. At Packt, we take the protection of our copyright and licenses very seriously. If you come across any illegal copies of our works in any form on the Internet, please provide us with the location address or website name immediately so that we can pursue a remedy.

Please contact us at copyright@packtpub.com with a link to the suspected pirated material.

We appreciate your help in protecting our authors and our ability to bring you valuable content.

Questions

If you have a problem with any aspect of this book, you can contact us at questions@packtpub.com, and we will do our best to address the problem.

Getting Started with Gradle

Consider a typical IT company development center scenario. Different teams are working together on one enterprise project with many components. Teams are working on server-side technologies, frontend technologies, the messaging layer, mobile development and there may be a separate team responsible for Quality Assurance. Every team is working as per their schedule, developing their own component(s), unit testing and committing code, and this cycle is repeated in multiple iterations. So far, everybody is happy as they are able to meet the deadlines as per the software release dates. Then comes the integration phase, when teams have to build the complete project and deploy the software (which could be WAR, JAR, or any service) to the integration/staging environment. And then the nightmare starts.

Although every team has successfully followed many best practices of software engineering such as committing code on a daily basis, unit testing of code and verifying the working software on a developer's test environment, but in the integration or staging environment the situation has suddenly changed. The team is stuck with configuration and interoperation issues, localization issues, environmental issues, and so on.

This might be a very common scenario for any project and the situation will become worse if they are not using any automated solution for the build and deployment process. Hence the need for an automated process or we can call a **Build Automation System** (**BAS**), which automates the manual task of building the project seamlessly and delivers the software in a repeatable, reliable, and portable fashion. BAS doesn't claim that there will be absolutely no issues or errors, but with BAS, the software can be managed in a better way, minimizing the probability of repeating the same error again and again.

Gradle is one of the advanced build automation tools available in the market. In the next 10 chapters, we will explore how to mitigate these problems with Gradle and with other related technologies. However, before we start learning Gradle, we need to understand what a BAS is and why we need it.

Understanding Build Automation System

The most common processes in building any software include compiling the source files, packaging the compiled output to a compressed format (ZIP, JAR or any other format), and adding the required resource files and configuration files to the packaging. Along with this, it may also include some other activities such as running static code analysis on the source code to provide feedback on the design and coding patterns, and another important area is Quality Assurance, which involves unit testing, integration testing, regression testing, and so on.

A BAS is part of the software life cycle, which automates the build and deployment phases of the software. The first phase is building the software, which is the process of creating the binaries or executables. The second phase is the deployment phase, wherein we need to install the software at a particular location. This phase also includes various other activities such as unpacking the bundle, localization of the software, configuring the software as per the environment and setting the environment-specific properties required to execute the software. The next important step is functional testing to check the behavior of the software. Once everything is fine, it makes a happy and smiley ending for you.

So, as a developer, writing the code and test cases is just one of the major tasks in **Software Development Life Cycle (SDLC)**. Build and deployment is also considered as another important phase in any software life cycle. If it is not managed properly, it could lead to major downtime and client dissatisfaction.

Build automation allows us to automate the manual steps in the build process. It also helps to eliminate the redundant tasks, mitigates the risks of manual intervention, keeps the history of the builds, and saves the cost and time spent in the manual process. The goal here is to create reproducible assets every time you run the build script, which will not be the case, if you manually execute the steps every time.

Many developers relate the build automation with **Continuous Integration (CI)**. Do not get confused. The CI allows executing the build process, performing deployment activities, and many more activities. It helps to create a workflow for build and deployment automation. It also helps to schedule the builds and provides on-demand execution of builds. The schedule could be once in every hour, once in four hours, nightly builds or on every user commit. Some of the well known CI tools are Jenkins, TeamCity, Bamboo, Hudson, Cruise Control, and so on, which are totally different from Build tools, such as Ant, Maven, and Gradle.

Need for BAS

Imagine that all the preceding mentioned steps in building a software need to be done manually, and every developer has to perform steps on different machines. Now you can realize the amount of effort wasted in figuring out problems with build issues rather than focusing on the actual business requirements. That's one of the reasons why we need a BAS. Following are some of the major activities, which we automate for the build system:

- Translating the source code into binaries
- Packaging the binaries with configuration files to create deployable artifacts
- Executing the test cases
- Publishing the artifacts to a common repository
- Deploying the artifacts to different environments (Development, QA, and Production)
- Incremental builds
- Status reports that summarize the current state of the build

Another reason to have a BAS is to reduce the operational complexities. If a new member joins the team and he has to perform the manual build of the software, it could be a nightmare for him, if there is no automation. Rather than concentrating on the business requirement, most of his time will be wasted on how to compile it, how to run unit tests, how to execute integration tests, and so on.

Actually, what he needs to know is where to commit the source code, where to put the resources, and what commands to execute to perform the build process. The build process should automatically perform all the tasks of compiling, packaging, running tests, uploading asserts and so on.

The more automated the build and deployment process, the faster you will get the deliverables to the client. It also helps with business continuity. In case of any system crash or network failure, you can rebuild and deploy the software on back up infrastructure in much less time.

Some developers believe that project automation is a waste of time and why should they put in extra effort as their IDE performs this job. They can build the JAR, WAR, or any other deliverable unit with the help of IDE and deploy the same. Since they can build, and test it quickly, it works very well on their local system. The problem starts when integration happens. Thus, an automated system is required to avoid any manual intervention (unless it is the only option left), and to make builds portable, predictable and efficient.

Gradle overview

Before getting into the details of Gradle, we need to understand some of the terminologies related to the build system.

There are two types of build tools, namely **imperative build tools** and **declarative build tools**. An imperative build tool tells the system what to do and how to do it. In other words, it provides a set of action statements or commands, which the system executes in the same order and performs those actions. You can take Ant as an example of the imperative build system.

Whereas, a declarative build tool instructs the system, telling it what you would like to achieve, and system will figure out how to interpret it. With a declarative approach, the user only needs to determine the *what*, not the *how*. This is one of the key innovations Maven brought to the build world, after Ant achieved some popularity, where we don't need to write each and every step of an action, and end up creating a very large and verbose build script. With Maven we need to write some configuration parameters for the build and the build system itself decides how to interpret it. Internally, the declarative layer is based on a powerful imperative layer, which can be accessed directly as required. Ant and Maven are very good and reliable build systems. They are innovative in all the areas for which they were designed and built. Each of them has introduced key innovations into the build space.

Gradle combines the good parts of both tools and provides additional features and uses Groovy as a **Domain Specific Language** (**DSL**). It has power and flexibility of Ant tool with Maven features such as build life cycle and ease of use.

Gradle is a general purpose, declarative build tool. It is general purpose because it can be used to build pretty much anything you care to implement in the build script. It is declarative, since you don't want to see lots of code in the build file, which is not readable and less maintainable. So, while Gradle provides the idea of conventions and a simple and declarative build, it also makes the tool adaptable and developers the ability to extend. It also provides an easy way to customize the default behavior and different hooks to add any third-party features.

Primarily, Gradle is a JVM-language build tool, but it also supports C, C++, Android, and so on. You will find more information about this at `https://docs.gradle.org/current/userguide/nativeBinaries.html`.

It provides automation for the different phases required in a Java project, such as compile, package, execute test cases, and so on. It has grouped its similar automation tasks into plugins. When you import any plugin to a Gradle script file, they always come with a set of predefined tasks. To get started with Gradle, you need to have basic knowledge of Java. It uses Groovy as its scripting language, which is another JVM language. We will discuss Groovy in the next chapter. As the build script is written in Groovy, it tends to be much shorter, expressive, and clearer than those written in Ant or Maven. The amount of boilerplate code is much less in Gradle with use of Groovy DSL. It also leverages Maven conventions for familiarity, while making it easy to customize to the needs of your project. Developers can add new functionality or extend the existing features at any time. They can override the existing tasks or plugins to provide the new functionality.

Installation and quick start

Gradle installation is quite simple. You can download the Gradle distribution from the Gradle home page at `https://www.gradle.org/downloads`, which is available in different formats.

Pre-requisites

Gradle requires a Java JDK or JRE to be installed, needing version 6 or higher (to check the Java version on your machine, use `java -version`). Some of the features might not work with JRE, so it is recommended to have JDK installed. Also, Gradle ships with its own Groovy library; therefore, Groovy does not need to be installed. Any existing Groovy installation is ignored by Gradle.

Gradle is available in three formats:

- `gradle-[version]-all.zip`: This contains the source code, the binaries, and the documentation

- `gradle-[version]-bin.zip`: This contains the binaries only

- `gradle-[version]-src.zip`: This contains the source code only, in case you want to extend the Gradle features

Alternatively, you can just download `gradle-[version]-bin.zip` file.

Once downloaded, you need to unpack the zip file and configure it as per your operating system.

Gradle for Windows

Following are the steps for installing Gradle on Windows:

1. Unpack the Gradle distribution on the hard drive.
2. Add Gradle's installed path (for example, `c:\gradle-2.4`) to the `GRADLE_HOME` variable. Note that this location should be the parent directory of the `bin` or the `lib` folder.
3. Add the `GRADLE_HOME/bin` to the `PATH` variable.

When you are ready to go ahead with Gradle, verify your installation by running the `gradle` command with the `--version` or `-v` command-line parameter.

```
> gradle -version

------------------------------------------------------------
Gradle 2.4
------------------------------------------------------------

Build time:   2015-05-05 08:09:24 UTC
Build number: none
Revision:     5c9c3bc20ca1c281ac7972643f1e2d190f2c943c

Groovy:       2.3.10
Ant:          Apache Ant(TM) version 1.9.4 compiled on April 29 2014
JVM:          1.7.0_79 (Oracle Corporation 24.79-b02)
OS:           Windows 8.1 6.3 amd64
```

Gradle for Mac/Linux

Following are the steps to install Gradle on the Mac/Linux operating system.

1. Unpack the Gradle distribution.
2. Add the following two lines in your initialization script (`~/.profile`).
3. Export `GRADLE_HOME = <Gradle_Installation_Dir>`
4. Export `PATH=$PATH:$GRADLE_HOME/bin`

Reload the profile by executing `source ~/.profile` and execute the `gradle -version` command. You will be able to see a similar output as mentioned in the previous section.

The Gradle JVM option

Gradle shares the same JVM options set by the environment variable `JAVA_OPTS`. If you don't want to use this setting and want to pass arguments specifically to the Gradle runtime, you can use the environment variable `GRADLE_OPTS`.

Suppose if `JAVA_OPTS=512MB` in your system and you want to increase the default maximum heap size to `1024MB` for Gradle application. You can set it like this:

`GRADLE_OPTS="-Xmx1024m"`

We can apply this setting in the project-specific build file. Alternatively, we can also apply this setting to all of the Gradle build by adding the variable to the Gradle startup script (this will be discussed later in this chapter).

Our first script

In the last section, we learned how to install Gradle. Now it's time create our very first Gradle script. This script will print `Hello Gradle- This is your first script` on the console. Just open a text editor, type in the following three lines, and save the file as `build.gradle`.

```
task helloGradle << {
    println 'Hello Gradle- This is your first script'
}
```

Then execute the `gradle helloGradle` command as follows:

```
$ gradle helloGradle
:helloGradle
Hello Gradle- This is your first script
BUILD SUCCESSFUL
Total time: 4.808 secs
```

So, what have we done here?

- We have a created a Gradle build script file called `build.gradle`. This is the default name given to a build file. You can give any name to the build file. However, to execute the script, you must use the `-b` option with your filename with the `gradle` command. Otherwise,the build will fail with the `Task '%TASK_NAME%' not found in root project '%PROJECT_NAME'."` `gradle [-b <file name>] [task1 task2 ….. taskn]` error.

- Try the `gradle -b <buildfile_name> helloGradle` command and you should get the same output.

- With the gradle command, we have executed a task called `helloGradle`, which prints a line in the console. So, the parameter we passed to the gradle command is the task name. You can execute one to any number of tasks with the Gradle command and these tasks will be executed in the same order as they appear in the command line.

 There is a way to define the default task using the `defaultTasks` keyword, which will be executed by default, if user does not mention any specific task to execute on the build file. We'll discuss this more in *Chapter 3, Managing Task*.

The Gradle command initializes the script, reads all tasks mentioned on the command-line, and executes tasks. Moreover, if any task has multiple dependencies, then dependent tasks are executed in alphabetical order unless those tasks themselves enforce the order. You can find more about task ordering in *Chapter 3, Managing Task*.

Remember that each Gradle build consists of three components: projects, tasks, and properties. Each build has at least one project and one or more tasks. The name of the project is the parent directory name in which the build file exists.

Gradle command Line arguments

Now that you have created the first working script, it is time to explore different command-line options supported by Gradle.

You have already seen the usage of -b option to specify a build script. We'll start with --help or -h or -? to list all the options available with the Gradle command line.

```
$ gradle -h
USAGE: gradle [option...] [task...]


-?, -h, --help          Shows this help message.
-a, --no-rebuild        Do not rebuild project dependencies.
-b, --build-file        Specifies the build file.
-c, --settings-file     Specifies the settings file.
--configure-on-demand   Only relevant projects are configured in this
build run. This means faster build for large multi-project builds.
[incubating]
--continue              Continues task execution after a task failure.
```

In the preceding output, -h or --help displays many more options. We have truncated the output.

You can execute the command on your systems and check all the options. Most of these are self-explanatory. We will discuss the usage of some of the most useful options in this section.

Now we'll add two more tasks, failedTask and test to the build.gradle script and save the file as sample_build.gradle. The task named failedTask is expected to always fail due to assertion failure and the test task is dependent on the previously created task helloGradle. A task can succeed (executing all statements in the task without any exception) or it can fail (due to any exception or error in any line of code mentioned in the task) thus stopping the execution of the script.

```
task failedTask << {
      assert 1==2
}


task test(dependsOn: helloGradle ) << {
      println 'Test case executed'
}
```

On executing the `gradle -b sample_build.gradle failedTask test` command, we observe that the `test` task is never executed. As Gradle executes tasks sequentially as they appear on the command-line, if a task fails to execute, all the remaining tasks will be ignored.

```
$ gradle -b sample_build.gradle failedTask test
:failedTask FAILED

FAILURE: Build failed with an exception.
...
BUILD FAILED


Total time: 6.197 secs
```

By default, Gradle stops the build process if any task fails to execute. This feature helps to get a quick feedback on the build process. If you do not want to stop execution of the build irrespective of any task failure and you want to continue with other tasks, then it can be done by using the `--continue` command-line option. This feature could be useful when we want to build a multimodule project, where some of the modules might fail due to compilation error or test failure. With the `–continue` option, we will get a complete status of all the modules.

```
$ gradle -b sample_build.gradle failedTask test --continue
:failedTask FAILED
:helloGradle
Hello Gradle- This is your first script
:test
Test case executed


FAILURE: Build failed with an exception.
```

As you can see in the preceding output, `failedTask` failed to execute. So the build is marked as FAILURE. However, this time the `test` task executed successfully. Also observe that the `helloGradle` task is executed before the `test` task. This is because we have defined the `test` task to be dependent on the `helloGradle` task. This is one of the ways you can create task dependencies. For now, don't get confused with task dependency. We will discuss the topic in detail in *chapter3, Managing Task*.

Now, what happens if the `helloGradle` task fails? Just add a line `assert 1==2` into the `helloGradle` task. The assert statement forces the task to fail. When you look at the following output, you will find that the test tasks is not executed as the dependent task failed:

```
$ gradle -b sample_build.gradle failedTask test --continue
:failedTask FAILED
:helloGradle
Hello Gradle- This is your first script
:helloGradle FAILED

FAILURE: Build completed with 2 failures.
```

In the preceding scenario, the test task is dependent on the `helloGradle` task. This means that, every time we execute the `test` task, the `helloGradle` task will be executed by default. In case you want to avoid the execution of the `helloGradle` task, you can use the `-x or --exclude-task` option.

```
$ gradle -b sample_build.gradle failedTask --continue test -x
helloGradle
:failedTask FAILED
:test
Test case executed
```

Another useful option is `--dry-run` or `-m`, which runs the build but does not execute the tasks. It is useful if you want to know the task execution order or you want to validate the script.

```
$ gradle --dry-run -b sample_build.gradle failedTask test
--continue
:failedTask SKIPPED
:helloGradle SKIPPED
:test SKIPPED
BUILD SUCCESSFUL
Total time: 4.047 secs
```

 `--dry-run` executes all the statements which are not part of any tasks and are defined outside of a task block. To verify this, add a `println` statement anywhere outside a task block definition and observe the result.

So far, you must have noticed that each output displays extra information apart from the task output and error messages. Try the command-line option -q or --quiet to display only the task output:

```
$ gradle -q -b sample_build.gradle failedTask --continue test
Hello Gradle- This is your first script
Test case executed
```

The options --debug (-d), --info (-i), --full-stacktrace (-S), and --stacktrace (-s) display the output with different log levels and stack traces. --debug is the most detailed log level. --full-stacktrace and --stacktrace show stack traces if the build fails with an exception. Try the previously executed command with these command-line options and observe the output:

```
$ gradle -d -b sample_build.gradle failedTask --continue test
```

Now we will explore the --daemon, --stop, and --no-daemon options. On my machine, it took around 3.6 seconds to execute the preceding script. For this simple script, most of the execution time was spent in the initialization of Gradle. When we execute a Gradle command, a new Java Virtual Machine is started, then Gradle-specific classes and libraries are loaded, and finally the actual build steps are executed. Initialization and execution of Gradle can be improved using the --daemon option. This is very useful if you are working in a test-driven development where you need to execute unit tests frequently or you need to run a particular task repeatedly.

To start a daemon, you can use the --daemon option. The daemon process automatically expires after 3 hours of idle time. To check whether the daemon is running on the system, use the ps command in the UNIX environment, or the Process explorer in Windows systems. Once you have started the daemon process, again execute the same Gradle task. You will find an improvement in the execution time.

Alternatively, you can use the gradle.properties file to set the system property org.gradle.daemon to enable the daemon. In this scenario, you don't need to specify the --daemon option when executing the tasks. To try it out, create a file called gradle.properties in the same directory where you created the sample_build. gradle file and add this line org.gradle.daemon=true. Now, run the gradle command and check whether the daemon process is running. The org.gradle. daemo is a property that we have set to configure the Gradle build environment. We'll discuss more on properties and system variables in *Chapter 6, Working with Gradle*.

To stop the daemon process, use the `gradle --stop` option. Sometimes, you may not want to execute Gradle tasks with the daemon process. Use the `--no-daemon` option with the task to ignore any running daemons.

```
$ gradle -b sample_build.gradle failedtask --continue test
--daemon

$ ps -ef | grep gradle
root    25395   2596 46 18:57 pts/1   00:00:04
/usr/local/java/jdk1.7.0_71/bin/java …..
org.gradle.launcher.daemon.bootstrap.GradleDaemon 2.4
/home/root/.gradle/daemon 10800000 93dc0fe2-4bc1-4429-a8e3-
f10b8a7291eb -XX:MaxPermSize=256m -XX:+HeapDumpOnOutOfMemoryError -
Xmx1024m -Dfile.encoding=UTF-8 -Duser.country=US -Duser.language=en -
Duser.variant

$ gradle --stop
Stopping daemon(s).
Gradle daemon stopped.
```

Although the Gradle daemon is recommended for the development environment, it might get corrupted occasionally. When Gradle executes user build scripts from multiple sources (for example, in the Continuous Integration environment), it might exhaust the daemon process and may cause memory leakage if resources are not handled properly. Therefore, it is recommended not to enable the daemon for staging or continuous integration environment. Apart from the command-line, Gradle can be executed in the **Graphical User Interface** (**GUI**) as well. In the next section, we'll discuss the graphical user interface supported by Gradle. The other important command-line options such as –D or `--system-prop`, -P or `--project-prop` will be discussed in *Chapter 6, Working with Gradle*, when we explore more on building Java applications with Gradle.

The Gradle GUI

Apart from the command-line arguments and tools, Gradle provides a graphical user interface. It can be launched with the help of the following command-line option:

```
$ gradle --gui
```

It launches a **graphical user interface (GUI)**, which can be used to execute Gradle tasks directly from the GUI.

Figure 1.1

It contains four tabs, which are explained as follows:

- **Task Tree**: The directory, under which you executed this command, is considered as the parent project directory. If the `build.gradle` file is present under this directory, task tree will list out all the tasks available in the `build.gradle` file. If the `build.gradle` file is not in this directory, it will list out only the default tasks. You can execute any task by double-clicking on the task name.

   Figure 1.1 displays `failedTask`, `helloGradle` and `test` tasks that we developed earlier along with the default Gradle tasks.

- **Favorites**: This works like your browser favorites, where you can save frequently used commands. Additionally, it provides an alias feature. In case you want to execute multiple tasks on the command line, you can add them here and give it a simple display name. For example, you can click on the plus sign and add the following tasks in the command-line textbox: `clean build`.

  Add `init` in the display name area. You will see that **init** appears in the **Favorites** area. Next time, just click on **init** to execute `clean build` tasks.

- **Command line**: This works like the console. Here you can execute single or multiple inline commands. It will execute the command and will display the result in the lower window.

- **Setup**: Even if you started the GUI from a specific project directory, you can change the directory using this tab. It allows you to change your current directory for executing commands. Along with that, it helps to change some general settings such as Log level, Stack Trace output, and so on. It also allows you to execute other Gradle versions through the custom Gradle Executor.

Start up script

Consider this scenario, for each of your Gradle projects you have a dependency on a local in-house jar files. Additionally, you want to set some common environment variables for each of your Gradle projects (such as GRADLE_OPTS).

A simple solution is to add the jar file in the dependency closure. An alternate solution could be to create one common build file and include this common file in each of the build files.

The simplest solution Gradle provides for these kinds of problems by introducing the initialization script.

Initialization scripts are no special files, but a Gradle script with the .gradle extension. However, this will execute every time before any of your build files execute.

 There can be more than one initialization script.

Some of the uses of the initialization script are as follows:

- Downloading some common jars for each of your projects
- Performing common environment configuration related to system details and/or user details.
- Registering listeners and loggers.

So, how does Gradle find these initialization script(s)? There are multiple ways to define the initialization script which are as follows:

- All the files with `.gradle` extension under `<USER_HOME>/.gradle/init.d` directory are treated as initialization scripts. Gradle will execute all the `.gradle` files under this directory before the execution of any Gradle build script.
- Files named `init.gradle` under `<USER_HOME>/.gradle/` are treated as an initialization script.
- All the files with the `.gradle` extension under `<GRADLE_HOME>/init.d/` directory.
- You can even specify any Gradle file as the initialization script with `-I <file name>` or `--init-script <file name>`.

 Even if multiple files are found at the location mentioned earlier, Gradle will execute all the files as initialization script before executing any project build script.

Following is a sample `init` script.

```
println "Hello from init script"
projectsLoaded {
  rootProject.allprojects {
    buildscript {
      repositories {
        maven {
          url "http://central.maven.org/maven2/"
        }
      }
      dependencies {
        classpath group: 'javax.mail', name: 'javax.mail-api',
          version: '1.4.5'
      }
    }
  }
}
```

Copy and paste the preceding code and save it as `init.gradle` file under any of the preceding mentioned paths. The `println` statement is intentionally added in this file to help you understand the execution cycle of the init script. Whenever you execute any Gradle script from a directory, you will see `Hello from init script`. Apart from printing `Hello from init script`, this script also downloads `javax.mail-api-1.4.5.jar` in the Gradle cache when the script is executed for the first time. It will not download this library again, unless there is a change in the file in the repository. If you don't understand what a cache is, don't worry. You will learn more about cache management in the later section of this chapter. Remember, sometimes defining too many configurations in the init script could be problematic. Specifically, debugging could be difficult because the projects are no longer self-contained.

Build life cycle

Gradle build has a life cycle, which consists of three phases: initialization, configuration, and execution. Understanding the build life cycle and the execution phases is crucial for Gradle developers. Gradle build is primarily a collection of tasks and a user can define the dependency between the tasks. So, even if two tasks depend on the same task, for example, Task C and Task B both depend on Task A, Gradle makes sure that Task A will execute only once throughout the execution of the build script.

Before executing any task, Gradle prepares a **Directed Acyclic Graph (DAG)** of all tasks for the build. It is directed because a task directly depends on another task. It is acyclic because, if Task A depends on Task B and if you make Task B depend on Task A, it will result in an error, as there can't be cyclic dependency between two tasks. Before executing the build script, Gradle configures the task dependency graph.

Let's quickly discuss the three build phases.

Initialization

User can create a build script for a single project as well as for a Multi-project build. During the initialization phase, Gradle determines which projects are going to take part in the build process, and creates a Project instance for each of these projects.

Configuration

This phase configures the project object. All the build scripts (in case the user is executing a multiproject build), which are part of the build process are executed without executing any task. This means whatever statements you have written outside of the task in the configuration block would be executed in the configuration phase. No tasks would be executed here; only the directed acyclic graph would be created for all tasks.

Execution

In this phase, Gradle executes all tasks as per the order given in the command line. However, if any dependencies exist between tasks, those relationships will be honored first before the command-line ordering.

Cache management

The main focus of any build tool is to not only automate the build and deployment processes, but also how to manage the cache effectively. No software works in isolation. Each software depends on some third-party libraries and/or in-house libraries.

Any good build tool should automatically take care of software dependencies. It should be able to download the dependencies automatically and maintain the versioning. When Ant was released, this feature was not available and developers need to manually download the dependencies and need to maintain their versioning on its own. Though it was later resolved by extending Ant with Ivy.

Gradle automatically downloads all dependencies given in the build file. It determines all the libraries needed for the project, downloads from the repositories, and stores them in its local cache. Next time when you run the build, it doesn't need to download those dependencies again (unless required) as it can reuse the libraries from the cache. It also downloads all the transitive dependencies.

Downloading the example code

You can download the example code files from your account at http://www.packtpub.com for all the Packt Publishing books you have purchased. If you purchased this book elsewhere, you can visit http://www.packtpub.com/support and register to have the files e-mailed directly to you.

Cache location

The first question arises regarding cache, in which location Gradle maintains its cache. Gradle uses `<USER_HOME>/.gradle/caches` as the default directory to store its local cache. It might contain more than one version directory if a developer has used multiple versions of Gradle to build the software. The actual cache is divided into two parts. All the jars that are downloaded from the repositories can be found under `modules-2/files-2.1`. Additionally, you will also find some binary files that will store the metadata about the downloaded binaries. If you look inside the `modules-2/files-2.1` directory, it has the path in the format `group/name/version/checksum`, which contains the actual binary. You can find out more about dependency management in detail in *Chapter 5, Dependency Management*.

Change Cache location

If you want to change the cache location to some other directory, other than default location, you need to set the following environment variables. You can set this variable in Windows as the environment variable and in the Unix/Linux in `.profile` file:

```
GRADLE_USER_HOME=<User defined location>
```

Cache features

Now, let's discuss some of the important features of the Gradle cache.

Reduce the traffic

One of the main features of Gradle cache management is to reduce the network traffic. When you build the application for the first time, Gradle downloads all the dependencies into a cache, so that next time onwards it can directly fetch it from the cache.

In case multiple repositories are configured in the build script and a JAR is found in the first repository, then Gradle won't search other repositories for the same JAR file. In another situation, if the JAR was not found in the first repository but was fetched from the second repository, then Gradle will store metadata information about the first repository, so that next time onwards the first repository won't be searched for the missing JAR, to save time and network traffic.

Dependency location

Whenever Gradle downloads dependencies from the repositories, it also stores the repository location in its metadata. It helps to detect the changes in case the binaries are removed from the repositories or their structure is changed.

Version integration

If a developer updates the Gradle version on his machine, and he has already downloaded libraries in an older cache, then it is reused. Gradle also provides tight integration with Maven's local repository. Gradle figures out whether an artifact has changed in the remote repository by comparing its checksum with the local cache. All those artifacts whose checksum matches are not downloaded. Apart from checksum, Gradle will consider an additional parameter to compare between the remote and local artifacts; Gradle uses the value of the HTTP header parameter *content-length* or the last modified date.

Switching off remote checking

With the `--offline` command-line option, a developer can ask Gradle to only look at the local cache, not in the remote cache. This could be useful if the user is working without any network connectivity. If Gradle can't find the JAR in the local cache, the build will fail.

Version conflicts

If a developer has not mentioned any specific version of dependency and there are multiple versions available for the download, Gradle, by default, always downloads the latest version of the artifact.

Gradle with IDE

So far, in this chapter, we have worked on creating some basic Gradle scripts. We will conclude this chapter by creating a Java application with Gradle. To create a Java application, we'll be using Eclipse IDE with the Gradle plugin.

With **Integrated Development Environment** (IDE), application development becomes much easier. In this section, we will explore how to install the Gradle plugin in Eclipse, create a simple Java application, explore Eclipse plugin tasks, and execute Gradle tasks from Eclipse.

Apart from Eclipse, another popular IDE is JetBrains IntelliJ IDEA. Gradle also supports IDEA plugin, which is very similar to the Eclipse plugin. However, in this book, we will focus only on the Eclipse plugin since it is freely available and is open source.

Installing the Gradle plugin in Eclipse

The Eclipse Integration Gradle project from the spring source (`https://github.com/spring-projects/eclipse-integration-gradle/`) helps the developer to work with Gradle in Eclipse. This tool offers support for:

- Working with multiprojects
- Using `Gradle Import Wizard` to import Gradle projects into Eclipse
- Using `New Gradle Project Wizard` to create new Gradle projects
- Using Dependency Management to configure the classpath of the Eclipse project
- Executing Gradle tasks using `Gradle Task UI`
- Integration with the Groovy Eclipse via DSLD (DSL Descriptors)

Following are the steps to install this plugin in Eclipse (3.7.2 or higher) from the update site:

1. Launch Eclipse. Navigate to **Help | Install New Software**.
2. In the **Install New Software** dialog, click on the **Add** button to add a new site.
3. Enter the **Location** as `http://dist.springsource.com/release/TOOLS/gradle` and **Name** as `Gradle`. You can enter any meaningful name you want.
4. Click on **OK** to add the repository.
5. Select the newly created Gradle repository from the repository list.
6. Check only the box next to **Extensions / Gradle Integration | Gradle IDE**. Click on **Next** (Refer to *Figure 1.2*).
7. On the next screen, click on **Next**.

8. Accept the terms and conditions and click on **Finish**. Eclipse should download and install Gradle IDE. Then restart Eclipse.

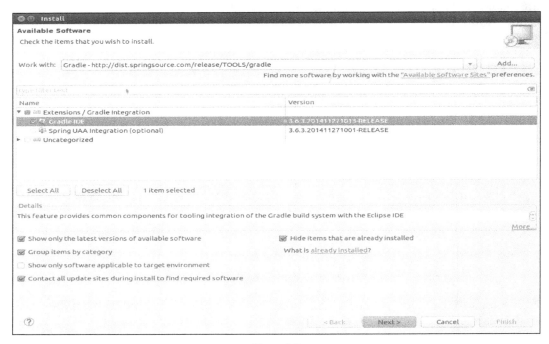

Figure 1.2

Working with the Gradle project in IDE

We have successfully installed Gradle plugin. Now, we'll create a simple Gradle project and we'll look into few Eclipse-related important files, for example, `.project` and `.classpath`. Then we will build the project using the Gradle Task UI.

Following are the steps to create a Gradle project:

1. In Eclipse, navigate to **File** | **New** | **Gradle** | **Gradle Project**.
2. In the **New Gradle Project** window, specify the project name as **FirstGradleProject** and select the sample project as **Java Quickstart**.
3. Click on **Finish** and wait for the build to be successful.

You will find the following console output:

```
:cleanEclipseClasspath UP-TO-DATE

:cleanEclipseJdt UP-TO-DATE

:cleanEclipseProject UP-TO-DATE

:cleanEclipse UP-TO-DATE

:eclipseClasspath

...

:eclipseJdt

:eclipseProject

:eclipse


BUILD SUCCESSFUL
```

The output clearly shows what is going on here. Gradle initially executes a series of clean tasks (cleanEclipseClasspath, cleanEclipse, and so on.), then downloads some jar files from the Maven repository and finally executes a few more tasks (eclipseJdt, eclipse, and so on) to complete the build process.

The autogenerated build.gradle file has the following contents:

```
apply plugin: 'java'
apply plugin: 'eclipse'

sourceCompatibility = 1.5
version = '1.0'
jar {
  manifest {
    attributes 'Implementation-Title': 'Gradle Quickstart',
      'Implementation-Version': version
  }
}

repositories {
  mavenCentral()
}

dependencies {
  compile group: 'commons-collections', name: 'commons-
    collections', version: '3.2'
```

```
    testCompile group: 'junit', name: 'junit', version: '4.+'
}

test {
  systemProperties 'property': 'value'
}

uploadArchives {
  repositories {
    flatDir {
      dirs 'repos'
    }
  }
}
```

This `build` file is, quite different from what we created earlier in this chapter. The Java and Eclipse plugin declarations were added in the beginning. Project properties such as `sourceCompatibility` and version were added. The repository was declared as `mavenCentral()`. Dependencies, common-collections, and JUnit were configured on `compile` and `testCompile` respectively. We'll learn each and every component in the next chapters; now, let's concentrate on the other artifacts created by the Gradle project.

If you browse the source code (look for the `src` folder) of the project, you'll find that the application was prepopulated with some Java source code and JUnit test cases.

Apart from the source code and build file, a few other files, namely, `.project`, and `.classpath` and a folder, namely, `.settings`, were added to this Java project. These are the default files created by Eclipse. As the name suggests, the `.project` file contains the metadata information about the project such as name, description and build specification. The `.classpath` file describes the Java dependency, external library dependencies, and other project dependencies. `.settings/org.eclipse.jdt.core.prefs` stores information such as the Java compiler version, source, and the target Java version. All these three files were created during the build process when the `eclipse` task was executed.

So, we claimed that the Eclipse plugin was responsible for creating all of the Eclipse IDE-specific files. To confirm, first execute the `gradle cleanEclipse` command from the project of the base folder:

```
$ gradle cleanEclipse
:cleanEclipseClasspath
:cleanEclipseJdt
```

```
:cleanEclipseProject
:cleanEclipse
```

BUILD SUCCESSFUL

The `cleanEclipse` task executed three more dependent tasks: `cleanEclipseClasspath` (removes the `.classpath` file), `cleanEclipseJdt` (removes the `.settings/org.eclipse.jdt.core.prefs` file), and `cleanEclipseProject` (removes the `.project` file).

Check whether all the three files got deleted from the project, and, finally, execute the `gradle eclipse` command to recreate those files.

```
$ gradle eclipse
:eclipseClasspath
:eclipseJdt
:eclipseProject
:eclipse
```

BUILD SUCCESSFUL

Now the question is if I have a Java project, how do I import that project in Eclipse IDE?

We have learned this already and you might have guessed it. It takes just three steps: add the Eclipse plugin into the build file (apply the `eclipse` plugin), execute Eclipse task (`gradle eclipse`), and finally import project using **Eclipse File | Import**.

Alternatively, you can use Gradle IDE. From Eclipse, select the project by navigating to **File | Import | Gradle | Gradle Project**, and then perform `Build Model` and finish. Use of Gradle IDE helps to avoid all the manual steps mentioned earlier.

We'll conclude this section by exploring Gradle Task UI, which enables us to execute tasks. Gradle task execution is supported by the standard Eclipse launching framework. This means that before we execute any task, we must create a standard Eclipse launch configuration. To create the launch configuration, navigate to **Gradle project | Run As |** and click on **Gradle Build**.

In the text area, enter the task names you want to execute, such as `clean build`. Then click on **Run** to execute the tasks. The launch configuration will be saved as the project name by default. In *Figure 1.3*, the configuration is saved as **FirstGradleProject**, which is the project name.

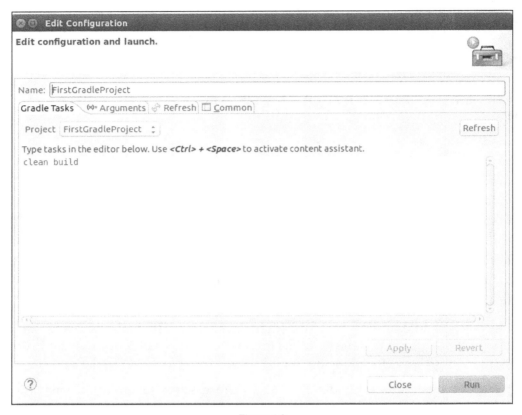

Figure 1.3

This launch configuration will be saved in Eclipse, so that it can be executed again. To launch the previously saved configuration, **FirstGradleProject**, you need to navigate to **Run As | Gradle Build**. This will once again, execute the `clean build` command.

Summary

In this chapter, we briefly discussed what a Build Automation System is, why do we need it, and why Gradle is a popular Build Automation System. You also learned how to install Gradle and we created our first Gradle script. Then we discussed the command-line options, GUI support, cache management, and startup scripts. Finally, we concluded the chapter working with Eclipse IDE with the Gradle Plugin to develop a simple Java application.

All the build scripts developed in this chapter were written in Groovy, but we have not talked about it. So, in the next chapter, we will learn some basic concepts of the Groovy programming language. Next chapter is meant mainly for developers who already have some basic knowledge of Java and object-oriented programming concepts.

2

Groovy Essentials for Gradle

In this chapter, we will learn some fundamental concepts of the Groovy programming language. This chapter briefly covers Groovy data types, control structures, object oriented concepts, collections, closures, and builders. This is just the tip of the iceberg. As this is not a Groovy book, we won't be able to cover all the topics. This chapter is meant for beginners who are coming from a Java background and have a basic understanding of **Object-oriented programming** (OOP) concepts. This will help them get started with Groovy. This chapter will also act as a tool box to proceed with Gradle scripting.

Overview

Groovy is a dynamic programming language for the Java Platform. You might be wondering why we specifically mention the Java platform. By the Java platform, it means Groovy code compiles into the bytecode, and bytecodes are executed on JVM similar to any other Java class. Along with the OOP features, it also provides the capability of scripting languages such as Python and Smalltalk, making them available to use in Groovy using a Java-like syntax.

As Groovy runs on JVM, it can be easily integrated with Java and nicely fits into the existing infrastructure. For example, the build and deployment of Groovy code is the same as the build and deployment of Java code, and you can easily mix Groovy and Java together by just adding another JAR file to the library. Groovy is not the only language that runs on JVM. Some of the other languages are Scala, Clojure, JRuby, Jython, and so on. In my opinion, if you have some Java background, Groovy is much easier to learn when compared with other languages. It has a very Java-like syntax to it, and most of the Java syntaxes are valid Groovy syntaxes. It just simplifies coding. Groovy is never intended to replace Java. It is intended to supplement Java to extend it to make it easier, and also it uses modern language features such as closures, builders, and metaprogramming.

The following are some of the key features of Groovy.

Integration with Java

Many people think Groovy is a scripting language. Yes, it provides scripting support, but it's not right to say Groovy is only a scripting language. Along with scripting, it perfectly fits into the OOP world. As mentioned earlier, Groovy also provides seamless integration with Java. Calling Java from Groovy is as simple as writing Groovy code. Every Groovy type is a subtype of `java.lang.Object`.

Minimum code

One good thing about Groovy is that it reduces the amount of code required to do some complex tasks, such as parsing XML files and accessing databases. With Groovy, you can always mix in Java code. If you've been using Java for a while, I think you'll appreciate the simplicity of using Groovy since you can program more functionality by writing less code.

Simpler I/O operations

I/O operations, one of the main pain points for the developer while working with Java, is made much simpler in Groovy. It's more fun to perform I/O operations in Groovy. Groovy provides simple properties to read/write from the file. It has added so many utility methods to the `java.io.File` class.

Integration with Ant

Like Java, Groovy provides seamless integration with Ant. Groovy has a helper class, `AntBuilder`, which gives Groovy the power of using Ant features to make the developer's life much simpler. Be it calculating the checksum of any file or copying the content of a directory from one location to another with any filter criteria. With Ant capabilities, Groovy makes developers more productive. In *Chapter 8, Migration,* we will discuss more on this topic.

Builder classes

Apart from AntBuilder, Groovy provides the capability of `NodeBuilder`, `MarkupBuilder`, and `SwingBuilder`. With the help of these Builders, the developer is able to achieve things in a much simpler way, as compared to life without the Builders. `MarkupBuilder` is useful while dealing with XML operations. `SwingBuilder` provides simplified API to the Swing framework that helps in building user-friendly GUI applications. `NodeBuilder` helps while working with object tree structure.

Closure

The inclusion of closures was a big selling point for Groovy. A closure in Groovy is an anonymous chunk of code that may take arguments, return a value, and reference and use variables declared in its surrounding scope. Closure has usually been associated with functional languages.

A Groovy closure is like a code block that is defined and then executed at a later point. It has some special properties such as implicit variables and free variables. We will discuss Closure in detail in later section of this chapter.

Of course, there are many more features to learn. We will discuss a few in this chapter. For more details refer to the Groovy documentation at `http://www.groovy-lang.org/`.

Groovy script for Hello World

We have discussed what Groovy is and some of its important features. Let us create a Hello World program and feel the magic with Groovy. Here we are assuming that Groovy is installed on the system, `GROOVY_HOME` is pointing to the installation directory and `<GROOVY_HOME>/bin` has been added to the PATH environment variable:

```
file: GroovyTest.groovy
  println "Hello Groovy"
```

And that's all. Yes, for a simple Groovy program, you don't need to declare any packaging, any main class, or any semicolons, only a simple `println` statement would create your first Groovy program.

To execute the program, use the following command:

```
$ groovy GroovyTest.groovy
  Hello Groovy
```

The `groovy` command is used to execute the Groovy script. The beauty of the Groovy script is that it can execute any file, not only files with the `.groovy` extension. Even you can write the preceding `println` statement in the `Test.text` file and use the groovy command to execute the file. File extension doesn't matter in groovy, but to make the file structures more readable, it is recommended to use `.groovy` extensions for Groovy files.

There is another way of executing Groovy files. You can compile Groovy files, generate class files like Java, and then execute the class files. Perform the following steps:

1. To compile and generate the class file, use the following command:

    ```
    $ groovyc GroovyTest.groovy
    ```

2. To run the class file generated, you need to execute the following command on Windows. If executing on Linux/Unix environment use $GROOVY_HOME:

    ```
    $ java -cp %GROOVY_HOME%/embeddable/groovy-all-2.3.1.jar;.
      GroovyTest
    ```

Executing a Groovy compiled file is same as executing the Java file. Developer needs to add groovy-all-<version>.jar in its classpath. You also need to make sure that the directory in which your compiled classes are present, it should be in the classpath. In the preceding example, we have added "." as the current directory to the classpath to find the GroovyTest.class file.

It doesn't matter which way you execute the Groovy scripts. In both the cases, Groovy scripts execute inside JVM only. Both the methods compile the Groovy scripts into bytecode. The groovy <filename> stores the classes into memory in a direct way, whereas compiling the script using the groovyc command creates a class file and stores it on disk, which you can later execute using Java command.

Data types

The first thing you learn about any programming language are the data types; how any programming language stores the data. Similar to the other programming languages, Groovy also offers a different set of data types for numerical, strings, char, and so on. As compared to Java, there are no primitive types present in Groovy. Groovy treats everything as an object, which makes Groovy a pure Object Oriented language. The problem with primitive data types is that developers can't perform any object-level operations, such as calling methods on them. Also, you can't store them as an object in maps and sets (collections that require objects). The following table shows primitive data types and wrapper types with default values:

Data type	Wrapper type	Default values
byte	Byte	0
short	Short	0
int	Integer	0

Data type	Wrapper type	Default values
long	Long	0L
float	Float	0.0f
double	Double	0.0d
char	Character	\u0000
boolean	Boolean	false
String	Not Applicable	null

Groovy gives you the flexibility to even declare variables using int, byte, short, and so on, which it internally converts into its respective classes, for example, int to Integer, char to Character, and so on.

String

You may be thinking, why are we discussing only String here? This is because Groovy provides different variants to represent String compared to Java, as shown in the following code:

```
def s1='This is single quote string.'

def s2="This is double quote string."

def s3="""This is multi line String.
You can write multiple lines here."""

def s4 ="Example of Gstring, You can refer to variable also like
${s1}"

def s5='''This is multi line String.
You can write multiple lines here.'''

def s6 =/ This is 'slashy' String.
It can also contains multiple lines $s1
/
```

Here, s1 contains String in single quotes. This String is fixed in size as we have written it.

The s2 variable contains String in double quotes similar to Java String.

Variable s3 contains String enclosed in three double quotes, which allows you to declare a multiline String.

In s4, String contains an embedded variable, which will be resolved to its value. This is formally known as GString. You can declare place holder using either ${variable} or $variable.

Another format Groovy supports is String declared inside / (slash). It also supports multiline Strings.

Dynamic typing in Groovy

Groovy provides support for both static typing and dynamic typing features. Static typing provides more checks at compile time, more memory optimization, and better support for the IDE used for Groovy. It also provides additional information about the type of variable or method parameters. However, the power of Groovy lies in dynamic typing. In many scenarios, you are not sure about the kind of value that would be stored in the variable or returned by the functions. In that scenario, Groovy provides flexibility to use dynamic typing. You can just define a variable or methods by using the def keyword, as shown in the following code:

```
def var1
var1 ='a'
println var1.class    // will print class java.lang.String
var1 = 1
println var1.class    // will print class java.lang.Integer
def method1() {/*method body*/}
```

Another use of dynamic typing is calling methods on objects that have no guaranteed type. This is often called **duck typing**. For example, consider the following scenario where a simple addition method is called on different data types such as Integer, List, and String. Based on different input parameters, each time the method returns different output.

```
def addition(a, b) { return a + b}
addition (1, 2)        // Output: 3
addition ([1,2], [4, 5]) // Output: [1, 2, 4, 5]
addition('Hi ', 3)     // Output: Hi 3
```

As you can see, when the addition method was invoked with an Integer as an argument, it performed an arithmetic addition. With list-type arguments, the addition method creates a new list by doing a union of two lists. Similarly, on string-type arguments, it does a simple concatenation. In this example, the + operator was interpreted as different method calls based on the input type arguments.

A major difference between Java and Groovy is that Groovy supports operator overloading.

So far so good. But what happens if the addition method is called on a user-defined object, say `Person`? This is shown in the following code:

```
class Person{
  String name

  @Override
  public String toString() {
    return "Person [name=" + name +"]";
  }
}

p1 = new Person()
p2 = new Person()
addition(p1, p2)  // Output: groovy.lang.MissingMethodException
```

This is expected because in the `Person` class we did not define the plus method. If we define the plus method in the `Person` class, the call to the addition (which invokes `p1 + p2` or `p1.plus(p2)`) method will be successful.

Another solution is to implement `methodMissing` method. This is a very powerful concept in Groovy. In the Gradle source code, you will find reference for this method many times.

So, instead of defining a plus method, we can define a `methodMissing` method as follows:

```
def methodMissing(String name, args) {
  if (name.startsWith("plus") ) {
// write your own implementation
    return "plus method intercepted"
  }
  else {
    println "Method name does not start with plus"
    throw new MissingMethodException(name, this.class, args)
  }
}
```

Now, if we call the addition method on the `Person` object, we will find `plus method intercepted` as the new output, as shown in the following code:

```
addition(p1, p2)  // Output: plus method intercepted
```

Classes, beans, and methods

This section introduces classes, methods, and beans. Groovy classes are similar to Java classes declared with the `class` keyword. Usually, a class definition starts with the package name, and then import package statements. One key difference with the Java counterpart is that Groovy imports six packages and two classes by default. So, if you create any class, these packages and classes are automatically available to you:

```
import java.lang.* // this is the only default import in Java
import java.util.*
import java.io.*
import java.net.*
import groovy.lang.*
import groovy.util.*
import java.math.BigInteger
import java.math.BigDecimal
```

Classes and methods in Groovy by default have public access, whereas in Java it is set to `package-private`. We will start with a sample Groovy class:

```
class Order {
  int orderNo
  Customer orderedByCustomer
  String description

  static main(args) {
    Order order1 = new Order();
    order1.orderNo = 1;
    order1.orderedByCustomer = new Customer(name: "Customer1",
      email: "cust1@example.com")
    order1.setDescription("Ordered by Customer1")
    println order1.orderByCustomer.showMail()
  }
}

class Customer{
  String name
  String email
  String address

  String showMail(){
  email
  }
}
```

Here we have created two classes, Order and Customer, with some fields; in the main method, we have created objects, and finally, called the showMail() method on the Customer object. Notice how objects are initialized with values. The Order object is created by the default constructor, then the object was initialized with the setter methods defined on fields.

However, for the Customer object, it is done with a constructor with named parameters. The Customer object is initialized with a property-value pair in the constructor. However, we haven't defined any parameterized constructors in the class definition. So how does it work?

We have created fields in the class with no access modifier. If fields are created with default access, then Groovy automatically creates a field with public getter and setter methods. If we specify any access modifier (public, private, or protected), then only fields will be created; no getter or setter method will be created. In our preceding example, orderNo, orderByCustomer, and description are declared with no access modifier. So, we were able to call the setDescription method on the Order object. Other fields are accessed by field names. In this scenario, Groovy calls the respective getter or setter methods internally on the fields. This feature is called **Property** in Groovy. So, each class in Groovy has properties and autocreated getter and setter methods for those properties. This is similar to the Java bean approach, where private fields are created with public getter and setter methods, but with less number of lines of code as, getter and setter methods are implicitly provided by Groovy. This is why, often, Groovy objects are referred to as **Plain Old Groovy Object (POGO)**.

Coming back to the constructor declaration, when the Customer object was created with named parameters, actually, a default constructor was created, and then, for each of the properties in the constructor, respective setter methods were called to initialize the properties.

Methods in Groovy are similar to Java, but the class method's visibility is set to public by default. To invoke a method on a class, we need to create an object of that class. In case of Groovy scripts where you do not provide any class definition, method invocation is done by calling the method by name. If a method supports a dynamic return type, then the method declaration should start with the def keyword.

Groovy also supports method invocation with default parameter values. In the following example, the sum method is defined with three parameters x, y, and z, with values of y and z as 10 and 1, respectively. The sum(1) and sum(1,2) methods should give results 12 and 4, respectively.

```
def sum(x,y=10,z=1) {x+y+z}
// x = 1
```

```
sum(1)
// x = 1, y= 2
sum(1, 2)
```

Groovy does not require an explicit return statement in methods. By default, the last evaluated expression is returned as the method output. In the preceding example, we have not mentioned `return x+y+z`. It would be returned by default.

Control structures

In this section, we will discuss the basic control structures, namely the `if...else` statement, the `switch` statement, the `for` loop, and the `while` loop.

The if-else condition

The `if...else` condition in Groovy is similar to Java with one exception, how Groovy evaluates the logical `if` condition. In the following example, the `if` condition is evaluated true for both Boolean and int values. In Groovy, non-zero integers, non-null values, nonempty strings, initialized collections, and a valid matcher are evaluated as Boolean true values. This is known as **Groovy Truths**. Let's take a look at the following code:

```
def condition1 = true
int condition2 = 0
if(condition1){
  println("Condition 1 satisfied")
  if(condition2){
    println("Condition 2 satisfied")
  }else{
    println("Condition 2 failed")
  }
}else{
  println("Condition 1 failed")
}
```

Groovy also supports ternary operators `(x? y: z)`, such as Java, which can be used to write the standard `if-else` logic:

```
(condition2> 0 )? println("Positive") : println("Negative")
```

Groovy also provides one additional operator known as the Elvis operator. It can be used as a shorter version of the ternary operator in the scenario, where the user wants to validate a variable against the null value. Consider the following example:

```
def inputName
String username = inputName?:"guest"
```

If inputName is not null username would be inputName else default value "guest" would be assigned to username

The switch statement

Groovy supports Class, Object, Range, Collection, Pattern, and Closure as classifiers in the switch statement. Anything that implements the isCase method can be used as a classifier in the switch statement. The following example shows a case defined for various classifiers. Just try different values of input and observe the output of the switch statement:

```
def checkInput(def input){
switch(input){
  case [3, 4, 5]   :   println("Array Matched"); break;
  case 10..15      :   println("Range Matched"); break;
  case Integer     :   println("Integer Matched"); break;
  case ~/\w+/      :   println("Pattern Matched"); break;
  case String      :   println("String Matched"); break;
  default          :   println("Nothing Matched"); break;
}
}
checkInput(3)   // will print Array Matched
checkInput(1)   // will print Integer Matched
checkInput(10)  // will print Range Matched
checkInput("abcd abcd") // will print String Matched
checkInput("abcd")  // will print Pattern Matched
```

Loops

Groovy supports both for (initialize; condition; increment) and for-each type looping. The for-each style is expressed as for(variable in Iterable) { body}. As loop works on an iterable object collection, it can be easily applied to array, range, collections, and so on. Let's take a look at the following code:

```
// Traditional for loop
for(int i = 0; i< 3; i++) {/* do something */ }
// Loop over a Range
for(i in 1..5) println(i)
```

```
// Array iteration
def arr = ["Apple", "Banana", "Mango"]
for(i in arr) println(i)
// for applied on Set
for(i in ([10,10,11,11,12,12] as Set)) println(i)
```

The `while` loop is similar to the Java `while` loop, though Groovy doesn't support the `do-while` style of looping. Let's demonstrate the `while` loop:

```
int count = 0
while(count < 5) {
  println count++
}
```

Collections

We assume you have basic knowledge on **Java Collection Framework (JCF)**, so we are not going to discuss the fundamentals of the collection framework. We start on what Groovy provides on collection framework and frequently used utility methods provided by different collection objects.

Groovy supports different collective data types to store group of objects, such as range, lists, sets, and maps. If you are already a Java programmer, you will find how easy it is in Groovy to play with collective data types as compared to Java. Apart from sets, lists, and maps, Groovy has introduced ranges, which was not available in Java.

Set

A set is an unordered collection of objects, with no duplicates. It can be considered as an unordered list with restrictions on uniqueness, and is often constructed from a list. Set can also contain at most one null element. As implied by its name, this interface models the mathematical set abstraction.

The following code snippet explains how to create a `Set`. Elements can be added or removed from the `Set` using the `add`, `addAll`, `remove`, or `removeAll` methods.

You might have learned a lot about `Set` in your math classes, where the instructor teaches you different set operations, such as union and intersection. Groovy also provides similar functionalities. The union of two sets contains all the unique elements and common elements present in both the sets without repetition. The intersection finds common elements between the two sets. The complement of `Set1` and `Set2` will contain all those elements of `Set1` that are not present in `Set2`.

Let's take a look at the following code:

```
// Creating a Set
def Set1 = [1,2,1,4,5,9] as Set
Set Set2 = new HashSet( ['a','b','c','d'] )

// Modifying a Set
Set2.add(1)
Set2.add(9)
Set2.addAll([4,5])          // Set2: [1, d, 4, b, 5, c, a, 9]

Set2.remove(1)
Set2.removeAll([4,5])       // Set2: [d, b, c, a, 9]

// Union of Set
Set Union = Set1 + Set2      // Union: [1, 2, 4, 5, 9, d, b, c, a]

// Intersection of Set
Set intersection = Set1.intersect(Set2)     // Intersection: [9]

// Complement of Set
Set Complement = Union.minus(Set1)      // Complement: [d, b, c, a]
```

List

As compared to Set, a List is an ordered collection of objects, and a List can contain duplicate elements. A List can be created using List list = [], which creates an empty list that is an implementation of java.util.ArrayList.

The following code snippet shows how to create a List, read values from the list, and list some utility methods on the List:

```
// Creating a List
 def list1 = ['a', 'b', 'c', 'd']
 def list2 = [3, 2, 1, 4, 5] as List

// Reading a List
println list1[1]         // Output: b
println list2.get(4)     // Output: 5
println list1.get(5)     //Throws IndexOutOfBoundsException

// Some utility method on List
//Sort a List
println list2.sort()     // Output: [1, 2, 3, 4, 5]
// Reserve a list
```

```
println list1.reverse()        // Output: [d, c, b, a]
// Finding elements
println ("Max:" + list2.max() + ":Last:" + list1.last())
// Output: Max:5:Last:d
```

Some of the `List` methods accept Closure. The following example shows how to find the first even number using the `find` method, and list of all the even numbers using the `findAll` method:

```
println list2.find({ it %2 == 0})    // Output: 2
println list2.findAll({it %2 == 0})  // Output: [2, 4]
```

Do not get confused by the "it" keyword inside the curly brackets. We will discuss this in the *Closure* section.

Map

Map is a key-value pair collection, where the key is unique. In Groovy, key-value pairs are delimited by colons. An empty Map can be created via [:]. By default, a Map is of the type `java.util.HashMap`. If the keys are of type String, you can avoid the single or double quotes in the Map declaration. For example, if you want to create a Map with `name` as the key and `Groovy` as the value, you can use the following notation:

```
Map m1 = [name:"Groovy"]
```

Here, [name: "Groovy"] is the same as ["name":"Groovy"]. By default, Map keys are Strings. But if you want to put some variable as the key, then use parentheses, as shown in the following code:

```
String s1 = "name"
Map m1 = [(s1):"Groovy"]
```

Alternatively, you can create a Map in the following way:

```
def m2 = [id:1,title: "Mastering Groovy" ] as Map
```

You can get the objects from the Map using key `m2.get("id")` or `m2["id"]`.

 If key is a String, then to get a value, you need to specify the key in double quotes (" "). If you do not specify the key in double quotes, it will treat it as a variable name and will try to resolve it.

Now we will discuss some of the utility methods (each, any, and every) of Maps, which accept Closures:

```
Map ageMap = [John:24, Meera:28,Kat:31,Lee:19,Harry:18]
```

To parse every entry of `Map`, you can use `each`. It takes either entry or key-value as a parameter, as shown in the following table:

`ageMap.each {key, value ->`
`  println "Name is "+key`
`  println "Age is " +`
`    value`
`}`
	`ageMap.each {entry  ->`
	`  println "Name is`
	`   "+entry.key`
	`  println "Age is " +`
	`    entry.value`
	`}`

If you want to validate the `Map` data, you can use either `.every` or `.any`, based on your requirements. The `.every` method checks and makes sure all records fulfil the mentioned condition, while `.any` just checks whether any one record fulfils the condition. For example, if you want to check whether there is any user who is more than 25 years old:

```
ageMap.any {entry -> entry.value > 25 }
```

It returns the output as a Boolean value; in this case, true, as Meera is 28.

If you want to check whether all the users are above 18:

```
ageMap.every {entry -> entry.value > 18 }
```

It will return false, as Harry is 18.

You can also use the `find` and `findAll` methods for `Map` in the same pattern as we used for `List` in the *List* section.

Range

Apart from Java collection types, Groovy also supports a new collective data type `Range`. It is defined as two values (generally starting point and ending point) separated by two dots.

To create a `Range`, use the following code:

```
def range1 = 1..10
Range range2 = 'a'..'e'
```

To read values from `Range`, use the following code:

```
range1.each { println it }
```

You can also use the `.any` and `.every` operators to validate range for your specific requirement. It checks for the condition and returns a Boolean value. Let's take a look at the following code:

```
range1.any { it > 5 }
range1.every { it > 0 }
```

For modifying the range interval, use the following code. If you want to modify range interval from default 1 to any other number, you can set it via step method. It returns a list:

```
List l1 = range1.step(2)    //Output: [1, 3, 5, 7, 9]
```

To fetch the starting element and ending element of a range, use the `From` and `To` element, as shown in the following code:

```
range1.getFrom()        //Output: 1
range1.getTo()          //Output: 10
```

The `isReverse()` method is used to check the range trend to see whether the range is constructed using `to value` (higher value) to `from value` (lower value):

```
range1.isReverse()         // Output: false
```

Closure

Closure has usually been associated with functional languages. Groovy provides a very easy way of creating closure objects. A Groovy Closure is like a code block written in curly braces. Many people associate Closure to be an anonymous function in Java.

Closure in Groovy may accept arguments and returns a value. By default, the last statement in a Groovy Closure is the `return` statement. It means that if you are not explicitly returning any value from Closure, it will by default, returns the output of the last statement of Closure. Commonly, we define a Closure like this {`argument list-> closure body`}. Here, an argument list is a comma separated value that Closure accepts. Arguments are optional. If no argument is specified, then one implicit untyped argument named `it` will be available in the Closure body. The argument `it` will be null if no argument is supplied during Closure invocation.

In the following example, for the first call of Closure `addTwo` the variable `it` is assigned is 2, but in the second call, `it` is assigned null:

```
def addTwo = {it+2 }
addTwo(2)           // Output: 4
addTwo()            // NullPointerException
```

Alternatively, you can even declare a variable of type Closure. In Groovy, Closures are a subclass of the `groovy.lang.Closure` type:

```
groovy.lang.Closure closure1 = { println it }
closure1("This will be printed") // Output: This will be printed
```

To separate the Closure body from the argument list, we use the `->` operator. The closure body consists of zero or more Groovy statements. Like methods, it can also reference and declare variables in its scope.

In the following code snippet, the `addOne` method was able to reference the `constantValue` variable in its scope, though it was defined outside of the Closure scope. Such variables are referred to as `free` variables. A variable which is defined within the curly braces of a Closure would be treated as a local variable:

```
int constantValue = 9
def addOne = { Integer a -> constantValue + a }

addOne(1)           // unnamed () invocation. Output: 10
addOne.call(1)      // call() invocation. Output: 10
addOne("One")       // MissingMethodException
```

In the preceding example, the argument of the Closure was of Integer type. With Closures, the statements within the curly braces are not executed until you explicitly invoke them, using either `call()` or by an `unnamed ()` invocation syntax of Closure. In our example, the closure is declared in the second line, but it's not evaluated at that time. It will be executed if the `call()` method is explicitly made on the Closure. This is an important differentiator between Closures and code blocks. They may look the same, but they are not. Closures are only executed if the `call()` method is invoked on the Closure; not during its definition time. Remember, Closures are first class objects in Groovy, and can be referred using untyped variables or by using Closure variables. In both the cases, it is derived from `groovy.lang.Closure`. This class has overloaded `call()` methods with no or multiple arguments to invoke Closures.

When `addOne` Closure was called with an Integer as an argument, it executed successfully. However, for String type as an argument, it throws an exception. Also observe that the compiler didn't complain when we passed a String as an argument to the `addOne` Closure. This is because all arguments are checked at runtime; there is no static type checking done by the compiler.

The doCall() method on this Closure is generated dynamically, which accepts only Integer as an argument. So any invocation other than Integer type will throw an exception. The doCall() method is the implicit method, which cannot be overridden and cannot be redefined. This method is always invoked implicitly when we invoke call method or unnamed () syntax on a Closure.

We will conclude Closure by discussing the concept of delegate. This feature is widely used in Gradle. For example, when we define a repository Closure or dependency Closure in the build script, those Closures are executed in the RepositoryHandler or DependencyHandler classes. These classes are passed to the closures as delegates. You can refer to the Gradle API for more details. Let us not complicate things here. We will try to understand the concept with simple examples.

Consider the following example, where we are trying to print a myValue variable, which is undefined in the class. Obviously, this call will throw an exception as this variable is not defined in the scope:

```
class PrintValue{
  def printClosure = {
    println myValue
  }
}
def pcl = new PrintValue().printClosure
pcl()    //Output: MissingPropertyException: No such property
```

There could be a situation where we want to execute this closure against another class. This class can be passed to the closure as a delegate:

```
class PrintHandler{
  def myValue = "I'm Defined Here"
}

def pcl = new PrintValue().printClosure
pcl.delegate = new PrintHandler()
pcl()

OUTPUT: I'm Defined Here
```

In this example, the PrintHandler class has defined the myValue variable. We have delegated and executed the closure against the PrintHandler class.

So far, it is working as expected. Now, what if `myValue` is redefined in the `PrintValue` class:

```
class PrintValue{
  def myValue = "I'm owner"
  def printClosure = {
    println myValue
  }
}
```

In this scenario, on executing the Closure, we will find the output as `I'm owner`. This is because, when closure was trying to resolve the `myValue` variable, it found the variable defined within the scope of the owner (the `PrintValue` class, where the Closure is defined), so it didn't delegate the call to the `PrintHandler` class. Formally, this is known as `OWNER_FIRST` strategy, which is the default strategy. The strategy resolves this way — the closure will be checked first, followed by the closure's scope, then the owner of the closure, and, finally, the delegate. Groovy is so flexible that it provides us with the capability to change the strategy. For example, to delegate the call to the `PrintHandler` class, we should specify the strategy as `DELEGATE_FIRST`:

```
def pcl = new PrintValue().printClosure
pcl.resolveStrategy = Closure.DELEGATE_FIRST
pcl.delegate = new PrintHandler()
pcl()
```

With the `DELEGATE_FIRST` strategy, the closure will try to resolve the property or methods to the delegate first and then the owner. The other important strategies are:

- `OWNER_ONLY`: It attempts to resolve the property or methods within the owner only and doesn't delegate.

- `DELEGATE_ONLY`: Closure will resolve the property references or methods to the delegate. It completely ignores the owner.

- `TO_SELF`: It will resolve the property references or methods to itself and go through the usual `MetaClass` look-up process.

This was indeed a very short description. I suggest you to refer to the Groovy documentation for more details at:
`http://docs.groovy-lang.org/latest/html/api/groovy/lang/Closure.html`.

Builder

Another important feature in Groovy is Builder. Groovy Builders allow you to create complex tree-like hierarchical object structures. For example, SwingUI or XML documents can be created very easily using the DSL or Closure-like features in Groovy, with the support of the `BuilderSupport` class and its subclasses, `MarkupBuilder` and `SwingBuilder`.

Let's try to understand with an example. We created the `Order` class earlier in this chapter. Assume we have a list of orders and we want to store the details in a file called `orders.xml`. So every `Order` object in our list should be saved as a node in the XML file. Each of these `Order` nodes, again should contain child nodes, grand children nodes, and so on. Creating this tree-like structure can be complex if we try to implement a DOM-like parser in Java:

```
<orders>
  <order>
    <no>1</no>
    <description>Ordered by customer 1</description>
    <customer>
      <name firstname='Customer1' />
      <email>cust1@example.com</email>
    </customer>
  </order>
  <order>
    <no>2</no>
    <description>Ordered by customer 2</description>
    <customer>
      <name firstname='Customer2' />
      <email>cust2@example.com</email>
    </customer>
  </order>
  ....
</orders>
```

But in Groovy, this is just few lines of code with some method calls combined with Closure and named parameters. In the following example, we have created a `builder` object from the `MarkupBuilder` class to create the XML document. Then we have defined `orders` as the root of the document. However, `builder` has no method defined as `orders`. So then, how does this work?

As mentioned earlier, the `MarkupBuilder` class is a subclass of the `BuilderSupport` class. `BuilderSupport` has methods such as `createNode`, `invokeMethod`, `nodeCompleted`, `setCurrent`, `setParent`, and a few more. In runtime, an object is created by calling the `createNode` method on the builder with the name `orders`. In a similar fashion, for each `order` object, `no`, `description`, and `customer` nodes are created. Finally, each `order` node is attached to the parent `orders` node by calling the `setParent` method of the builder object:

```
def builder = new groovy.xml.MarkupBuilder(new FileWriter("orders.
xml"))

builder.orders{
  for(i in orderlist){
    order{
      no(i.orderNo)
      description(i.description)
      customer{
        name(firstname : i.orderedBy.name)
        email(i.orderedBy.email)
      }
    }
  }
}
```

Summary

In this chapter, we discussed some basic fundamental concepts. We learned about concepts of classes, methods, beans, collection frameworks, and closures. We also developed a markup builder to produce XML files. This was indeed a very short introduction to Groovy. However, in my opinion this introduction should be good enough to write Gradle scripts for your projects.

From the next chapter onwards, we will start exploring the core features of Gradle. In the next chapter, we will learn task management in Groovy. We will take a close look at the different in-built tasks supported by Gradle. We will also learn about task dependencies and task configurations. Then we will create some custom tasks for build scripts.

3
Managing Task

In this chapter, we will discuss the basic unit of Gradle build script, that is, Task. We will have a detailed look into the Task framework, how to create your own tasks, overwrite tasks provided by Gradle, tasks configurations, and creating custom tasks using different approaches provided by Gradle. We will also discuss the task dependencies. This chapter will also give insight view of controlling the execution of tasks, how to enable or disable task execution, and skip task execution based on some conditions. Gradle provides one additional feature known as incremental build support, which skips the execution of tasks if it is up to date, that is, if there are no changes in the input and output of the tasks. It helps in reducing the build time of the scripts if you are running the build repeatedly. We will try to understand this feature with some examples. Gradle supports this functionality by default. We will see how to extend this feature to user-defined tasks. Additionally, we will also explore the `Project` object provided by Gradle to control the build scripts.

Build script basics

A build script is nothing but a set of actions that execute in some predefined order and perform certain operations. In Gradle, we call these actions or group of actions a **Task**, which is part of the parent entity called **Project**. The atomic unit of execution in the Gradle build file is called a Task. The outcome of the build file might be some assets such as JAR, WAR, and so on, or it might perform certain operations such as deployment of assets and configuration of assets. Each build file that is `build.gradle` represents at least one project. It might contain more than one project also in case of multiproject or multimodule build. We will discuss multiproject build in *Chapter 6, Working with Gradle*. The execution of the build represents the execution of the `Project` object, which internally calls different tasks to perform the operations.

When you execute any build script, Gradle instantiates the `org.gradle.api.Project` object for the build file and gives an implicit project object. You can use this object to access the Project API in the build file either through `project.<methodname | property>` or simply `<methodname | property>`. For example; to print the name of the project in your build file, you can use the following code:

```
println "Project name is "+project.name
println "Project name is "+name // here project object is implicit
println "Project name is $project.name"
println "Project name is $name"
```

All the preceding statements will return the same output, that is, the project name. The project name is the name of the parent directory of the `build.gradle` file. Consider that `build.gradle` is under the `Chapter3` directory; thus, the output of the preceding statements would be `Project name is Chapter3`. You can change the name of the project by providing `rootProject.name=<New Project Name>` in the `settings.gradle` file. We will discuss further usage of the `settings.gradle` file in *Chapter 6, Working with Gradle*.

 To get the output `Project name is Chapter3`, you need to write the statements outside of a task block. If you write it inside a task, and if we are using the name or $name variable, it will show the task name. This is because inside a task block, the scope of the name variable will be different.

The following are some of the properties of the project object, which can be used to configure the build file using the getter and setter methods:

* `name // readonly`, you can only change using `settings.gradle`
* `parent // readonly`
* `version`
* `description`

Some of the properties are read-only, which are directly set by Gradle runtime.

Gradle also provides some default tasks, which can be used without applying any plugin such as copy task and zip task. It is also possible to define your own custom properties and custom tasks for the **project** object.

For each task in the build file, Gradle instantiates one of the implementations of Task object. There are different implementations of the Task interface; you can find further details of it at `https://docs.gradle.org/current/javadoc/org/gradle/api/Task.html`. Similar to the `Project` object, you can also control tasks programmatically using the Task API. You will see more details on this when we will create custom tasks using Groovy in a later section. In summary:

- A task is a collection of actions and properties. It can depend on some other tasks

- A task can accept input and return output

- A task also provides certain predefined properties such as name and description enabled

We will start with a simple build file example to explain the existing project properties, provide custom properties, create tasks, and so on.

Consider the file location /Chapter3/build.gradle:

```
// Section 1: Project object existing properties
version = '1.0'
description = 'Sample Java Project'
// Section 2: Project level custom properties
ext {
  startDate="Jan 2015"
}
ext.endDate = "Dec 2015"
println "This is project configuration part, description is
  $description"
// Section 3: Task
task sampleTask1 {
  // Section 3.1: Task existing properties
  description = "This is task level description"
  // Section 3.2: Task level custom properties
  ext {
    taskDetail=" This is custom property of task1"

  }
println "This is sampleTask1 configuration statements, taskDetail
  is $taskDetail"

// Section 3.3: Task actions
doFirst {
println "Project name is $project.name, description is
  $project.description"
```

```
    println "Task name is $name, description is $description"
       println "Project start date is $startDate"
     }
     doLast {
         println "Project endDate is $endDate"
     }

  }
  // Section 4: Task
  task sampleTask2 {
     println "This is sampleTask2 configuration statements"

  doFirst {
  println "Task getProjectDetailsTask properties are:
  "+sampleTask1.taskDetail
     }
  }
```

To execute the preceding build.gradle file:

```
$ gradle sampleTask1 sampleTask2

This is project configuration part, description is Sample Java
Project

This is sampleTask1 configuration statements, taskDetail is  This is
  custom property of task1

This is sampleTask2 configuration statements

:sampleTask1

Project name is chapter3, description is Sample Java Project

Task name is sampleTask1, description is This is task level
  description

Project start date is Jan 2015

Project endDate is Dec 2015

:sampleTask2

Task getProjectDetailsTask properties are:  This is custom property
  of task1

BUILD SUCCESSFUL


Total time: 6.892 secs
```

In the preceding example, in Section 1, we have overwritten some of the existing properties of the project object. In Section 2, we have added custom properties to the project object. Note that the syntax of adding custom properties is to add the `<name=value>` pair inside the `ext` closure, or we can define it as `ext.<propertyname> = value`. Then, we have added two tasks to this build script in Section 3 and 4 and added custom properties to the `sampleTask1` task. To add/update properties of the project, you do not need to add the `def` keyword. `def` is used to define the user-defined variables. However, here we are defining project properties. If you use `def startDate=<Value>`, it would be treated as a variable not a project property.

We are able to print the `startDate` and `endDate` in `sampleTask1` as we added these two as project properties, which can be directly accessed throughout the build file. To call task methods or to use task properties outside the task, we can use `task.<property name>` or `task.<method name>`. As in the preceding example, inside the `sampleTask2` task, we are printing `sampleTask1.taskDetail`.

There are multiple ways to specify the properties of any project. We will see this in detail when we discuss properties in *Chapter 6*, *Working with Gradle*.

Task configuration

We discussed in first chapter that a build file consists of three phases: initialization, configuration, and execution, which are explained briefly as follows:

*   Initialization creates the project object.
*   The configuration phase configures the project object, creates **DAG (Directed Acyclic Graph)** based on task dependencies. It also executes the project and the task configuration statements.
*   The execution phase finally executes the actions mentioned in the task body.

The task API mainly defines two types of closures: `doFirst`(Closure closure) and `doLast`(Closure closure), which internally calls `doFirst(Action action)` and `doLast(Action action)`. You can mention either one or both of them.

 Statements mentioned outside of these actions are part of your configuration, which are executed during the configuration phase.

To verify the configuration phase of a task, you can execute the build script using the `--dry-run` or `-m` option. The `--dry-run` (or `-m`) option only goes through the initialization and configuration phase, not the execution phase. Try to execute the preceding build file with the `--dry-run` option and you will find all the configuration statements printed on the console:

```
$ gradle --dry-run
This is project configuration part, description is Sample Java
Project
This is sampleTask1 configuration statements, taskDetail is  This is
custom property of task1
This is sampleTask2 configuration statements
:help SKIPPED


BUILD SUCCESSFUL
```

In Gradle 2.4 version, there are some performance improvements implemented in the configuration phase. For more details, refer to the release note at `https://docs.gradle.org/2.4/release-notes#significant-configuration-time-performance-improvements`.

Task execution

As mentioned earlier, a task is nothing but a single or group of actions that is executed to perform certain operations. You can add multiple actions to `doFirst` or `doLast` closures if needed. The `doFirst` closure will always execute before the `doLast` closure. You can add the actions to the task even after task definition.

For example, add the following statements after the `sampleTask2` task is mentioned in the preceding script.

```
sampleTask2.doFirst { println "Actions added separately" }
sampleTask2.doLast { println " More Actions added " }
```

The preceding statement will add two more additional actions to `sampleTask2`. Gradle provides one short notation for `doLast`, which is `<<`.

In Groovy, `<<` is the left shift operator to append elements to a list:

```
task sampleTask3 << {
        println "Executing task3"
}
sampleTask3.doFirst {println "Adding doFirst action" }
```

Try to execute `sampleTask3` and review the output:

```
$ gradle sampleTask3

...

:sampleTask3
Adding doFirst action
Executing task3


BUILD SUCCESSFUL
```

If multiple tasks are mentioned on the command line, they will be executed in the order defined (unless some dependency is applied on the tasks).

Task dependency

When we talk about build lifecycle or test lifecycle of any build tool, what does actually happen internally? It does not execute only one task; it basically executes a group of tasks, which are defined in a certain order and this order is nothing but the task dependencies. Consider the example of building any Java project. You can build a Java project by executing the `gradle build` task. This will do everything, such as compiling the source code, package classes into JAR file and copy the JAR file to a location. Does it mean that all these processes are only part of the **build** task? The message we want to convey here is that Gradle's `build` task does not execute only one task, but it executes the series of tasks from `compileJava`, `classes`, `compileTestJava` and so on until the building of the JAR file.

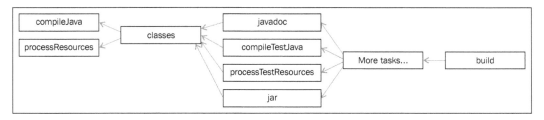

Figure 3.1

The preceding figure is nothing but the representation of the DAG after applying the Java plugin. It represents different tasks and how they are dependent on each other.

If a task, Task1, depends on another task, Task2, then Gradle makes sure that Task2 is always executed before Task1. In the preceding example, the **compileJava**, **classes**, and **jar** tasks will always execute before the build task. A task can depend on one or more tasks. Two or more tasks can also depend on the same prerequisite task. For example, in the preceding DAG the **javadoc**, **compileTestjava**, and **jar** tasks depends on the **classes** task. It does not mean that the **classes** task will execute three times. It will execute only once in the **build** lifecycle. If a task has already been executed due to some other dependency, it will not execute again. It will just inform the other dependent task about its status so that dependent task will continue to execute without calling it again.

In the build file, a task dependency can be defined in any of the following ways:

```
task task1(dependsOn: task2)
task task1(dependsOn: [task2,task3]) // in case of more than one
  dependency
task1.dependsOn task2, task3  //Another way of declaring
  dependency
```

Many plugins provide tasks with default dependencies. As we have seen in the preceding diagram, the `classes` task has the `compileJava` dependency. If you add any other dependency (for example, `task1`) to the `classes` task, it will append the task (`task1`) with the `compileJava` task. This means, executing the `classes` task will execute both `compileJava` and `task1`. To exclusively override the existing dependencies with a new set of dependencies, use the following syntax:

```
classes {dependsOn = [task1, task2]
}
```

Here, executing the `classes` task will execute both `task1` and `task2` as dependent tasks and it will ignore the `compileJava` task.

Task ordering

If **Task1** depends on **Task2**, then Gradle makes sure that **Task2** will always execute before **Task1**. However, it does not make sure the ordering of tasks. That is, it will not ensure that **Task2** will execute immediately before **Task1**. Between the execution of **Task2** and **Task1**, other tasks might be executed.

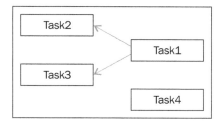

Figure 3.2

As shown in the preceding diagram, **Task1** depends on **Task2** and **Task3**. **Task4** is an independent task. If you execute `gradle Task1 Task4`, the execution flow will be **Task2, Task3, Task1**, and then **Task4**, as if a task depends on multiple tasks. Gradle executes the dependent tasks in alphabetical order.

Along with `dependsOn`, Gradle provides some additional categories of ordering. For example, after the execution of the last task, you might want to clean the temporary resources, which were created during the build process. To enable this type of ordering, Gradle provides the following options:

- `shouldRunAfter`
- `mustRunAfter`
- `finalizedBy` (more strict in nature)

Let's take a look at the following example. Create the `build_ordering.gradle` file:

```
(1..6).each {
  task "sampleTask$it" << {
        println "Executing $name"
    }
  }

sampleTask1.dependsOn sampleTask2
sampleTask3.dependsOn sampleTask2

sampleTask5.finalizedBy sampleTask6
sampleTask5.mustRunAfter sampleTask4
```

In the script, we have created six tasks named `sampleTask` with an integer suffix. Now, to understand task ordering, execute the preceding build script with different task names:

$ gradle -b build_ordering.gradle sampleTask1

This will execute `sampleTask2` and `sampleTask1`:

```
$ gradle -b build_ordering.gradle sampleTask1 sampleTask3
```

This will execute `sampleTask2`, `sampleTask1`, and `sampleTask3`. Task `sampleTask2` will execute only once:

```
$ gradle -b build_ordering.gradle sampleTask5
```

This will execute `sampleTask5` and `sampleTask6`.

Note that the `sampleTask5` task will not execute `sampleTask4`, since the `mustRunAfter` ordering will come into effect when both tasks (`sampleTask4` and `sampleTask5`) are part of the execution process. This is explained in the following command. Here, you have also seen the use of the `finalizedBy` operation. It provides the concluded by order, that is, `sampleTask5` should be immediately followed by `sampleTask6`:

```
$ gradle -b build_ordering.gradle sampleTask5 sampleTask4
```

This will execute `sampleTask4`, `sampleTask5`, and `sampleTask6` in sequence. This is because `sampleTask5` must run after `sampleTask4`, and `sampleTask5` should be concluded by `sampleTask6`.

The difference between `mustRunAfter` and `shouldRunAfter` is that `mustRunAfter` is strict ordering, whereas `shouldRunAfter` is lenient ordering. Consider the following code:

```
sampleTask1.dependsOn sampleTask2
sampleTask2.dependsOn sampleTask3
sampleTask3.mustRunAfter sampleTask1
```

In this case, for the first two statements, the execution order is `sampleTask3`, `sampleTask2`, and then `sampleTask1`. The next statement `sampleTask3.mustRunAfter sampleTask1`, which says `sampleTask3` must execute after `sampleTask1` introduces cyclic dependency. Thus, the execution of `sampleTask1` will fail:

```
$ gradle -b build_ordering.gradle sampleTask1
FAILURE: Build failed with an exception.

* What went wrong:
Circular dependency between the following tasks:
:sampleTask1
\--- :sampleTask2
```

```
        \--- :sampleTask3
              \--- :sampleTask1 (*)

(*) - details omitted (listed previously)
. . .
```

If you replace `mustRunAfter` with `shouldRunAfter`, then it will not throw any exception and will ignore strict ordering in this scenario.

Task operations

If you are tired of typing complete task names in the command-line; here is a good option for you. If you have defined task names in camel case (*camelCase*) format, you can just execute the task by mentioning the first letter of each word. For example, you can execute the `sampleTask1` task with shorthand `sT1`:

```
$ gradle -q -b build_ordering.gradle sT1 sT2
```

This will execute `sampleTask1` and `sampleTask2`.

If the shorthand of camel case matches more than one task, it will result in ambiguity:

```
  $ gradle -q -b build_ordering.gradle sT


FAILURE: Build failed with an exception.


* What went wrong:
Task 'sT' is ambiguous in root project 'Chapter3'. Candidates are:
'sampleTask1', 'sampleTask2', 'sampleTask3', 'sampleTask4',
'sampleTask5', 'sampleTask6'.


* Try:
Run gradle tasks to get a list of available tasks. Run with --
stacktrace option to get the stack trace. Run with --info or --debug
option to get more log output.
```

Now, we will explore some other task operations such as conditional execution, build optimization, and force execution.

Conditional execution

There are different scenarios when you want to execute some tasks based on certain properties. For example, you have a property named environment in the build file. If the value of the property is set to prod, you want to execute production specific tasks and if it is qa, you want to execute test-specific tasks. Create a build file build_condition.gradle with the following code snippet:

```
ext {
  environment='prod'
// can set this value from property file or command line using -
Pname=value option
}

task prodTask << {
  println 'Executing prod tasks '+ environment
}
prodTask.onlyIf {project.hasProperty('environment') &&
project.environment=='prod' }

task qaTask << {
  println 'Executing qa tasks '+ environment
}
qaTask.onlyIf { project.hasProperty('environment') &&
project.environment== 'qa '}
```

Execute the preceding build file with both the tasks:

```
$ gradle -b build_condition.gradle prodTask qaTask
:prodTask
Executing prod tasks prod
:qaTask SKIPPED

BUILD SUCCESSFUL
```

Here, Gradle skipped qaTask and executed only prodTask based on the environment property set in the build file. You can also remove the environment value in the preceding ext closure and directly set the property from the command-line option and try to execute the following commands:

```
$ gradle -b build_condition.gradle -Penvironment=qa qaTask prodTask
:qaTask
Executing qatasks qa
:prodTask SKIPPED

BUILD SUCCESSFUL
```

There might be another scenario when a task is outdated and you do not want to execute it, even if some other task depends on this task. This feature is supported by the `enabled` option in the task configuration phase:

```
task sampleTask12 << {
println " This task is disabled"
}
task sampleTask13 (dependsOn: sampleTask12) << {
println "This task depends on sampleTask12"
}
sampleTask12.enabled = false
```

$ gradle -b build_enabled.gradle sT12 sT13

:sampleTask12 SKIPPED

:sampleTask13

This task depends on task12

BUILD SUCCESSFUL

Note that you can set `enabled` in the configuration phase itself. It should not be part of the `doFirst` or `doLast` closure:

```
task sampleTask12 {
   //enabled = false     // valid statement
   doLast {
      enabled = false   // Invalid statement
      println 'Task execution'
   }
}
```

In the preceding example, if we try to set `enabled = false` in the `doLast` closure, the task will not execute. Build will fail with the `Cannot call Task. setEnabled(boolean) on task ':sampleTask12' after task has started execution` error.

Build optimization

Consider a scenario where your `build` file consists of 10 tasks, which execute as per the task dependencies order. Out of 10 tasks, five tasks are modifying five different files on the filesystem. Let's say these five files are some property files and these build tasks are setting some values to the property:

```
envproperty.txt
  env=prod
sysproperty.txt
  memory=1024
......
```

After first execution, the property files are modified with the respective values. When you run the `build` script again, although the files are already modified, the build script modifies those files again.

Gradle provides a mechanism of skipping the execution of these kinds of tasks based on the input and output parameters of the task, which is also known as **incremental build**. It helps in reducing the build time. You might have observed when you apply Java plugin and build your project couple of times, some tasks are marked with UP-TO-DATE keyword (execute without -q option). This means there is no change in the input and output compared to the last execution of these tasks and those tasks are ignored.

By default, Gradle provides this feature to its in-built tasks. You can also enhance your tasks with this capability, with the help of inputs and outputs of the task. Task inputs and outputs are of type `TaskInputs` and `TaskOuputs`. We will explain this behavior with help of one example:

Consider the `PropDetails.xml` file:

```xml
<properties>
  <property>
    <filedetail>
      <name>envproperty.txt</name>
      <key>env</key>
      <value>prod</value>
    </filedetail>
  </property>
  <property>
    <filedetail>
      <name>sysproperty.txt</name>
      <key>memory</key>
```

```
      <value>1024</value>
    </filedetail>
  </property>
</properties>
```

Consider the `build_optimization.gradle` file:

```
task updateExample {
ext {
propXml = file('PropDetails.xml')
}
File envFile = file('envproperty.txt')
File sysFile = file('sysproperty.txt')

inputs.file propXml
outputs.files (envFile, sysFile)

doLast {
println "Generating Properties files"
def properties = new XmlParser().parse(propXml)
properties.property.each { property ->
def fileName = property.filedetail[0].name[0].text()
def key = property.filedetail[0].key[0].text()
def value = property.filedetail[0].value[0].text()
def destFile = new File("${fileName}")
destFile.text = "$key = ${value}\n"
}
}
}
```

```
$ gradle -b build_optimization.gradle updateExample
```

If you run this task for the first time, it will read the `PropDetail.xml` file and will create two files `envproperty.txt` and `sysproperty.txt` with `key=value` pair mentioned in the `property` file. Now, if you run this command again, you will see the following output:

:updateExample UP-TO-DATE

BUILD SUCCESSFUL

This implies that there is no change in the input and output of this task; thus, there is no need to execute the task again.

Try to change either the XML file or the generated property files or delete the output files. If you run the `Gradle` command again, this time, the task will execute and it will recreate the files. Gradle internally generates snapshots of input parameters and output parameters (Gradle generates a hash code to avoid duplicates) and stores it. Next time onwards, Gradle generates the snapshots of input and output parameters, and if both are the same, it avoids the execution of tasks.

Also, an important point to remember, if no output is defined for tasks, then it will not be considered for optimization (UP-TO-DATE). The task will always execute. There can be a scenario where the output of a task is not a file or a directory, it could be some other logical build steps or system-related check. In this situation, you can use the `TaskOutputs.upToDateWhen()` method or the `outputs.upToDateWhen` closure to check the specific scenario and mark tasks UP-TO-DATE.

To skip the optimization technique and force full execution of the task, the `--rerun-tasks` command line option can be used. It will execute the task forcefully, even if it is UP-TO-DATE.

```
$ gradle -b build_optimization.gradle updateExample --rerun-tasks
```

The `--rerun-tasks` option will always execute the task without checking the input and output parameters.

Task rules

We discussed the `methodMissing` concept in Groovy. You can define some method patterns in Groovy, which can respond to method calls at runtime with the predefined patterns. Task rules provide the same flexibility with tasks. It allows executing a task, which does not exist. Gradle checks the task rule and creates the task if the rules have been defined. We will see the usage with the help of a simple example. For example, you have different assets, which are synced from different repository servers. Rather than creating different tasks for each sync, you can create the task rule as follows:

```
tasks.addRule("Pattern: sync<repoServer>") { String taskName ->
  if (taskName.startsWith("sync")) {
    task(taskName) << {
      println "Syncing from repository: " + (taskName -
'sync')
      }
    }
}
```

Here you can call different tasks for each repository servers as `gradle sync<repoServer>` and it will sync the assets from that repository.

A very common example of task rules can be found in the Java plugin. Add `apply plugin: 'java'` as the first line in the `build` file and run the following command:

```
$ gradle -b build_rule.gradle tasks
```

```
...............

Rules
-----

Pattern: clean<TaskName>: Cleans the output files of a task.
Pattern: build<ConfigurationName>: Assembles the artifacts of a
configuration.
Pattern: upload<ConfigurationName>: Assembles and uploads the artifacts
belonging to a configuration.
Pattern: sync<repoServer>


To see all tasks and more detail, run with --all.


BUILD SUCCESSFUL


Total time: 4.021 secs
```

As of now, do not worry much about the plugin. We will discuss plugins in detail in *Chapter 4, Plugin Management*.

In the above output, you can find the rules defined in the Java plugin. Gradle provides three in-built rules `clean<TaskName>`, `build<sConfigurationName>`, and `upload<ConfigurationName>` and the newly created `sync<repoServer>` rule. For all the tasks that are available in your `build` file (Java plugin tasks and user-defined tasks), you can execute one additional task using `clean<TaskName>`. For example, you have assemble, classes, and jar tasks available in the Java plugin. Apart from executing normal clean task, which deletes the build directory, you can also execute tasks such as `cleanClasses,` `cleanJar`, and so on, which cleans only the result of one particular task.

Gradle's in-built tasks

For day-to-day build-related activities, Gradle provides a variety of tasks. We will take a look at some of Gradle's in-built tasks.

The Copy Task

This task is used to copy file(s) or directories from one location to the other:

```
task copyTask(type: Copy) {
  from "."
  into "abc"
  include('employees.xml')
}
```

In copyTask, we have configured the from location and into location, and have also added the condition to include only employees.xml.

The Rename Task

This task is an extended version of the copy task, which is used to rename files or directories:

```
task copyWithRename(type: Copy) {
  from "."
  into "dir1"
  include('employees.xml')
  rename { String fileName ->
  fileName.replace("employees", "abc")
  }
}
```

In the copyWithRename task, an additional rename closure was added.

The Zip task

This task is used to zip a group of file(s) or directories and copy the zip to the destination directory:

```
task zipTask(type: Zip) {
  File destDir = file("dest")
  archiveName "sample.zip"
  from "src"
  destinationDir destDir
}
```

In the `ziptask` task, another `destinationDir` configuration was added. You can refer to the online documentation for more a detailed API for these tasks.

 Note that here we have not mentioned any actions for these tasks. Tasks themselves know what to do. We only need to configure the tasks to define them.

Most of the time, you use tasks that are part of plugins. Mostly, a plugin is a group of tasks bound together for some specific functionality. For example; we use the `java` plugin to build the Java project, the `war` plugin to create web archives, and so on. When you apply the `java` plugin to a build script, Java tasks are automatically included. We will discuss about plugins in detail in *Chapter 4, Plugin Management*.

To execute the Java tasks, we do not need to mention even the configurations. For these tasks, Gradle applies conventions, that is, the default configuration. If a project follows a certain convention, it can directly execute these tasks without any configurations. If not, it should define its own configurations. To add the `java` plugin to a `build` file, just add the following line of code:

```
apply plugin: 'java'
```

By default, the `java` plugin assumes that the project's source files are located at `src/main/java`. If the source files are present in this directory, you can execute the `gradle compileJava` or `gradle build` task without any configuration. We will discuss more on Java plugins and tasks in the next chapter.

Until now in this chapter, we have got some idea about how to create tasks and how to use Gradle's in-built tasks. In the next section, we will explore how to create custom tasks.

Custom tasks

Gradle supports a variety of tasks for build automation, either from Gradle's in-house plugins or from third-party plugins. As we know the software adage, change is the only constant thing in software; the requirements and complexity change over the time. Many a times we come across different automation requirements for which no task or plugin is available in Gradle. In such cases, you can extend Gradle by adding custom tasks to the build.

A custom task is an enhanced task, which you add to Gradle to fulfill custom requirements. It can have input, output, configurations and more. Its scope is not only limited to the build file where it is defined; it can be reused in other projects by adding custom task JAR in the classpath. You can write custom tasks in Groovy, Java, and Scala. In this section, we will create custom task examples in Groovy.

Gradle provides different ways to add custom tasks in the build script:

- The build file
- The buildSrc directory inside the project directory
- Create a standalone Groovy project

A custom task is a Java or Groovy class that extends from DefaultTask. We can use the @TaskAction annotation to define the task actions. You can add multiple actions in a single task. They will execute in the order they are defined. Let's start with a simple custom task in the build file.

Consider the file located at Chapter3/Customtask/build.gradle:

```
println "Working on custom task in build script"

class SampleTask extends DefaultTask {
  String systemName = "DefaultMachineName"
  String systemGroup = "DefaultSystemGroup"
  @TaskAction
  def action1() {
    println "System Name is "+systemName+" and group is
      "+systemGroup
  }
  @TaskAction
    def action2() {
      println 'Adding multiple actions for refactoring'
    }

}

task hello(type: SampleTask)

hello {
  systemName='MyDevelopmentMachine'
  systemGroup='Development'
}
hello.doFirst {println "Executing first statement "}
hello.doLast {println "Executing last statement "}
```

The output of the following file will be:

```
$ gradle -q hello
Executing first statement
System Name is MyDevelopmentMachine and group is Development
Adding multiple actions for refactoring
Executing last statement

BUILD SUCCESSFUL
```

In the preceding example, we have defined a custom task type, SampleTask. We have added two action methods action1() and action2(). You can add more actions as per the requirement. We have added two task variables systemName and systemGroup with some default values. We can reinitialize these variables in the project scope again while configuring the task (hello). Gradle also provides the flexibility to add more actions to a task with the help of the doFirst and doLast closures like any other task.

Once a task type is defined, you can create a task by using task <taskname>(type: <TaskType>).

You can configure the task in configuration closure either while declaring the task or as a separate closure, as mentioned in the preceding file.

Using buildSrc

If you want to keep the custom task code separate from the build file, but you do not want to create a separate project for it, you can achieve this by adding the custom task in the buildSrc directory.

Create a buildSrc directory in the project base directory and create the following mentioned folder hierarchy: buildSrc/src/main/groovy/ch3/SampleTask.groovy.

Move the preceding SampleTask class in the file. You also need to import two packages: org.gradle.api.DefaultTask and org.gradle.api.tasks.TaskAction. Now, the build file is left with the following code snippet:

```
task hello(type: com.test.SampleTask)
hello {
  systemName='MyDevelopmentMachine'
  systemGroup='Development'
}
hello.doFirst {println "Executing first statement "}
hello.doLast {println "Executing last statement "}
```

On executing the `hello` task, you will find the same output that was displayed earlier.

After execution, you will find the following folder structure in the project. Note that you do not need to compile the `SampleTask` class. All the required steps would be performed by Gradle. It will compile the classes, create JAR, and will automatically add the required class to the build class path. You can just define the task and execute it.

```
├── build.gradle
└── buildSrc
    ├── build
    │   ├── classes
    │   │   └── main
    │   │       └── ch3
    │   │           └── SampleTask.class
    │   ├── libs
    │   │   └── buildSrc.jar
    │   └── tmp
    │       ├── compileGroovy
    │       │   └── groovy-java-stubs
    │       └── jar
    │           └── MANIFEST.MF
    └── src
        └── main
            └── groovy
                └── ch3
                    └── SampleTask.groovy

14 directories, 5 files
```

Figure 3.3

The limitation is that the `SampleTask` task is only available in the current project and its subprojects only. You cannot use this task in other projects.

The standalone task

To overcome the limitations of the `buildSrc` way of creating custom tasks, you need to create an independent Groovy project. Move the `SampleTask` class in a new project (`SampleTaskProj`), and then compile and package the project. You can even use Gradle to build this Groovy project. Just add `build.gradle` with the following statements to the `SampleTaskProj` project:

```
apply plugin: 'groovy'
apply plugin: 'eclipse'
version=1.0 // to generate jar with version
dependencies {
compile gradleApi() // It creates dependency on the API of current
  Gradle version
compile localGroovy() // it will use the Groovy shipped with
  Gradle
// these dependencies comes along with groovy plugin
}
```

If you are creating the project in Eclipse, you can run the following command to generate the Eclipse classpath:

```
$ gradle clean cleanEclipse eclipse
```

Now, execute the `gradle build` command to build the project. A JAR file will be created in the build directory. To use the tasks, in the build file (think of it as a new `build.gradle` file in another project), we need to reference the JAR file path in the **repositories** closure.

Create a new project and update the `build.gradle` file with the following content:

```
buildscript {
repositories {
  // relative path of sampleTaskProject jar file
  flatDir {dirs "../SampleTaskProj/build/libs"}
}
dependencies {
classpath group: 'ch3', name: 'SampleTaskProj',version: '1.0'
}
}
task hello(type: ch3.SampleTask)

hello {
  systemName='MyDevelopmentMachine'
  systemGroup='Development'
}

hello.doFirst {println "Executing first statement "}
hello.doLast {println "Executing last statement "}
```

Execute the `hello` task again and you will find the same output:

```
$ gradle hello
:hello
Executing first statement
Adding multiple actions for refactoring
System Name is MyDevelopmentMachine and group is Development
Executing last statement

BUILD SUCCESSFUL
```

Summary

In this chapter, we have discussed Gradle task in detail. We learned how to create simple tasks in Gradle and add actions to it. Along with it, we looked into task dependencies. We also looked into strict ordering of tasks if needed, using `mustRunAfter` and `FinalyzedBy`. We also discussed incremental build feature in Gradle, which improves build execution time. One of the important extensions is the custom task. We also saw how to create custom tasks and reuse the same task across different projects.

As mentioned, a task could fulfill a simple build requirement. However, requirements keep growing and we need more number of tasks. It is also required to group certain related tasks to perform a specific behavior. This grouping of tasks is done in a plugin. A plugin is a group of different tasks bonded together. So, our next chapter is dedicated to plugin management. We will discuss how to bind tasks to a plugin and how to utilize plugins to enhance build capabilities.

4
Plugin Management

In the last chapter, we discussed Gradle task, which is the atomic unit of execution in Gradle. In most cases, a task provides only a single unit of work in modules. We can choose to bundle tasks together and execute them in a certain order to provide the complete functionality. This grouping of tasks along with properties and configuration is called a plugin. A plugin is the logical grouping of tasks, which may have a life cycle. You can configure plugins to alter the behavior based on the requirements. You can extend it to provide additional features. At a broader level, Gradle provides two types of plugins; script plugin and binary plugin. Gradle treats a build script as a script plugin and you can use other build scripts in a project by importing build scripts into the current project.

Binary plugins are plugins, that we create using programming languages such as Java or Groovy. Gradle provides in-built binary plugins for different build functionalities. There are different approaches to creating a binary plugin in Gradle, which we will discuss in the Custom Plugin section. First, we will explore the script plugin.

The script plugin

A script plugin is nothing but a Gradle file, which we import into other build files. It is the same as modularizing your code across different classes. When a build file size exceeds to a certain limit or diverse functionalities are clubbed to a single file, it might be a better option to divide the cohesive tasks into different build files. Then, you can import these files to the main build file to use the new functionalities.

To import the build file you can use the following code:

```
apply from: <Path of otherfile.gradle>
```

Here, the path could be a local file or a location relative to the project directory or a valid URL. However, if you mention the URL, the downside is that the file will be downloaded each time. Once the build file is imported, you can use the tasks defined in the build file without any additional configuration.

If you are adding multiple build files in the main build file, make sure you do not have tasks with the same name in the imported build files. During import, if Gradle finds two tasks with the same name, it will throw the following exception:

```
* What went wrong:
A problem occurred evaluating script.
> Cannot add task ':<TASK_NAME>' as a task with that name already
exists.
* Try:
Run with --stacktrace option to get the stack trace. Run with --info
or --debug option to get more log output.
```

Consider the following directory structure:

```
/Chapter4/scriptplugin.gradle

    task scriptPluginTask1 << {
      println "this is scplugin1"
    }
```

```
/Chapter4/build.gradle

    apply from: 'scriptplugin.gradle'

    task mainTask << {
      println "This is main task"
    }
```

Execute the following command:

```
$ gradle mainTask scriptPluginTask1
:mainTask
This is main task
:scriptPluginTask1
this is scplugin1

BUILD SUCCESSFUL
```

Here, we have defined the `scriptPluginTask1` in the `scriptplugin.gradle` file and have imported this build file in the main script `build.gradle`. Thus, importing the `scriptplugin.gradle` file into `build.gradle` will make `scriptPluginTask1` available in the main build file and you can call it directly without mentioning any build filename.

The binary plugin

Binary plugins are classes that implement the **Plugin** interface, which you can embed into the build script. Alternatively, you can create a separate project, package it into a jar file and add that jar file as a classpath entry to a project. The second approach makes it more reusable. Each binary plugin has one ID to uniquely identify it. To use a binary plugin, you need to include it using the `apply plugin` statement:

```
apply plugin: '<pluginid>'
```

For example, to use the Java plugin, you can write the following code:

```
apply plugin: 'java'
```

You can also use the class type to add plugins. For example, if you are creating a custom class, `DisplayPlugin`, as a plugin, you can apply the following code:

```
apply plugin: DisplayPlugin
```

Before using this approach make sure you import this class in the build file using the import statement. All the Gradle core plugins are available to you by default. You do not need any additional configuration to use them. For third-party or community plugins, you need to make sure they are available in the classpath before you use them. You can do this by adding the plugin in the classpath using the `buildscript{}` closure. When you apply any plugin to a build file, all the tasks that are part of the plugin are automatically added. You can directly use the task with the default configurations or you can customize the task configuration, if needed.

Gradle's in-built plugins

Gradle provides different in-built plugins to automate the build process. Gradle not only provides different plugins to build a project, but also provides plugins to test the project, for code analysis, for IDE support, for web container support, and so on.

The following are some of the frequently used plugins in different categories. You will find more details on core plugins in the Gradle documentation at `https://docs.gradle.org/current/userguide/userguide`.

Build and Test plugins

These plugins also support the testing features to execute Junit and TestNG tests:

- The Java plugin
- The Groovy plugin
- The Scala plugin
- The War plugin

Code analysis plugins

The following are the code analysis plugins:

- The Checkstyle plugin
- The FindBugs plugin
- The Sonar plugin
- The Sonar Runner plugin
- The PMD plugin

IDE plugins

The following are IDE plugins:

- The Eclipse plugin
- The IDEA plugin

These are some of the frequently used plugins. Apart from the core plugins, you can also find third-party plugins at https://plugins.gradle.org/. It allows the publication of binary plugins with the support of the Gradle Plugin Publishing plugin. Consider spending some time learning how to publish a plugin and how to use the Plugin Publishing plugin. In the following chapters, we will learn a few core plugins. In the next section, we will explore the Java plugin.

The Java plugin

In *Chapter 1, Getting Started with Gradle*, we already created a Java project called FirstGradleProject. However, the discussion was only limited to the Eclipse plugin tasks. We did not discuss anything about the Java plugin. The Java plugin is part of the Gradle core API, which enables us to build a Java project with supporting tasks such as compiling the Java code, testing the code, assembling binaries to create libraries, and more. It supports conventions over configuration. This means, if we use this plugin, some default configuration is already available to the developer, such as the location of the source code, the location of the compiled class file, and the jar naming convention. Unless we want to override these configurations, we do not need to write a lot of code to work with the default tasks and properties.

To apply the Java plugin, we add a single statement to the build file:

```
apply plugin: 'java'
```

Internally, the apply method of the Java plugin is invoked with the **project** object as the argument and the build script is enabled in order to use all the tasks and properties provided by the Java plugin. To understand the Java plugin, we will create a new Java application (project name Ch04-Java1) similar to the Java project FirstGradleProject, which we developed in *Chapter 1, Getting Started with Gradle*. We will add two new classes, Customer and Order; we will also add a new JUnit or TestNG library dependency to support unit testing functionality for the project.

With the help of this example, we will explore different Java plugin conventions. To be precise, we will try to understand how different tasks work and which default conventions are supported by the Java plugin. Then, in the next section, we will learn how to customize different properties, so that we can create our own configuration in the build file.

Conventions

To understand conventions, let us start with the Java plugin tasks. Once we have applied the Java plugin to display all the available tasks in the project (project name Ch04-Java1), we can use the tasks command:

```
$ gradle tasks --all

...


Build tasks
----------

assemble - Assembles the outputs of this project. [jar]
```

```
build - Assembles and tests this project. [assemble, check]
buildDependents - Assembles and tests this project and all projects
that depend on it. [build]
buildNeeded - Assembles and tests this project and all projects it
depends on. [build]
classes - Assembles classes 'main'.
   compileJava - Compiles Java source 'main:java'.
   processResources - Processes JVM resources 'main:resources'.
clean - Deletes the build directory.
jar - Assembles a jar archive containing the main classes. [classes]
testClasses - Assembles classes 'test'. [classes]
   compileTestJava - Compiles Java source 'test:java'.
   processTestResources - Processes JVM resources 'test:resources'.


...


Documentation tasks
-------------------
javadoc - Generates Javadoc API documentation for the main source
code.[classes]


...


Verification tasks
-----------------
check - Runs all checks.
test - Runs the unit tests.


Rules
-----
Pattern: clean<TaskName>: Cleans the output files of a task.
Pattern: build<ConfigurationName>: Assembles the artifacts of a
configuration.
Pattern: upload<ConfigurationName>: Assembles and uploads the
artifacts belonging to a configuration.


To see all tasks and more detail, run with --all.


BUILD SUCCESSFUL
```

The preceding output displays different build tasks, test tasks, documentation tasks, and other available tasks in the Java plugin. The output also shows the task dependencies between different tasks. For example, task classes internally depend on the compileJava and processResources tasks, which compile and process the source code and resources from src/main/java and src/main/resources, respectively. Similarly, the compileTestJava task and processTestResources task compile and process resources from src/test/java and src/test/resources, respectively. The output of all these tasks is compiled classes and resources, which will be created under the build directory by convention and will be added to the classspath during the execution of the program. Now, let us explore, with an example, what these tasks mean and which conventions are available by default.

To compile classes only under src/main, we should use the task classes. The compiled classes will be created under build/classes/ directory.

```
$ gradle classes
:compileJava
:processResources UP-TO-DATE
:classes


BUILD SUCCESSFUL
```

The testClasses task compiles and processes test classes and resources, and additionally, executes the classes task. In the following output, you can see that the compileJava, processResources, and classes tasks were executed again but the tasks were marked as UP-TO-DATE. This is because there was no change in the input and output of those tasks, as we have already executed the classes task in the last command. After successful execution, you will find a test directory created under the build/classes folder:

```
$ gradle testClasses
:compileJava UP-TO-DATE
:processResources UP-TO-DATE
:classes UP-TO-DATE
:compileTestJava
:processTestResources UP-TO-DATE
:testClasses


BUILD SUCCESSFUL
```

The other important task is the `test` task. This task helps to execute unit test code written under the `src/test` directory. After successful execution, you will find the test results created under the `build/test-results` directory:

```
$ gradle test
:compileJava UP-TO-DATE
:processResources UP-TO-DATE
:classes UP-TO-DATE
:compileTestJava UP-TO-DATE
:processTestResources UP-TO-DATE
:testClasses UP-TO-DATE
:test
```

BUILD SUCCESSFUL

You have the `assemble` task or the `jar` task to package classes and resources into a jar file. The `jar` task will only create jar files, whereas, the assemble task helps you to produce other artifacts, including jar. For example, when you apply the war plugin, the `jar` task is disabled and is replaced with the war task. By default, the JAR file is named `<project-name>.jar` and is created under `build/libs`. If you have not set the `<project-name>` in the build file, you will get the jar name `<project-folder-name>.jar`. This is not good practice if the jar file does not contain any version. You can add the version to the jar file by adding the version property to your project in the build file, which will generate `<name>-<version>.jar`. In our example, the project name is `Ch04-Java1` and the version property is set to `1.0` in the build file. Therefore, the jar file will be named `Ch04-Java1-1.0.jar`. Execute the following command and you will find the jar file under `build/libs`:

```
$ gradle assemble
:compileJava UP-TO-DATE
:processResources UP-TO-DATE
:classes UP-TO-DATE
:jar
:assemble
```

BUILD SUCCESSFUL

 No test classes will be packaged in the JAR file.

Another task is the `build` task, which executes the `check` and `assemble` tasks together. The `clean` task deletes all the artifacts created by another task. It actually deletes the complete `build/` folder. This means, the `clean` task deletes the output generated by all the tasks, that is, `check` and `assemble`. To delete a task-specific output, we can apply the `clean<TaskName>` rule. For example, to delete only the jar file created by the `build` task, we can execute the `gradle cleanJar` command.

All the tasks in the Java plugin execute based on conventions such as source directory location, build folder name, test result folder, and so on. To understand this in a better way, the following example shows some of the conventions supported by Gradle:

```
task displayJavaPluginConvention << {

    println "Lib Directory: $libsDir"
    println "Lib Directory Name: $libsDirName"
    println "Reports Directory: $reportsDir"
    println "Test Result Directory: $testResultsDir"

    println "Source Code in two sourcesets: $sourceSets"
    println "Production Code: ${sourceSets.main.java.srcDirs}"
    println "Test Code: ${sourceSets.test.java.srcDirs}"
println "Production code output: ${sourceSets.main.output.classesDir}
& ${sourceSets.main.output.resourcesDir}"
println "Test code output: ${sourceSets.test.output.classesDir} &
${sourceSets.test.output.resourcesDir}"
}
```

The output displays various conventions supported by the Java plugin. You can find the complete list in the official Gradle documentation at https://docs.gradle.org/current/userguide/java_plugin.html.

```
$ gradle displayJavaPluginConvention
:displayJavaPluginConvention
Lib Directory: <path>/build/libs
Lib Directory Name: libs
Reports Directory: <path>/build/reports
Test Result Directory: <path>/build/test-results
Source Code in two sourcesets: [source set 'main', source set 'test']
Production Code: [<path>/src/main/java]
Test Code: [<path>/src/test/java]
```

```
Production code output: <path>/build/classes/main &
<path>/build/resources/main
Test code output: <path>/build/classes/test &
<path>/build/resources/test
```

BUILD SUCCESSFUL

Sometimes, these default configurations might not suffice. We might need to configure some default properties to support our requirements. In the next section, we will explore how to configure some of the default configurations.

Configuration

In the previous example, we learned about the default properties or conventions available in the Java plugin. Now, we will configure some of these properties. This is important when we want to change the build directory name, the libs folder name, or the source file location of the project.

The source- related configuration changes can be set in the sourceSets closure. The upcoming code snippet (project name Ch04-Java2) shows that the source code location has been modified from src/main/java to src/productioncode for the source code location and src/test/java to src/testcode for the test code location, respectively. As a result, compiled classes will now be stored in classes/productioncode and classes/testcode locations for the source and test code, respectively. This will not replace the source directory from main to productioncode, but Gradle will now look for source code in both main and productioncode directories and for test code in both test and testcode directories. If you want Gradle to look for the source code only in the productioncode directory, you can set the java.srcDirs property.

These Java plugin conventions are written in the JavaPluginConvention and BasePluginConvention classes. One such property, testResultsDirName, can also be set in the build file:

```
buildDir = 'buildfolder'
libsDirName = 'libfolder'

sourceSets {
  main {
    java {
      srcDir 'src/productioncode/java'
    }
    resources {
      srcDir 'src/productioncode/resources'
    }
  }
```

```
test{

  java {
    srcDir 'src/testcode/java'
  }
  resources {
    srcDir 'src/testcode/resources'
  }
  }
}

testResultsDirName = "$buildDir/new-test-result"
sourceSets.main.output.classesDir
"${buildDir}/classes/productioncode/java"
sourceSets.main.output.resourcesDir
"${buildDir}/classes/productioncode/resources"
sourceSets.test.output.classesDir
"${buildDir}/classes/testcode/java"
sourceSets.test.output.resourcesDir
"${buildDir}/classes/testcode/resources"
```

These changes will make sure that `buildfolder`, `libfolder`, and `test-result` folders have been replaced with `buildfolder`, `libfolder`, and `new-test-result` folders.

Figure 4.1 shows the directory structure of the `src` folder and new the `buildfolder`:

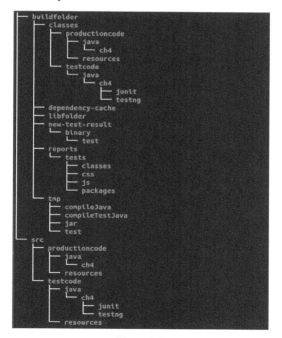

Figure 4.1

All these new changes can be verified by executing the previously created `displayJavaPluginConvention` task. After executing the task, you will find the output updated with new configurations:

```
$ gradle displayJavaPluginConvention
:displayJavaPluginConvention
Lib Directory: <path>/buildfolder/libfolder
Lib Directory Name: libfolder
Reports Directory: <path>/buildfolder/reports
Test Result Directory: %path%/buildfolder/new-test-result
Source Code in two sourcesets: [source set 'main', source set 'test']
Production Code: [<path>/src/main/java,
<path>/src/productioncode/java]
Test Code: [<path>/src/test/java, <path>/src/testcode/java]
Production code output:
<path>/buildfolder/classes/productioncode/java &
<path>/buildfolder/classes/productioncode/resources
Test code output: <path>/buildfolder/classes/testcode/java &
<path>/buildfolder/classes/testcode/resources


BUILD SUCCESSFUL
```

The custom plugin

In this section, we will discuss how to create a custom plugin. A plugin can be created by implementing the `org.gradle.api.Plugin<T>` interface. This interface has one method named `apply(T target)`, which must be implemented in the plugin class. Typically, we write a plugin for the Gradle projects. In that situation, T becomes the Project. However, T can be any type of object.

The class that implements the plugin interface can be placed in various locations, such as:

- The same build file
- The `buildSrc` directory
- A standalone project

This is similar to creating a custom task that we discussed in the last chapter. When we define a plugin in the same build file, the scope is limited to the defining project only. This means, this plugin cannot be reused in any other projects. This is not a good idea, if we want to distribute our plugin for other projects. For a multiproject Gradle build, the plugin code can be placed in the buildSrc folder of the root project or build file of the root project. All the subprojects will have access to this custom plugin. The most elegant way to create a plugin is to create a standalone Groovy project, create a jar file from it and share the plugin across projects and teams. Now, we will explore how to create a custom plugin with examples.

The build file

In the following example, we have added a FilePlugin class, which implements a Plugin interface in the build file. In the apply method, we have added two tasks, copy and move. These tasks are simple tasks, which print a line in the console. Now, we need to add this plugin to the build file if we want to execute the copy or move tasks. In this example, the plugin name is FilePlugin. We add this plugin using the apply plugin statement. Without adding the plugin, you will find Could not find property 'copy' on root project 'PROJECT_NAME'. if you try to execute the copy task:

```
apply plugin: FilePlugin

class FilePlugin implements Plugin<Project> {
  void apply(Project project) {
    project.task('copy') << {
      println "Task copy is running"
        //....
      }
    project.task('move') << {
      println "Task move is running"
      //...
    }
  }
}
copy.doLast { println "Copy Task ending .." }
```

On executing the copy task (for the Ch04_CustomPlugin1 project) from the command-line, we find the following two lines printed in the console as expected:

```
$ gradle copy
:copy
Task copy is running
Copy Task ending ..
BUILD SUCCESSFUL
```

The buildSrc directory

Similar to Task, to keep the plugin code separate from the build file, we can create a buildSrc folder inside the project root directory and any common code, task or plugin can be placed in this folder. In the following example, the Plugin is created in the buildSrc folder, which can be reused in the root build file and in all the subprojects. We have created a FilePlugin.groovy class under buildSrc/src/main/groovy. This class implements the plugin interface and adds two tasks: the copy task and the move task in the apply method. This FilePlugin.groovy class is similar to what we have done in the previous example. For this example, we will create a project Ch04_CustomPlugin2. Additionally, in the FilePlugin.groovy class, we need to add the package declaration and import statements (import org. gradle.api.*).

During build execution, this plugin class will be compiled automatically by Gradle and added to the classpath of the project. As the plugin definition is not in the build file, we need a mechanism to declare plugin information in the build file. This is done by importing the Plugin class and adding the plugin with the apply plugin statement. The following snippet shows the content of the main build file. In the file, additionally, we have added a doLast method in the copy task just for logging purposes:

```
import ch4.FilePlugin
apply plugin: FilePlugin

copy.doLast {
println "This is main project copy dolast"
}
```

Next, we create two subprojects: project1 and project2. Each project has a simple build file. This build file is similar to the main build file. The build file imports and applies the FilePlugin and adds a doLast method to the copy task for logging. The content of build.gradle of project1 is shown in the following code. The build file of project2 is also similar to this:

```
import ch4.FilePlugin
apply plugin: FilePlugin

copy.doLast {
  println "Additional doLast for project1"
}
```

We need another settings.gradle file, which includes the subprojects in the main project:

```
include 'project1', 'project2'
```

Do not get confused with the `settings.gradle` file. We will discuss multiproject builds in detail in *Chapter 6, Working with Gradle*.

For convenience, the directory structure of the `Ch04_CustomPlugin2` project is displayed in Figure 4.2:

Figure 4.2

When we execute the `copy` task, we find three copy tasks being executed: one from the main project and two other copy tasks from subprojects `project 1` and `project 2`.

```
$ gradle copy
:buildSrc:compileJava UP-TO-DATE
:buildSrc:compileGroovy
:buildSrc:processResources UP-TO-DATE
:buildSrc:classes
:buildSrc:jar
:buildSrc:assemble
:buildSrc:compileTestJava UP-TO-DATE
:buildSrc:compileTestGroovy UP-TO-DATE
:buildSrc:processTestResources UP-TO-DATE
:buildSrc:testClasses UP-TO-DATE
:buildSrc:test UP-TO-DATE
:buildSrc:check UP-TO-DATE
:buildSrc:build
:copy
Task copy is running
This is main project copy dolast
:project1:copy
```

```
Task copy is running

Additional doLast for project1

:project2:copy

Task copy is running

Additional doLast for project2


BUILD SUCCESSFUL
```

The Standalone project

In the last section, we placed the plugin code in the `buildSrc` directory and we used the plugin in the root build file and all the subprojects build files. It was just one step towards modularizing the plugin code from the build logic. However, this plugin is not reusable in other projects. Ideally, a plugin should be created in a standalone Groovy project. Then we create a JAR file and include that JAR file in the classpath of other build files. In this section, we will explore how to create a standalone plugin project.

We will start by creating a simple Groovy project. We will add a plugin class `FilePlugin.groovy` and two tasks `CopyTask` and `MoveTask` in the `src/main/groovy`. We will also add a properties file in the resource folder. The snapshot of the project (`Ch04_CustomPlugin3`) is displayed in Figure 4.3:

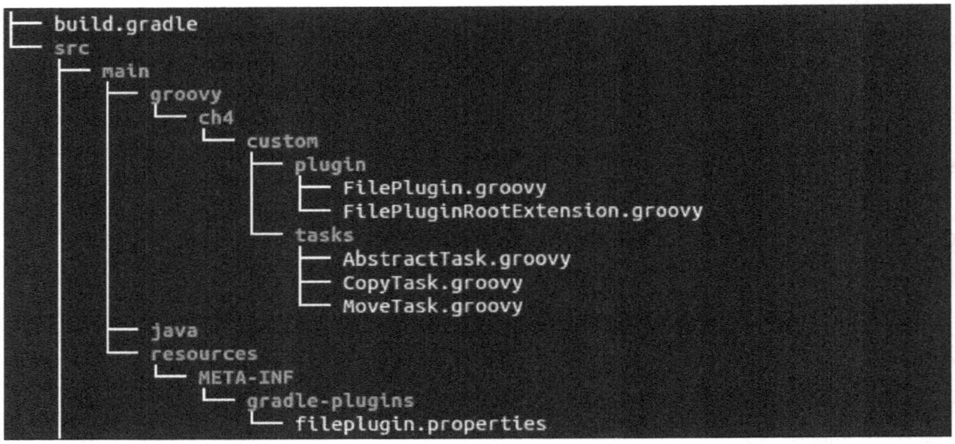

Figure 4.3

The `FilePlugin.groovy` class creates two tasks named `copy` and `move` by referring to the `CopyTask` and `MoveTask` classes. These tasks are created by calling the `create(...)` method on the `TaskContainer` object with the `taskname` and `task` classes as method parameters. Both tasks extend `DefaultTask` and define their own implementation. This is just an example of creating a custom task that we learned about in the last chapter. We have created one more additional task `customTask`, which will print the `sourceFile` property value. The `sourceFile` property is defined using the extension object. Plugin extensions are plain old Groovy objects used to add properties to plugins. You can provide properties/configuration information to `Plugins` using `extension` objects. You can create more than one extension object in the plugin to group the related properties together. Gradle adds a configuration closure block for each extension object.

The code snippet of the `FilePlugin.groovy` class is as follows:

```groovy
package ch4.custom.plugin

import org.gradle.api.Plugin
import org.gradle.api.Project
import org.slf4j.Logger
import org.slf4j.LoggerFactory
import ch4.custom.tasks.CopyTask
import ch4.custom.tasks.MoveTask

class FilePlugin implements Plugin<Project> {

  @Override
  public void apply(Project project) {

    def extension = project.extensions.create("simpleExt",
      FilePluginRootExtension)

    project.tasks.create("copy", CopyTask.class)
    project.tasks.create("move", MoveTask.class)
    project.task('customTask') << {
    println "Source file is "+project.filePluginExtension.sourceFile
    }
  }
}
```

The following is the source code for the `AbstractTask`, `CopyTask`, `MoveTask`, and `extension` classes.

File: `AbstractTask.groovy`

```
package ch4.custom.tasks

import org.gradle.api.DefaultTask
import org.gradle.api.tasks.TaskAction

class AbstractTask extends DefaultTask {

}
```

File: `CopyTask.groovy`

```
package ch4.custom.tasks

import org.gradle.api.tasks.TaskAction

class CopyTask extends AbstractTask {

  @TaskAction
  def action1() {
    println "Copy Task Running"
  }
}
```

File: `MoveTask.groovy`

```
package ch4.custom.tasks

import org.gradle.api.tasks.TaskAction

class MoveTask extends AbstractTask {

  @TaskAction
  def action1() {
    println "Move Task Running"
  }

}
```

File: `FilePluginRootExtension.groovy`

```
package ch4.custom.plugin

class FilePluginRootExtension {

  def sourceFile = "/home/tmp"
  def destinationFile

}
```

Now, we need a plugin ID so that Gradle can find this plugin information. This is done by creating a properties file under `src/main/resources/META-INF/gradle-plugins`. The name of the file becomes the plugin ID. In our example, we have named the file `fileplugin.properties`. So, the plugin ID is `fileplugin`. In any other build file, we can now apply the plugin as:

```
apply plugin: 'fileplugin'
```

In the `fileplugin.properties` file, we need to add the `implementation-class` property, which maps to the main plug in the implementing class:

```
implementation-class=ch4.custom.plugin.FilePlugin
```

That's all you need. Now, we can build this project to create a jar file and then we can use this jar in any other project. In our example, the jar file is named `Ch04_CustomPlugin3-1.0.jar`. If you wish to publish a plugin in `https://plugins.gradle.org/`, you need to make sure the plugin ID is unique. In such cases, you might want to rename `fileplugin.properties` to something like `mastering.gradle.ch4.properties` to ensure uniqueness of the plugin ID.

Once the jar file is created, the plugin can be used in any other build file. The code snippet shows how the `buildscript` closure can define a local directory as the repository. The plugin jar file can be included in the classpath by the dependencies closure. In the example, we are using the plugin from the local directory. Ideally, we should publish the plugin jar to a private or public repository and reference it via the Maven or Ivy URL:

```
buildscript {
  repositories {
    flatDir {dirs "../Ch04_CustomPlugin3/build/libs/"}
  }
dependencies {
  classpath group: 'ch4.custom.plugin', name:
    'Ch04_CustomPlugin3',version: '1.0'
}
```

```
  }
  apply plugin: 'fileplugin'

  copy.doLast {
    println "This is from project $project.name"
  }
```

We have added a dolast in the copy task, which prints the project name. Try to execute the following command:

```
$ gradle copy cT
:copy
Copy Task Running
This is from project UsingPlugin
:customTask
Source file is /home/tmp

BUILD SUCCESSFUL

Total time: 3.59 secs
```

From the output, you can understand that the copy task has two statements. One we mentioned in plugin definition and the other we added in the build.gradle file. The output of the customTask prints the default value of the source file, which is /home/tmp. This value was set in the FilePluginRootExtension.groovy class. If you want to update the property to some other value, add the following configuration closure in the build file:

```
  filePluginExtension {
    sourceFile = "/home/user1"
  }
```

After adding the preceding closure, try to execute the following command:

```
$ gradle cT
:customTask
Source file is /home/user1

BUILD SUCCESSFUL

Total time: 3.437 secs
```

Now, the output is changed to the new value mentioned in the filePluginExtension closure.

Summary

In this chapter, we have mainly discussed two topics: the Java plugin and the custom plugin. In the Java plugin, we learned about the default convention and properties supported by Gradle. Then we discussed how to customize and configure these properties. In the custom plugin, we showed different ways to create a plugin. However, there are so many plugins to discuss in Gradle. We will be discussing a few important plugins in *Chapter 6, Working with Gradle* and *Chapter 7, Continuous Integration*. However, we will not be able to cover all the plugins in this book. We request readers to refer to the Gradle documentation for more details.

In the next chapter, we will cover another important topic in Gradle, which is dependency management. We will learn about various repository configurations in the build file, different dependency resolution strategies, publishing artifacts in the repositories, and more.

5
Dependency Management

One of the most important features of any software is managing dependencies. As we know, no software works in isolation and we usually depend on third-party or open source libraries. The libraries are required during the compile and runtime execution and they have to be available in the classpath. Gradle has excellent support for dependency management. We just need to write few lines of code in the build file and Gradle internally does all the heavy lifting of managing configurations.

In this chapter, we will go into details of **dependency management** of Gradle. We will discuss the different features such as how to manage project dependencies, resolving conflicts, and resolution strategies. We will also discuss how to publish artifacts in different repositories.

Overview

Dependency management is one of the most the important features of any build tool. It helps to manage software dependencies in a better way. If you are using **Ant**, which initially did not support any dependency management, you need to write the name of each and every dependent jar file and its location to `build.xml`. For small applications that do not have many dependencies, this approach might work well. However, for enterprise applications, where software depends on hundreds of other libraries, which internally can depend on some other libraries (transitive dependencies), this approach of configuring each and every jar file in your `build.xml` could work but it requires huge effort to maintain it. Also, managing their version conflicts would be really a big pain for any developer and could turn the build process into a nightmare. To resolve these drawbacks in Ant, Maven came with an internal dependency management solution.

Later, Ant also integrated with Apache Ivy (a dependency management solution) to provide the same feature. Gradle came with its own dependency management implementation. It helps to define first-level dependencies, logically group them into different configurations, define multiple repositories and also provide tasks to publish assets after the execution of the build file. It also supports Ivy, Maven, and flat file repositories. In this chapter, along with dependency management, we will also look into repositories configurations and asset publications, that is, how to configure different repositories and upload assets to repositories.

Dependency configurations

Before starting with dependency configuration, let's discuss how to publish packaged software in Java. You package and publish either in `.jar` or `.war` or `.ear` file formats to a repository. The goal is to share these assets within the teams in an organization or with open source developers. Consider a scenario where you are publishing a utility project (`messageutil.jar`) to a repository. Although the publication process mostly depends on an organization's policy, the common practice is, all the assets that you plan to publish should be **versioned** and stored in a central repository, so that all other teams can share it. This versioning helps to track different versions of libraries. With versioned libraries, you can also revert to old versions in case of any functionality issues. Whenever you publish any asset to the repositories, always make sure it is versioned. To know more about versioning look at this link: `http://semver.org/`.

Dependency types

Other than internal or external JAR files, a project can also depend on:

- The files located on the filesystem
- Some other projects (in case of a multiproject build) in the same build
- The Gradle API (for custom tasks and plugins)
- The Groovy version used by Gradle (for custom tasks and plugins)

We saw an example of the Gradle API and the Groovy version used in the previous chapters when we developed custom tasks and plugins. Project dependency will be discussed in *Chapter 6, Working with Gradle*. In this chapter, we will discuss other module dependencies on global and local repositories, and file dependencies on the local system.

We will start dependency management with a simple example. Consider you are building a project, `SampleProject`, which depends on a third-party library `log4j-1.2.16.jar`.

To build the project, you need this jar file at compile time. Gradle provides a very easy and systematic way to define dependencies of the project using the **dependencies** closure in the following way:

```
dependencies {
  <configuration name> <dependencies>
}
```

Gradle groups dependencies to different configurations. If you apply **Java Plugin** to a project, it provides six different configurations, which are listed in the following table:

Names	Details
compile	The dependencies mentioned here are added to the classpath during compilation of the source code (src/main/java)
runtime	The dependencies mentioned here are required at runtime during execution of the source code (src/main/java)
testCompile	The dependencies mentioned here are added to the classpath during compilation of the test code (src/main/test)
testRuntime	The dependencies mentioned here are required at runtime during execution of the test code (src/main/test)
archives	This is used to tell the build file about the artifacts generated by the project
default	This contains the artifacts and dependencies used at runtime

To define the preceding dependencies, you need to pass the following details to Gradle's dependency manager:

- JAR file group (or namespace)
- JAR filename
- JAR file version
- classifier (in case JAR has classifier-like-specific JDK version)

The dependencies can be defined in one of the following ways:

- An individual dependency:
  ```
  compile group: 'log4j', name: 'log4j', version: '1.2.16'
  ```

- A Dependency as an Arraylist:
  ```
  compile 'log4j:log4j:1.2.16','junit:junit:4.10'
  ```

- A Dependency as a Configuration Closure:

```
compile ('log4j:log4j:1.2.16') ) {
    // extra configurations
}
```

- A Dependency as a Configuration Closure with key-value format:

```
compile (group:'log4j',name:'log4j',version:'1.2.16') {
    // extra configurations
}
```

> In case of a flat directory (local or remote filesystem), the dependency group name is not required.

To configure project dependencies, you need to mention all the libraries in the `dependencies` closure. So the build file will look like this:

```
apply plugin: 'java'
repositories {
  mavenCentral()
}
dependencies {
  compile group: 'log4j', name: 'log4j', version: '1.2.16'
}
```

Do not get confused with the `repositories` closure we have added in the example. We will discuss about this in the next section.

Repositories

The job is half done when we say dependencies are identified and defined. How Gradle will know where to get these dependencies from? Here comes the concept of `repositories`. Gradle provides the `repositories` closure to define repositories from where dependencies can be downloaded. You can configure any number of repositories and also any type of repositories in your project. For dependencies listed in the `dependencies` closure, Gradle searches repositories in sequential order. If it finds a library or a dependency in one of the repositories (if multiple repositories are configured), it skips searching other repositories. In the next section, we will learn how to configure different repositories.

Repositories configuration

You can use the following methods to configure repositories. Gradle allows you to use more than one configuration in a build file.

- **Maven Central repository**: This configuration is used to directly download your dependencies from the **Maven Central repository**. You do not need to remember the repository URL. You can directly add `mavenCentral()` to the `repositories` closure as mentioned here:

```
repositories {
  mavenCentral()
}
```

- **Maven JCenter repository**: Gradle also connects directly to the `jCenter` repository by using `jcenter()` inside the repositories.

```
repositories {
  jcenter()
}
```

- **Maven local Repository**: There might be a scenario where the local Maven cache contains all the required dependencies and you do not want to connect to the Maven central repository. Instead, you will need to use jars from Maven's local cache. In this scenario, you can use `mavenLocal()` in the `repositories` closure. By default, Maven's local cache path would be `<USER_HOME>/.m2/repository`. If you want to change it to another location, you can configure the path in `settings.xml` under `<USER_HOME>/.m2` or `<USER_HOME>/.m2/conf`. Having this configuration makes it easy to build a "SNAPSHOT" version of another project locally and include that version.

```
repositories {
  mavenLocal()
}
```

- **Ivy repository**: If you want to refer to the Ivy repository, you can define it as follows:

```
repositories {
  ivy {
    url "http://<ivyrepositorylocation>"
    layout "ivy"  // valid values are maven, gradle, ivy
  }
}
```

You can also define the custom layout for your Ivy repository. There is not an equivalent `ivyLocal()` because Ivy does not allow local publishing of artifacts such as Maven.

- **Organization repository**: No matter how many open source repositories are there, you will always need a private repository for software development as you are the owner of this repository and changes can be tracked and managed better by private repositories. To use your organization's private repository, you can configure the `Repositories` location in the following format:

```
repositories {
  maven {
    url "http://private.repository/path"
    credentials {
      username 'guest'
      password '123123'
    }
  }
  ivy { // For Ivy repositories
  url "http://private.repository/path"
  }
}
```

If your private repository needs authentication, you can provide the credentials as well. You can add the credentials to `~/.gradle/gradle.properties` as well and use it from there, because it is not a good practice to add credentials directly to the build file.

For Maven's format repositories, there is always metadata attached with the jar as `pom.xml`. There might be a scenario in which POM file and JAR file are located at two different locations. In such cases, you can mention both locations as follows:

```
repositories {
  maven {
    url "http://private.repository/pompath"
    artifactUrls "http://private.repository/jardir"
  }
}
```

 If the URL mentioned earlier contains the JAR file, Gradle will download the JAR file from that location; otherwise, it will search in `artifactUrls`. You can mention more than one `artifactUrls`.

- **Flat directory repository**: There might be a case when you refer a repository in the local filesystem (not the `mavenLocal()` location). This situation could arise when some other projects or teams are creating jars at a different location and publishing those jars to a central location. You want your project to refer to these local directories only for dependency. This can be achieved by using the following code:

```
repositories {
  flatDir {
  dirs '/localfile/dir1', '/localfile/dir2'
  }
}
```

This is not the recommended approach as this will result in inconsistencies. The recommended approach is to always use the private or global repository.

Dependency resolution

We have seen the standard way of defining dependency and repository, which can help you to quick start with the concepts. It's time for a deep dive, and understand how to customize the standard configuration, which can suit your specific requirements.

Transitive dependency

Suppose your application depends on `commons-httpclient-3.1.jar`, which is a first-level dependency. However, this JAR again depends on the following other JARs, `commons-codec-1.2.jar` and `commons-logging-1.0.4.jar`.And if we try to find more details, `commons-logging jar` again depends on some other JARs.

Here, `commons-httpclient-3.1` is a first-level dependency; the two previously mentioned JARs are second-level dependencies, and so on. However, with Gradle, you do not need to manage all these levels of dependencies. Imagine the complexity, if you have to figure out and mention each level of dependency in the build file. This can be very tedious and time consuming. And it becomes more painful if you encounter some version conflicts.

With Gradle, you do not need to bother about any such dependency-related issues. Gradle provides complete automation for the dependency management. You just define the first-level dependency and Gradle will take care of all the transitive dependencies. By default, it will download all the transitive dependencies until the last level.

Exclude transitiveness

For some scenarios, you might not want to depend on Gradle to fetch all transitive dependencies. Rather, you want to have complete control to download only the libraries that you have mentioned in the build file. To switch off a transitive feature, you can set the transitive flag off in the build file (build_transitive.gradle):

```
apply plugin:'java'
repositories {
  mavenCentral()
}
dependencies {
  compile group:'commons-httpclient', name:'commons-httpclient',
    version:'3.1', transitive: false
}
```

Clean the Gradle cache (~/.gradle/caches) and try to build the project again. This time it will download only one JAR that is commons-httpclient-3.1.jar:

$ gradle -b build_transitive.gradle build

….. .

:compileJava

Download https://repo1.maven.org/maven2/commons-httpclient/commons-httpclient/3.1/commons-httpclient-3.1.pom

Download https://repo1.maven.org/maven2/commons-httpclient/commons-httpclient/3.1/commons-httpclient-3.1.jar

:processResources UP-TO-DATE

…….

This feature could be useful if you need some other version of second-level dependencies, or the second-level dependency is missing in the repository and you want to manually copy that.

Selective exclude

There might be a scenario when you want to partially use transitive feature, that is, you do not want to stop Gradle from getting transitive dependencies, but you know it might result in a version conflict. So, you might want some specific jars to be excluded from the second or next-level of dependencies. To selectively exclude dependencies from the second-level onwards, you can use the following configuration:

```
dependencies{
  compile('commons-httpclient:commons-httpclient:3.1') {
```

```
    exclude group:'commons-codec' // exclude by group
    // exclude group:'commons-codec',module:'commons-codec'
  }
}
```

> The exclude criteria requires group as the mandatory field, but the module can be optional.

Version conflicts

Version conflict is a very common scenario in which the project depends on a specific JAR but of different versions. For example, your project depends on commons-httpclient-3.1 JAR and commons-codec-1.1 JAR. The commons-httpclient-3.1 JAR has a transitive dependency on the commons-codec-1.2 JAR. During the build process, Gradle will find the dependency on two different versions of the same JAR. Your build file (build_versionconflict.gradle) will look like this:

```
apply plugin:'java'

repositories {
  mavenCentral()
}
dependencies {
  compile group:'commons-httpclient', name:'commons-httpclient',
version:'3.1'
  compile group:'commons-codec',name:'commons-codec',
version:'1.1'
}
```

> Issues due to version conflicts take a considerable amount of time even to get noticed.

Gradle supports different strategies to resolve the version conflicts scenarios, they are as follows:

- **Latest version**: By default Gradle applies the **get latest** strategy to resolve version conflicts issues if it finds different versions of the same JAR file. In the preceding scenario, it will skip version 1.1 and download the commons-codec JAR of version 1.2.

After executing the `gradle -b build_versionconflict.gradle clean build` command, the output will be as follows:

```
Download https://repo1.maven.org/maven2/commons-codec/commons-codec/1.1/commons-codec-1.1.pom
```

```
Download https://repo1.maven.org/maven2/commons-codec/commons-codec/1.2/commons-codec-1.2.pom
```

......

```
Download https://repo1.maven.org/maven2/commons-codec/commons-codec/1.2/commons-codec-1.2.jar
```

```
:processResources UP-TO-DATE
```

......

```
BUILD SUCCESSFUL
```

- **fail on conflict**: The Get latest strategy might not work always. Sometimes, rather than getting the latest version, you might want the build to fail for further investigation. To enable this, you apply the `failOnVersionConflict()` configuration by adding the following closure:

```
configurations.all {
resolutionStrategy {
  failOnVersionConflict()
}
}
```

You can update your build file with the preceding configuration. If you want this strategy for all the builds, you can add this to your `init` script.

- **Force specific version**: In conflict situations, another alternative could be, rather than failing the build, you can download specific version of a JAR. This can be achieved by using **force flag**:

```
dependencies {
  compile group:'commons-httpclient', name:'commons-httpclient', version:'3.1'
  compile group:'commons-codec',name:'commons-codec', version:'1.1', force:true
}
```

Now, try to execute the `gradle -b build_versionconflict.gradle build` and observe the output:

```
Download https://repo1.maven.org/maven2/commons-codec/commons-codec/1.1/commons-codec-1.1.pom
```

```
Download https://repo1.maven.org/maven2/commons-codec/commons-
codec/1.1/commons-codec-1.1.jar

:processResources UP-TO-DATE

:classes

....

BUILD SUCCESSFUL
```

Dynamic dependency

To make the build flexible on the jar version, you can use the `latest.integration` placeholder, or you can define a version range such as `1.+`. With this option, you do not have to stick to a specific version. With the `1.+` or `2.+` format, it will fix the major version to 1 or 2 (it could be any number) and it will pick the latest of the minor version (for example, 1.9 or 2.9).

```
compile group:'commons-codec',name:'commons-codec', version: '1.+'
compile group:'commons-codec',name:'commons-codec', version:
'latest.integration'
```

You can use either one to get the latest dependency.

Customizing the dependency

Whenever Gradle searches for dependencies in the repository, first it searches for a module descriptor file (for example, `pom.xml` or `ivy.xml`). Gradle parses this file and downloads the actual JAR file and its dependencies mentioned in the module descriptor. There might be a case when a module descriptor file is not present. In this case, Gradle directly looks for the JAR file and downloads it.

Gradle enables you to play with your dependencies in different ways. Not only you can download other file formats such as ZIP and WAR, you can also mention different classifiers, if needed.

Download file other than JAR

By default, Gradle downloads file with the `.jar` extension. Sometimes, you might need to download either a ZIP file or a WAR file, which does not have any module descriptor. In this scenario, you can explicitly mention the extension of the file:

```
Dependencies {
    runtime group: 'org.mywar', name: 'sampleWeb', version: '1.0',
        ext: 'war'
}
```

Dependency on files with classifiers

Sometimes you release the artifacts with special notation (known as classifiers) such as `sampleWeb-1.0-dev.war` or `sampleWeb-1.0-qa.jar`. To download artifacts with classifiers, Gradle provides the `classifier` tag:

```
dependencies {
    runtime group: 'org.mywar', name: 'sampleWeb', version: '1.0',
        classifier: 'qa', ext:'war'
}
```

Replacing transitive dependencies

If you do not want to download the existing transitive dependencies and want to replace them with your customized transitive dependencies, Gradle provides the following way:

```
dependencies {
    compile module(group:'commons-httpclient', name:'commons-
        httpclient', version:'3.1') {
        dependencies "commons-codec:commons-codec:1.1@jar"
    }
}
```

Here we have used `@jar`, which can be used as a replacement for the `ext` tag that is used in the preceding example. This code snippet will not download the existing transitive dependencies of `commons-httpclient`, but it will download the JAR mentioned inside the curly braces.

Custom configuration for dependency

When we apply the Java plugin, Gradle automatically gives you some default configurations such as compile and runtime. We can extend this feature and use our own configuration for dependencies. This is an excellent way to group dependencies only needed at build time to achieve particular tasks such as code generators (depending on a templating library), xjc, cxf wsdl to Java, and so on. We can group them under our user-defined configurations. Before using custom configurations under the dependency closure, we need to define it inside the configuration closure. The following is the code snippet of the `build_customconf.gradle` file:

```
apply plugin: 'java'
version=1.0
configurations {
```

```
    customDep
  }
  repositories {
    mavenCentral()
  }
  dependencies {
    customDep group: 'junit', name: 'junit', version: '4.11'
    compile group: 'log4j', name: 'log4j', version: '1.2.16'
  }

  task showCustomDep << {
    FileTree deps  = project.configurations.customDep.asFileTree
    deps.each {File file ->
      println "File names are "+file.name
    }
  }
}
```

The following is the output of the preceding code:

```
$ gradle -b build_customconf.gradle showCustomDep
:showCustomDep
....
Download https://repo1.maven.org/maven2/junit/junit/4.11/junit-4.11.jar
Download https://repo1.maven.org/maven2/org/hamcrest/hamcrest-core/1.3/
hamcrest-core-1.3.jar
File names are junit-4.11.jar
File names are hamcrest-core-1.3.jar


BUILD SUCCESSFUL
```

Dependency reports

Gradle provides a very convenient way to list out all of the project dependencies from the first level to the *n*th level. It includes all your **transitive dependencies**, including manually changed, overridden, and forced dependencies. The dependency tree groups dependencies by configurations such as compile, testCompile, and so on. The following is the code snippet from the `build_depreport.gradle` file:

```
apply plugin: 'java'
version=1.0
repositories {
  mavenCentral()
}
```

```
    dependencies {
      compile group: 'log4j', name: 'log4j', version: '1.2.16'
      compile 'commons-httpclient:commons-httpclient:3.1'
      compile 'dom4j:dom4j:1.6.1'
    }
$ gradle -b build_depreport.gradle dependencies
...
Root project
....


+--- log4j:log4j:1.2.16
+--- commons-httpclient:commons-httpclient:3.1
|    +--- commons-logging:commons-logging:1.0.4
|    \--- commons-codec:commons-codec:1.2
\--- dom4j:dom4j:1.6.1
     \--- xml-apis:xml-apis:1.0.b2


default - Configuration for default artifacts.
+--- log4j:log4j:1.2.16
+--- commons-httpclient:commons-httpclient:3.1
|    +--- commons-logging:commons-logging:1.0.4
|    \--- commons-codec:commons-codec:1.2
\--- dom4j:dom4j:1.6.1
     \--- xml-apis:xml-apis:1.0.b2


runtime - Runtime classpath for source set 'main'.
+--- log4j:log4j:1.2.16
+--- commons-httpclient:commons-httpclient:3.1
|    +--- commons-logging:commons-logging:1.0.4
|    \--- commons-codec:commons-codec:1.2
\--- dom4j:dom4j:1.6.1
     \--- xml-apis:xml-apis:1.0.b2


testCompile - Compile classpath for source set 'test'.
+--- log4j:log4j:1.2.16
+--- commons-httpclient:commons-httpclient:3.1
```

```
|    +--- commons-logging:commons-logging:1.0.4
|    \--- commons-codec:commons-codec:1.2
\--- dom4j:dom4j:1.6.1
     \--- xml-apis:xml-apis:1.0.b2


testRuntime - Runtime classpath for source set 'test'.
+--- log4j:log4j:1.2.16
+--- commons-httpclient:commons-httpclient:3.1
|    +--- commons-logging:commons-logging:1.0.4
|    \--- commons-codec:commons-codec:1.2
\--- dom4j:dom4j:1.6.1
     \--- xml-apis:xml-apis:1.0.b2


BUILD SUCCESSFUL
```

It will show until the child level of all the dependencies for all configurations. You might be surprised to see why other configurations such as runtime and testRuntime are being displayed, though only compile configuration was defined. The following table shows the relationship between different configurations:

Dependency	Extends
compile	-
runtime	compile
testCompile	compile
testRuntime	runtime, testCompile
default	runtime

If you want to list out dependencies for only one configuration, you can mention that using –configuration <configuration name>:

```
$ gradle -b build_depreport.gradle dependencies –configuration compile
:dependencies


Root project


compile - Compile classpath for source set 'main'.
+--- log4j:log4j:1.2.16
+--- commons-httpclient:commons-httpclient:3.1
```

```
|     +--- commons-logging:commons-logging:1.0.4
|     \--- commons-codec:commons-codec:1.2
\--- dom4j:dom4j:1.6.1
     \--- xml-apis:xml-apis:1.0.b2
```

```
BUILD SUCCESSFUL
```

Dependency-specific details

Sometimes you might get issues while downloading some transitive dependencies and you do not know which dependency is downloading that JAR file.

Suppose while executing the preceding `build_depreport.gradle` script, you are getting issues while fetching the `commons-logging` JAR file. It is not the first-level dependency and you do not know which first-level dependency is responsible for this. To get that detail, use the `dependencyInsight` command:

```
$ gradle -b build_depreport.gradle dependencyInsight -dependency
commons-logging -configuration runtime
```

```
:dependencyInsight
```

```
commons-logging:commons-logging:1.0.4
\--- commons-httpclient:commons-httpclient:3.1
     \--- runtime
```

```
BUILD SUCCESSFUL
```

If you do not specify the `-configuration` option, it will apply the `compile` configuration by default. The other options are `runtime`, `testCompile`, and so on, as mentioned in the preceding example.

Publishing artifacts

Until now, we have discussed a lot about dependencies. How we can define project dependencies, customize them, and configure repositories to download libraries. Now, let's try to build the artifacts (JAR, WAR, and so on) and publish it to **Artifact repositories** (could be a local filesystem, remote location, or Maven repository) to make it available to all the other teams to share.

Default artifacts

When we apply the Java plugin, Gradle adds some default configuration to the project such as compile, runtime, testCompile. The Java plugin also adds one more configuration `archive`, which is used to define the artifacts of your project. Gradle provides the default artifact with some of the plugins. For example, Java, Groovy plugin publishes JAR as a default artifact, `war plugin` publish WAR as a default artifact. This JAR can be uploaded or published to a repository using the `uploadArchives` task.

The following code snippet shows how to configure the repository to upload archives using the `build_uploadarchives.gradle` file:

```
apply plugin: 'java'
version=1.0

repositories {
  mavenCentral()
}
dependencies {
  compile group: 'log4j', name: 'log4j', version: '1.2.16'
  compile 'commons-httpclient:commons-httpclient:3.1'
  compile 'dom4j:dom4j:1.6.1'
}
uploadArchives {
  repositories {
    maven {
      credentials {
        username "guest"
        password "guest"
      }
      url "http://private.maven.repo"
    }
    //flatDir {dirs "./temp1" }
  }
}
```

Instead of the Maven repository, we can also use the flat directory as a repository. In the preceding example, replace the Maven closure with flatDir (`flatDir {dirs "./temp1" }`) configuration. Now, if you execute the `gradle uploadArchives` command, you will find the JAR file published in the `temp1` directory.

Custom artifacts

For each configuration, Gradle provides `Upload<configuration name>`, by default, which assembles and uploads the artifacts in the specified configuration. The `UploadArchives` task provided by the Java plugin uploads the default artifact (`jar`) to the repository.

Sometimes, you might need to generate some additional artifacts with the JAR file such as the ZIP and XML files. This can be done by archive task to define an artifact.

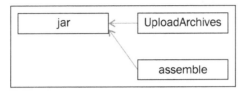

Figure 5.1

In the preceding figure, the **assemble** task depends on the **jar** task, which is nothing but the default artifact of your Java plugin project. You can configure additional artifacts using the `archives` configuration. The input to the archive configuration can be an artifact itself or a task which creates an artifact.

Let's take a look at the following two examples:

Generate additional XML file along with your JAR file

In this example, we will generate additional XML file with the JAR file and upload it to the repository. The following is the content of the `CustomArtifact/build.gradle` file:

```
apply plugin: 'java'
archivesBaseName="MySample" // to customize Jar Name
version=1.0
repositories {
  mavenCentral()
}
def confFile = file('configurations.xml') // artifact2
artifacts {
  archives confFile
}
uploadArchives {
```

```
repositories {
    flatDir {dirs "./tempRepo"}
}
}
```

Here, we have added `configurations.xml` as a separate XML file to the archive so that we can upload the file, along with the the the JAR file, to the repository.

After executing Gradle's `uploadArchives` command, you will find the following files in the `tempRepo` directory:

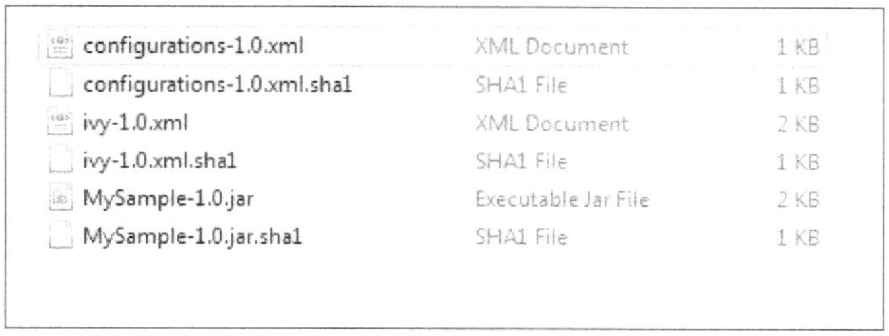

configurations-1.0.xml	XML Document	1 KB
configurations-1.0.xml.sha1	SHA1 File	1 KB
ivy-1.0.xml	XML Document	2 KB
ivy-1.0.xml.sha1	SHA1 File	1 KB
MySample-1.0.jar	Executable Jar File	2 KB
MySample-1.0.jar.sha1	SHA1 File	1 KB

Figure 5.2

Gradle also generates checksum and a deployment descriptor (here, `ivy-1.0.xml`) along with the artifact.

In the following section, we will learn how to upload a ZIP file as an artifact.

Generate an additional ZIP file along with your JAR file

If you want to upload an additional ZIP file along with the JAR file, then you can mention the additional archives in the `artifacts` closure. The following is the `CustomArtifact/build_zip.gradle` file:

```
apply plugin: 'java'
archivesBaseName="MySample" // to customize Jar Name
version=1.0
repositories {
  mavenCentral()
}
task zipSrc(type: Zip) {
  from 'src'
}
artifacts {
  archives zipSrc
}
```

```
uploadArchives {
  repositories {
    flatDir {dirs "./temp1" }
  }
}
```

After executing the `gradle -b build_zip.gradle uploadArchives` command, verify the files in the `temp1` directory:

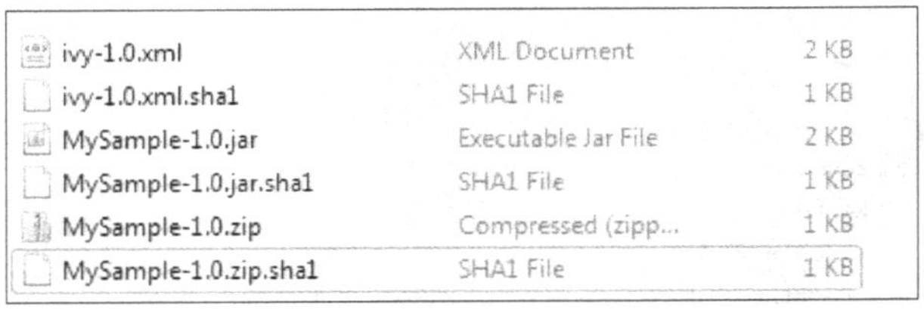

ivy-1.0.xml	XML Document	2 KB
ivy-1.0.xml.sha1	SHA1 File	1 KB
MySample-1.0.jar	Executable Jar File	2 KB
MySample-1.0.jar.sha1	SHA1 File	1 KB
MySample-1.0.zip	Compressed (zipp...	1 KB
MySample-1.0.zip.sha1	SHA1 File	1 KB

Figure 5.3

Here, an additional `MySample-1.0.zip` is generated with the JAR file. You may have noticed that we did not make any additional call to the `zipSrc` task, which is required to create the ZIP file. Gradle applies a declarative approach here. Whatever archives you have configured in the `artifacts` closure, Gradle will create those artifacts. Within this closure, you can assign different type of tasks, such as JAR, ZIP, TAR (`org.gradle.api.tasks.building.AbstractArchiveTask`), or any file to be archived.

Custom configuration

In the same way as custom dependency, you can also define custom configurations for your artifacts. Consider the following example (`CustomArtifacts/build_customconf.gradle`):

```
apply plugin: 'java'

archivesBaseName="MySampleZip" // to customize Jar Name
version=1.0
configurations {
  zipAsset
}
repositories {
  mavenCentral()
}
task zipSrc(type: Zip) {
  from 'src'
```

```
}
artifacts {
  zipAsset zipSrc
}
uploadZipAsset {
  repositories {
    flatDir {dirs "./temp1" }
  }
}
```

Now, execute the `gradle -b build_customconf.gradle uploadZipAsset` command to create and upload files to the repository. In the example, we have defined a custom configuration `zipAsset`. We used that configuration inside the artifacts closure. As mentioned in the preceding example, Gradle automatically provides the `upload<configname>` task for each configuration. Thus, we have the `cuploadZipAsset` task available to upload the required ZIP file to the repository.

The maven-publish plugins

In the previous section, we discussed the Maven plugin and other repositories configuration. Here, we will discuss the new plugin (`maven-publish plugin`) introduced by Gradle.

To have more control over the publication process, Gradle provides the `'maven-publish'` plugin. With the help of the following examples, you will see how it can help us in publication using the `MavenPublish/build.gradle` file:

You can configure publications by using following closure:

```
publishing {
  publications {
    customPublicationName(MavenPublication) {
      // Configure the publication here
    }
  }
}
```

The following is the file `MavenPublish/build.gradle`.

```
apply plugin: 'java'
apply plugin: 'maven-publish'

publishing {
  publications {
```

```
    mavenJava(MavenPublication) {
      from components.java
      groupId 'org.mygroup'
      artifactId 'MySampleProj'
      version '1.0'
    }
  }

}
```

This plugin adds the following tasks:

- publish: This publishes all the publications produced by this project
- publishToMavenLocal: This publishes all the Maven publications produced by this project to the local Maven cache

When you add the preceding mentioned publications closure inside publishing, it will add two additional tasks, generatePomFileFor<publicationName>Public ation and public<publicationName>PublicationToMavenLocal. You can find additional tasks in task list as follows:

- generatePomFileForPluginPublication: This generates the Maven POM file for publication 'plugin'
- publishPluginPublicationToMavenLocal: This publishes Maven publication 'plugin' to the local Maven repository

To publish the artifacts in the local Maven repository, execute the following command:

```
$ gradle -i publishToMavenLocal


:publishMavenJavaPublicationToMavenLocal
Executing task ': publishMavenJavaPublicationToMavenLocal'
(up-to-date check took 0.001 secs) due to:
  Task has not declared any outputs.
Publishing to repository
org.gradle.api.internal.artifacts.repositories.DefaultMavenLocal
ArtifactRepository_Decorated@4a454218
[INFO] Installing
/Chapter5/sent/MavenPublish/build/libs/MavenPublish.jar to
<%USER_HOME>/.m2/repository/org/mygroup/MySampleProj/1.0/
MySampleProj-1.0.jar
: publishMavenJavaPublicationToMavenLocal (Thread[main,5,main])
completed. Took 1.079 secs.


BUILD SUCCESSFUL
```

If you browse the local Maven repository, you will also find that the POM file has the following content:

```
<?xml version="1.0" encoding="UTF-8"?>
<project xsi:schemaLocation="http://maven.apache.org/POM/4.0.0
http://maven.apache.org/xsd/maven-4.0.0.xsd"
xmlns="http://maven.apache.org/POM/4.0.0"
xmlns:xsi="http://www.w3.org/2001/XMLSchema-instance">
  <modelVersion>4.0.0</modelVersion>
  <groupId>org.mygroup</groupId>
  <artifactId>MySampleProj</artifactId>
  <version>1.0</version>
</project>
```

By default, it produces the JAR file for the Java project. If you want to add additional artifact along with JAR, you can customize the preceding configuration by adding additional artifact declaration in the following format.

Here is the sample code for `MavenPublish/build_zip.gradle`:

```
apply plugin: 'java'
apply plugin: 'maven-publish'

task zipSrc(type: Zip) {
  baseName = 'SampleSource'
  from 'src'
}

publishing {
  publications {
    mavenJava(MavenPublication) {
      from components.java
      groupId 'org.mygroup'
      artifactId 'MySampleProj'
      version '1.0'

      artifact zipSrc {
        classifier "sources"
      }
      // artifact can be <Jar,Zip tasks which will generate
        jar,zip file>

    }
  }
}
```

```
$ gradle -b build_zip.gradle - i publishToMavenLocal

. . .

Publishing to repository
org.gradle.api.internal.artifacts.repositories.DefaultMavenLocalArtif
actRepository_Decorated@434d54de
[INFO] Installing
/Chapter5/MavenPublish/build/libs/MavenPublish.jar to
<USER_HOME>/.m2/repository/org/mygroup/MySampleProj/1.0/MySampleProj-
1.0.jar
[INFO] Installing
/Chapter5/MavenPublish/build/distributions/SampleSource-source-
.zip to <USER_HOME>
/.m2/repository/org/mygroup/MySampleProj/1.0/MySampleProj-1.0-source-
.zip
:publishPluginPublicationToMavenLocal (Thread[main,5,main])
completed. Took 0.85 secs.

. . .


BUILD SUCCESSFUL
```

Now, in the local repository, along with the JAR file, you will also find an additional ZIP file.

> Remember that for each additional artifact that you are publishing, you will need to mention a classifier. Gradle allows only one artifact without a classifier.

Publishing to the local-hosted repository

To publish artifacts to the local-hosted repository with help of the maven-publish plugin, we can use the same configuration, which we discussed in the Maven plugin. The repositories closure is exactly the same as before, but it has to be surrounded by a publishing closure. You can define the closure as follows:

```
Publishing {
  repositories {
    maven {
      name "localRepo"
      url "http://local.maven.repo"
      credentials { // if required
        username = 'username'
        password = 'password'
      }
```

```
      }
    }
  }
```

You can even publish to a local file repository by mentioning the URL `./localrepo`. Maven will automatically create a directory structure for you and you can find artifacts under `localrepo/<group>/<version>/artifact-<version>.jar`.

If you mention the name attribute in the `maven { .... }` closure, Gradle will automatically create a new task with the name `publishPluginPublicationTo<name>Repository`:

```
publishing {
  repositories {
    maven {
      name "localRepo"
      url "./localrepo"
    }
  }
}
```

Now, you will be able to use the `publishMavenJavaPublicationToLocalRepoRepository` task or simply the `publish` task to publish to the repository; such as `gradle -b build_localrepo.gradle publish`.

Custom POM

By default, Gradle generates the POM file for the artifact with default parameters. If you want to modify POM with additional details, you can utilize the `pom.withXml` closure. You can add any number of new nodes to the XML file and also update some of the existing details. Remember that `groupId`, `artifactId` and `version` are read only. You cannot modify these details. Consider the file `build_custompom.gradle`.

```
apply plugin: 'java'
apply plugin: 'maven-publish'
publishing {
  publications {
    mavenCustom(MavenPublication) {
      from components.java
      groupId 'org.mygroup'
      artifactId 'MySampleProj'
      version '1.0'
```

```
        pom.withXml {
          def root = asNode()
          root.appendNode('name', 'Sample Project')
          root.appendNode('description', 'Adding Additional details')
          def devs = root.appendNode('developers')
          def dev = devs.appendNode('developer')
          dev.appendNode('name', 'DeveloperName')
          }
        }
      }
    }
```

Now, execute the `publishToMavenLocal` task and you will find `pom.xml` generated in the repository.

Summary

This chapter covered details of dependency management provided by Gradle. We looked into dependency configuration, strategies involved in dependency resolution, and configuring transitive dependencies. We also learned different versions of conflict strategies provided by Gradle and how we can configure it to get the most out of it.

We also talked about repositories. We covered how you can use different repositories such as flat file, local **Maven Repository**, and remote repositories hosted on the HTTPS server. Finally, we discussed the publication of the project. With the help of different plugins, you can publish artifacts to a central location such as the local or remote **Maven Repository**. We also discussed how we can utilize the new maven-publish plugin and how to configure it, so that it fits into our own requirement.

In the next chapter, we will discuss few important plugins such as War and Scala. We'll also discuss other important concepts such as File management, Multi-Project, and Properties management.

6
Working with Gradle

This chapter covers some more plugins such as **War** and **Scala**, which will be helpful in building web applications and Scala applications. Additionally, we will discuss diverse topics such as **Property Management**, **Multi-Project build**, and **logging** aspects. In the *Multi-project build* section, we will discuss how Gradle supports multi-project build through the root project's build file. It also provides the flexibility of treating each module as a separate project, plus all the modules together like a single project. In the final section of this chapter, we will learn the automated testing aspects with Gradle. You will learn to execute unit tests with different configurations. In this section, we will learn about testing concepts with the examples of two commonly used testing frameworks, JUnit and TestNG.

The War plugin

The War plugin is used to build web projects, and like any other plugin, it can be added to the build file by adding the following line:

```
apply plugin: 'war'
```

War plugin extends the Java plugin and helps to create the war archives. The war plugin automatically applies the Java plugin to the build file. During the build process, the plugin creates a war file instead of a jar file. The war plugin disables the jar task of the Java plugin and adds a default war archive task. By default, the content of the war file will be compiled classes from src/main/java; content from src/main/webapp and all the runtime dependencies. The content can be customized using the war closure as well.

In our example, we have created a simple `servlet` file to display the current date and time, a `web.xml` file and a `build.gradle` file. The project structure is displayed in the following screenshot:

```
├── build.gradle
└── src
    └── main
        ├── java
        │   └── ch6
        │       └── DateTimeServlet.java
        └── webapp
            ├── META-INF
            │   └── MANIFEST.MF
            └── WEB-INF
                ├── lib
                └── web.xml

8 directories, 4 files
```

Figure 6.1

The `SimpleWebApp/build.gradle` file has the following content:

```
apply plugin: 'war'

repositories {
  mavenCentral()
}

dependencies {
  providedCompile "javax.servlet:servlet-api:2.5"
  compile("commons-io:commons-io:2.4")
  compile 'javax.inject:javax.inject:1'
}
```

The `war` plugin adds the `providedCompile` and `providedRuntime` dependency configurations on top of the Java plugin. The `providedCompile` and `providedRuntime` configurations have the same scope as `compile` and `runtime` respectively, but the only difference is that the libraries defined in these configurations will not be a part of the `war` archive. In our example, we have defined `servlet-api` as the `providedCompile` time dependency. So, this library is not included in the `WEB-INF/lib/` folder of the `war` file. This is because this library is provided by the servlet container such as Tomcat. So, when we deploy the application in a container, it is added by the container. You can confirm this by expanding the `war` file as follows:

```
SimpleWebApp$ jar -tvf build/libs/SimpleWebApp.war
    0 Mon Mar 16 17:56:04 IST 2015 META-INF/
   25 Mon Mar 16 17:56:04 IST 2015 META-INF/MANIFEST.MF
```

```
   0 Mon Mar 16 17:56:04 IST 2015 WEB-INF/

   0 Mon Mar 16 17:56:04 IST 2015 WEB-INF/classes/

   0 Mon Mar 16 17:56:04 IST 2015 WEB-INF/classes/ch6/

1148 Mon Mar 16 17:56:04 IST 2015 WEB-
INF/classes/ch6/DateTimeServlet.class

   0 Mon Mar 16 17:56:04 IST 2015 WEB-INF/lib/

185140 Mon Mar 16 12:32:50 IST 2015 WEB-INF/lib/commons-io-2.4.jar

 2497 Mon Mar 16 13:49:32 IST 2015 WEB-INF/lib/javax.inject-1.jar

 578 Mon Mar 16 16:45:16 IST 2015 WEB-INF/web.xml
```

Sometimes, we might need to customize the project's structure as well. For example, the webapp folder could be under the root project folder, not in the src folder. The webapp folder can also contain new folders such as conf and resource to store the properties files, Java scripts, images, and other assets. We might want to rename the webapp folder to WebContent. The proposed directory structure might look like this:

```
├── build.gradle
├── src
│   └── main
│       └── java
│           └── ch6
│               └── DateTimeServlet.java
├── WebContent
│   ├── conf
│   │   └── app.properties
│   ├── META-INF
│   │   └── MANIFEST.MF
│   ├── resources
│   │   ├── images
│   │   └── js
│   └── WEB-INF
│       ├── lib
│       └── web.xml
```

Figure 6.2

We might also be interested in creating a war file with a custom name and version. Additionally, we might not want to copy any empty folder such as images or js to the war file.

To implement these new changes, add the additional properties to the build.gradle file as described here. The webAppDirName property sets the new webapp folder location to the WebContent folder. The war closure defines properties such as version and name, and sets the includeEmptyDirs option as false. By default, includeEmptyDirs is set to true. This means any empty folder in the webapp directory will be copied to the war file. By setting it to false, the empty folders such as images and js will not be copied to the war file.

The following would be the contents of `CustomWebApp/build.gradle`:

```
apply plugin: 'war'

repositories {
  mavenCentral()
}
dependencies {
  providedCompile "javax.servlet:servlet-api:2.5"
  compile("commons-io:commons-io:2.4")
  compile 'javax.inject:javax.inject:1'
}
webAppDirName="WebContent"

war{
  baseName = "simpleapp"
  version = "1.0"
  extension = "war"
  includeEmptyDirs = false
}
```

After the build is successful, the war file will be created as `simpleapp-1.0.war`. Execute the `jar -tvf build/libs/simpleapp-1.0.war` command and verify the content of the war file. You will find the `conf` folder is added to the war file, whereas `images` and `js` folders are not included.

You might also find the Jetty plugin interesting for web application deployment, which enables you to deploy the web application in an embedded container. This plugin automatically applies the War plugin to the project. The Jetty plugin defines three tasks; `jettyRun`, `jettyRunWar`, and `jettyStop`. Task `jettyRun` runs the web application in an embedded Jetty web container, whereas the `jettyRunWar` task helps to build the war file and then run it in the embedded web container. Task `jettyStop` stops the container instance. Covering more on war configuration is beyond the scope of the book, so for more information please refer to the Gradle API documentation. Here is the link: `https://docs.gradle.org/current/userguide/war_plugin.html`.

The Scala plugin

The **Scala** plugin helps you to build the Scala application. Like any other plugin, the Scala plugin can be applied to the build file by adding the following line:

```
apply plugin: 'scala'
```

The Scala plugin also extends the Java plugin and adds a few more tasks such as compileScala, compileTestScala, and scaladoc to work with Scala files. The task names are pretty much all named after their Java equivalent, simply replacing the java part with scala. The Scala project's directory structure is also similar to a Java project structure where production code is typically written under src/main/scala directory and test code is kept under the src/test/scala directory. Figure 6.3 shows the directory structure of a Scala project. You can also observe from the directory structure that a Scala project can contain a mix of Java and Scala source files. The HelloScala.scala file has the following content. The output is Hello, Scala... on the console. This is a very basic code and we will not be able to discuss much detail on the Scala programming language. We request readers to refer to the Scala language documentation available at http://www.scala-lang.org/.

```
package ch6

object HelloScala {
    def main(args: Array[String]) {
        println("Hello, Scala...")
    }
}
```

To support the compilation of Scala source code, Scala libraries should be added in the dependency configuration:

```
dependencies {
    compile('org.scala-lang:scala-library:2.11.6')
}
```

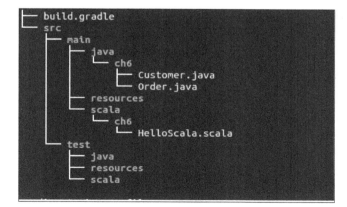

Figure 6.3

As mentioned, the Scala plugin extends the Java plugin and adds a few new tasks. For example, the `compileScala` task depends on the `compileJava` task and the `compileTestScala` task depends on the `compileTestJava` task. This can be understood easily, by executing `classes` and `testClasses` tasks and looking at the output.

`$ gradle classes`
`:compileJava`
`:compileScala`
`:processResources UP-TO-DATE`
`:classes`
 	
`BUILD SUCCESSFUL`
	`$ gradle testClasses`
	`:compileJava UP-TO-DATE`
	`:compileScala UP-TO-DATE`
	`:processResources UP-TO-DATE`
	`:classes UP-TO-DATE`
	`:compileTestJava UP-TO-DATE`
	`:compileTestScala UP-TO-DATE`
	`:processTestResources UP-TO-DATE`
	`:testClasses UP-TO-DATE`
	
	`BUILD SUCCESSFUL`

Scala projects are also packaged as `jar` files. The `jar` task or `assemble` task creates a `jar` file in the `build/libs` directory.

```
$ jar -tvf build/libs/ScalaApplication-1.0.jar
0 Thu Mar 26 23:49:04 IST 2015 META-INF/
94 Thu Mar 26 23:49:04 IST 2015 META-INF/MANIFEST.MF
0 Thu Mar 26 23:49:04 IST 2015 ch6/
1194 Thu Mar 26 23:48:58 IST 2015 ch6/Customer.class
609 Thu Mar 26 23:49:04 IST 2015 ch6/HelloScala$.class
594 Thu Mar 26 23:49:04 IST 2015 ch6/HelloScala.class
1375 Thu Mar 26 23:48:58 IST 2015 ch6/Order.class
```

The Scala plugin does not add any extra convention to the Java plugin. Therefore, the conventions defined in the Java plugin, such as lib directory and report directory can be reused in the Scala plugin. The Scala plugin only adds few `sourceSet` properties such as `allScala`, `scala.srcDirs`, and `scala` to work with source set. The following task example displays different properties available to the Scala plugin. This example is similar to the convention example task that we created in *Chapter 4, Plugin Management*.

The following is a code snippet from `ScalaApplication/build.gradle`:

```
apply plugin: 'java'
apply plugin: 'scala'
apply plugin: 'eclipse'

version = '1.0'

jar {
  manifest {
  attributes 'Implementation-Title': 'ScalaApplication',
    'Implementation-Version': version
  }
}

repositories {
  mavenCentral()
}

dependencies {
  compile('org.scala-lang:scala-library:2.11.6')
  runtime('org.scala-lang:scala-compiler:2.11.6')
  compile('org.scala-lang:jline:2.9.0-1')
}

task displayScalaPluginConvention << {
  println "Lib Directory: $libsDir"
  println "Lib Directory Name: $libsDirName"
  println "Reports Directory: $reportsDir"
  println "Test Result Directory: $testResultsDir"

  println "Source Code in two sourcesets: $sourceSets"
  println "Production Code: ${sourceSets.main.java.srcDirs},
    ${sourceSets.main.scala.srcDirs}"
  println "Test Code: ${sourceSets.test.java.srcDirs},
    ${sourceSets.test.scala.srcDirs}"
  println "Production code output:
    ${sourceSets.main.output.classesDir} &
      ${sourceSets.main.output.resourcesDir}"
  println "Test code output: ${sourceSets.test.output.classesDir}
    & ${sourceSets.test.output.resourcesDir}"
}
```

The output of the task `displayScalaPluginConvention` is shown in the following code:

```
$ gradle displayScalaPluginConvention

...

:displayScalaPluginConvention
Lib Directory: <path>/ build/libs
Lib Directory Name: libs
Reports Directory: <path>/build/reports
Test Result Directory: <path>/build/test-results
Source Code in two sourcesets: [source set 'main', source set 'test']
Production Code: [<path>/src/main/java], [<path>/src/main/scala]
Test Code: [<path>/src/test/java], [<path>/src/test/scala]
Production code output: <path>/build/classes/main & <path>/build/
resources/main
Test code output: <path>/build/classes/test & <path>/build/resources/test


BUILD SUCCESSFUL
```

Finally, we will conclude this section by discussing how to execute Scala application from Gradle; we can create a simple task in the build file as follows.

```
task runMain(type: JavaExec){
  main = 'ch6.HelloScala'
  classpath = configurations.runtime + sourceSets.main.output +
    sourceSets.test.output
}
```

The `HelloScala` source file has a main method which prints `Hello, Scala...` in the console. The `runMain` task executes the main method and displays the output in the console:

```
$ gradle runMain

....

:runMain
Hello, Scala...


BUILD SUCCESSFUL
```

Logging

Until now we have used `println` everywhere in the build script to display the messages to the user. If you are coming from a Java background you know a `println` statement is not the right way to give information to the user. You need logging. Logging helps the user to classify the categories of messages to show at different levels. These different levels help users to print a correct message based on the situation. For example, when a user wants complete detailed tracking of your software, they can use debug level. Similarly, whenever a user wants very limited useful information while executing a task, they can use quiet or info level. Gradle provides the following different types of logging:

Log Level	Description
ERROR	This is used to show error messages
QUIET	This is used to show limited useful information
WARNING	This is used to show warning messages
LIFECYCLE	This is used to show the progress (default level)
INFO	This is used to show information messages
DEBUG	This is used to show debug messages (all logs)

By default, the Gradle log level is LIFECYCLE. The following is the code snippet from `LogExample/build.gradle`:

```
task showLogging << {
  println "This is println example"
  logger.error "This is error message"
  logger.quiet "This is quiet message"
  logger.warn "This is WARNING message"
  logger.lifecycle "This is LIFECYCLE message"
  logger.info "This is INFO message"
  logger.debug "This is DEBUG message"
}
```

Now, execute the following command:

```
$ gradle showLogging
```

```
:showLogging
This is println example
This is error message
This is quiet message
```

```
This is WARNING message
```

```
This is LIFECYCLE message
```

```
BUILD SUCCESSFUL
```

Here, Gradle has printed all the logger statements upto the lifecycle level (including lifecycle), which is Gradle's default log level. You can also control the log level from the command line.

-q	This will show logs up to the quiet level. It will include error and quiet messages
-i	This will show logs up to the info level. It will include error, quiet, warning, lifecycle and info messages.
-s	This prints out the stacktrace for all exceptions.
-d	This prints out all logs and debug information. This is most expressive log level, which will also print all the minor details.

Now, execute gradle showLogging -q:

```
This is println example
```

```
This is error message
```

```
This is quiet message
```

Apart from the regular lifecycle, Gradle provides an additional option to provide stack trace in case of any exception. Stack trace is different from debug. In case of any failure, it allows tracking of all the nested functions, which are called in sequence up to the point where the stack trace is generated.

To verify, add the assert statement in the preceding task and execute the following:

```
task showLogging << {
println "This is println example"
..
assert 1==2
}
```

```
$ gradle showLogging -s
```

```
......
```

```
* Exception is:
```

```
org.gradle.api.tasks.TaskExecutionException: Execution failed for
task ':showLogging'.
```

```
at org.gradle.api.internal.tasks.execution.ExecuteActionsTaskExecuter.
executeActions(ExecuteActionsTaskExecuter.java:69)
        at
....
org.gradle.api.internal.tasks.execution.SkipOnlyIfTaskExecuter.
execute(SkipOnlyIfTaskExecuter.java:53)
        at org.gradle.api.internal.tasks.execution.
ExecuteAtMostOnceTaskExecuter
.execute(ExecuteAtMostOnceTaskExecuter.java:43)
        at org.gradle.api.internal.AbstractTask.executeWithoutThrowingTask
Failure(AbstractTask.java:305)
...
```

With `stracktrace`, Gradle also provides two options:

- `-s` or `--stracktrace`: This will print truncated stracktrace
- `-S` or `--full-stracktrace`: This will print full stracktrace

File management

One of the key features of any build tool is I/O operations and how easily you can perform the I/O operations such as reading files, writing files, and directory-related operations. Developers with Ant or Maven backgrounds know how painful and complex it was to handle the files and directory operations in old build tools; sometimes you had to write custom tasks and plugins to perform these kinds of operations due to XML limitations in Ant and Maven. Since Gradle uses Groovy, it will make your life much easier while dealing with files and directory-related operations.

Reading files

Gradle provides simple ways to read the file. You just need to use the File API (application programing interface) and it provides everything to deal with the file. The following is the code snippet from `FileExample/build.gradle`:

```
task showFile << {
  File file1 = file("readme.txt")
  println file1    // will print name of the file
  file1.eachLine {
    println it  // will print contents line by line
  }
}
```

To read the file, we have used file(<file Name>). This is the default Gradle way to reference files because Gradle adds some path behavior ($PROJECT_PATH/<filename>) due to absolute and relative referencing of files. Here, the first println statement will print the name of the file which is readme.txt. To read a file, Groovy provides the eachLine method to the File API, which reads all the lines of the file one by one.

To access the directory, you can use the following file API:

```
def dir1 = new File("src")
println "Checking directory "+dir1.isFile() // will return false
  for directory
println "Checking directory "+dir1.isDirectory() // will return
true for directory
```

Writing files

To write to the files, you can use either the append method to add contents to the end of the file or overwrite the file using the setText or write methods:

```
task fileWrite << {
  File file1 = file ("readme.txt")

  // will append data at the end
  file1.append("\nAdding new line. \n")

  // will overwrite contents
  file1.setText("Overwriting existing contents")

  // will overwrite contents
  file1.write("Using write method")
}
```

Creating files/directories

You can create a new file by just writing some text to it:

```
task createFile << {
  File file1 = new File("newFile.txt")
  file1.write("Using write method")
}
```

By writing some data to the file, Groovy will automatically create the file if it does not exist.

To write content to file you can also use the leftshift operator (<<), it will append data at the end of the file:

```
file1 << "New content"
```

If you want to create an empty file, you can create a new file using the createNewFile() method.

```
task createNewFile << {
  File file1 = new File("createNewFileMethod.txt")
  file1.createNewFile()
}
```

A new directory can be created using the mkdir command. Gradle also allows you to create nested directories in a single command using mkdirs:

```
task createDir << {
  def dir1 = new File("folder1")
  dir1.mkdir()

  def dir2 = new File("folder2")
  dir2.createTempDir()

  def dir3 = new File("folder3/subfolder31")
  dir3.mkdirs() // to create sub directories in one command
}
```

In the preceding example, we are creating two directories, one using mkdir() and the other using createTempDir(). The difference is when we create a directory using createTempDir(), that directory gets automatically deleted once your build script execution is completed.

File operations

We will see examples of some of the frequently used methods while dealing with files, which will help you in build automation:

```
task fileOperations << {
  File file1 = new File("readme.txt")
  println "File size is "+file1.size()
  println "Checking existence "+file1.exists()
  println "Reading contents "+file1.getText()
  println "Checking directory "+file1.isDirectory()
  println "File length "+file1.length()
  println "Hidden file "+file1.isHidden()
```

```
    // File paths
    println "File path is "+file1.path
    println "File absolute path is "+file1.absolutePath
    println "File canonical path is "+file1.canonicalPath

    // Rename file
    file1.renameTo("writeme.txt")

    // File Permissions
    file1.setReadOnly()
    println "Checking read permission "+ file1.canRead()+" write
    permission "+file1.canWrite()
    file1.setWritable(true)
    println "Checking read permission "+ file1.canRead()+" write
    permission "+file1.canWrite()

}
```

Most of the preceding methods are self-explanatory. Try to execute the preceding task and observe the output. If you try to execute the `fileOperations` task twice, you will get the exception `readme.txt` `(No such file or directory)` since you have renamed the file to `writeme.txt`.

Filter files

Certain file methods allow users to pass a regular expression as an argument. Regular expressions can be used to filter out only the required data, rather than fetch all the data. The following is an example of the `eachFileMatch()` method, which will list only the Groovy files in a directory:

```
task filterFiles << {
  def dir1 = new File("dir1")
  dir1.eachFileMatch(~/.*.groovy/) {
    println it
  }
  dir1.eachFileRecurse { dir ->
    if(dir.isDirectory()) {
      dir.eachFileMatch(~/.*.groovy/) {
        println it
      }
    }
  }
}
```

The output is as follows:

```
$ gradle filterFiles


:filterFiles
dir1\groovySample.groovy
dir1\subdir1\groovySample1.groovy
dir1\subdir2\groovySample2.groovy
dir1\subdir2\subDir3\groovySample3.groovy


BUILD SUCCESSFUL
```

Delete files and directories

Gradle provides the `delete()` and `deleteDir()` APIs to delete files and directories respectively:

```
task deleteFile << {
  def dir2 = new File("dir2")
  def file1 = new File("abc.txt")
  file1.createNewFile()
  dir2.mkdir()
  println "File path is "+file1.absolutePath
  println "Dir path is "+dir2.absolutePath
  file1.delete()
  dir2.deleteDir()
  println "Checking file(abc.txt) existence: "+file1.exists()+"
and Directory(dir2) existence: "+dir2.exists()
}
```

The output is as follows:

```
$ gradle deleteFile
:deleteFile
File path is Chapter6/FileExample/abc.txt
Dir path is Chapter6/FileExample/dir2
Checking file(abc.txt) existence:  false and Directory(dir2) existence:
false


BUILD SUCCESSFUL
```

The preceding task will create a directory `dir2` and a file `abc.txt`. Then it will print the absolute paths and finally delete them. You can verify whether it is deleted properly by calling the `exists()` function.

FileTree

Until now, we have dealt with single file operations. Gradle provides plenty of user-friendly APIs to deal with file collections. One such API is **FileTree**. A FileTree represents a hierarchy of files or directories. It extends the `FileCollection` interface. Several objects in Gradle such as `sourceSets`, implement the `FileTree` interface. You can initialize FileTree with the `fileTree()` method. The following are the different ways you can initialize the `fileTree` method:

```
task fileTreeSample << {
  FileTree fTree = fileTree('dir1')
  fTree.each {
    println it.name
  }
  FileTree fTree1 = fileTree('dir1') {
    include '**/*.groovy'
  }
  println ""
  fTree1.each {
    println it.name
  }
  println ""
FileTree fTree2 = fileTree(dir:'dir1',excludes:['**/*.groovy'])
  fTree2.each {
    println it.absolutePath
  }
}
```

Execute the `gradle fileTreeSample` command and observe the output. The first iteration will print all the files in `dir1`. The second iteration will only include Groovy files (with extension `.groovy`). The third iteration will exclude Groovy files (with extension `.groovy`) and print other files with absolute path.

You can also use FileTree to read contents from the archive files such as ZIP, JAR, or TAR files:

```
FileTree jarFile = zipTree('SampleProject-1.0.jar')
jarFile.each {
  println it.name
}
```

The preceding code snippet will list all the files contained in a `jar` file.

Property management

We cannot make a software available on different operating systems, or different environments without configuring it dynamically. One approach to configure software is by using the properties file or environment properties. The following are the different ways Gradle provides to configure properties to `build.gradle`:

- `ext` closure
- `gradle.properties`
- Command line
- Custom properties file

ext closure

We saw many examples in *Chapter 3, Managing Task*, of adding custom properties to a project using the `ext` closure. Thus, we will not discuss the topic in this chapter.

gradle.properties

Gradle provides a default mechanism of reading the properties file using `gradle.properties`. You can add the `gradle.properties` file in any of the following locations:

- `<USER_HOME>/.gradle`: `gradle.properties` defined under this directory would be accessible to all the projects. You can use this file to define global properties and you can access these properties using `$project.<propertyname>`. If you have defined GRADLE_USER_HOME to some other directory, then Gradle will skip the `<USER_HOME>/.gradle` directory and will read `gradle.properties` from the GRADLE_USER_HOME directory. By default `<USER_HOME>/.gradle` would be considered to read the `gradle.properties` file. If properties are defined in `<USER_HOME>/.gradle/gradle.properties`, but are not set by the user, it leads to an exception. If this is not desired, such properties should be checked using the `hasProperty` method of `project`, and if not set, it should be initialized with a default value. This property file may also be used for storing passwords.

- `<ProjectDir>: gradle.properties` defined under this directory would be accessible to the current project. You cannot access these properties from any other project. So, all the project-specific properties can be defined in the project's `gradle.properties` file.

  Along with project-level properties, you can also define system-level properties in the `gradle.properties` file. To define system-level properties, you can append properties with `systemProp`. So `systemProp.sProp1=sVal1` will set `sProp1` as a system-level property with the value `sVal1`.

We will see an example in the next section.

The command line

You can define runtime properties on the command line also using the `-P` and `-D` options. Using `-P`, you can define project-specific properties. Using `-D`, you can define system-level properties. To access system-level properties, you can use `System.properties['<propertyname>']`. Note that, command line properties override `gradle.properties`. When you configure properties in multiple places, the following order applies and the last one gets the highest priority:

- `gradle.properties` in project `build` dir.
- `gradle.properties` in Gradle user home.
- System properties set on the command line.

The Custom properties file

You might want to use the custom filename for your properties file, for example, `login.properties` or `profile.properties`. To use the custom properties, simply read the file using `FileInputStream` and convert it to the properties object:

```
task showCustomProp << {
  Properties props = new Properties()
  props.load(new FileInputStream("login.properties"))
  println props
  println props.get('loginKey1')
}
```

The preceding code will read the `login.properties` file, and the first `println` statement will print all the properties while the second `println` statement will display the value of the `loginKey1` property.

Let's take a look at a comprehensive example. We will create one `gradle.properties` file in the `<USER_HOME>/.gradle` directory and another `gradle.properties` file in the project directory:

`<USER_HOME>/.gradle/gradle.properties`

globalProp1=globalVal1

globalProp2=globalVal2

`Chapter6/PropertyExample/Proj1/gradle.properties`

Proj1Prop1=Proj1Val1

Proj1Prop2=Proj1Val2

systemProp.sysProp1=sysVal1

Here is our build script, `Chapter6/PropertyExample/Proj1/build.gradle`:

```
task showProps << {
  println "local property "+Proj1Prop1
  println "local property "+Proj1Prop2
  println "local property via command line: "+projCommandProp1
  println "global property "+globalProp1
  println "global property "+globalProp2
  println "System property "+System.properties['sysProp1']
  println "System property via command line:
    "+System.properties['sysCommandProp1']
}
```

Now, execute the following command:

**$gradle -PprojCommandProp1=projCommandVal1
-DsysCommandProp1=sysCommandVal1 showProps**

:showProps

local property Proj1Val1

local property Proj1Val2

local property via command line: projCommandVal1

global property globalVal1

global property globalVal2

System property sysVal1

System property via command line: sysCommandVal1

BUILD SUCCESSFUL

Here, you can see that the first two lines contain the properties defined in the project's `gradle.properties` file. The third line shows the property, which the user initialize with the `-P` option. The fourth and fifth lines show the properties defined in `<USER_HOME>/.gradle/gradle.properties`. The sixth line shows the system properties defined in the project's `gradle.properties` file, and finally, the example shows the system property passed in the command line using the `-D` option.

Multi-project build

We have explored many features of Gradle such as tasks, plugins, and dependency management. We have seen many examples of the build script involving in-built tasks, custom tasks, and dependencies between the tasks. Yet, we have not covered one of the main features of Gradle, which is **Multi-Project Build**. Until now we have seen build files for a single project. A single project build file represents only one project or one module. It is a very common scenario in any software world that it starts with a single module initially and as the software matures and grows over time, it turns into a big project. Then we need to divide it again into different submodules, but overall, we build the project using one file only. Gradle provides the capability of treating different modules as a different project, which can be grouped under a root project. It also gives the flexibility of building a submodule independently without building the complete project.

Multi-project is not a new concept. The only additional capability Gradle provides is to build the modules separately as an individual subproject, and whenever required, you can build the entire module using the root project. The subproject has all the properties and features, which a project object has in Gradle. You can define modular dependencies to other projects. Gradle allows you to define subproject tasks' dependencies to other subprojects. You can build only one subproject (and its dependencies) to optimize the build performance time and so on.

The Multi-project structure

Consider a simple user management Java application, which authenticates and authorizes the user, allows the user to manage his profile, and perform transactions. Let's say we divided this into three different subprojects or modules: login module, profile module, and transaction module.

One more question might arise, when we have already defined three subprojects why do we need the root project `UserManagement`, as it does not contain any source code? One of the purposes of the root project is to coordinate among the subprojects, define dependencies between the projects, if any, define common behaviors to avoid duplicate build configurations in each project, and more.

The purpose of these three modules is to work on them independently, build them separately, and if required, publish its artifacts without any dependency.

The directory structure will look like the following diagram:

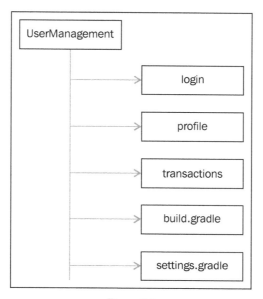

Figure 6.4

Here, we have created three subprojects: **login**, **profile**, and **transaction**, each module with its own src/main/java hierarchy. We have grouped the subprojects under the root project **UserManagement**. Additionally, the root project contains one **build. gradle** file and a **settings.gradle** file.

The **settings.gradle** file is one of the key files in multi-project build. This file needs to be present in the root project's directory. It lists all the subprojects. The content of the **settings.gradle** file is shown in the following code:

```
settings.gradle:
include 'login', 'profile', 'transactions'
```

Here, we have included all the subprojects, which are part of the root project. On executing the following command, we get all the project details as output:

```
$ gradle projects
......

Root project 'UserManagement'
+--- Project ':login'
```

```
+--- Project ':profile'
\--- Project ':transactions'
......
```

```
BUILD SUCCESSFUL
```

The output displays the root project `UserManagement`, and all the subprojects which are under the root project. Now, try to delete the `settings.gradle` file or remove the include statements in the `settings.gradle` file and run this command again. This time, it will display only root project details. The `settings.gradle` is an important file, which makes the root project aware of all the subprojects it should include. It is also possible to declare multiple levels of subprojects using `'subproject:subsubproject'`, `'subproject:subsubproject:subsubsubproject'`, and so on.

We talked about three phases of the Gradle build life cycle: initialization, configuration, and execution. Using the `settings.gradle` file during the initialization phase, Gradle adds all the subproject instances to the build process. You can also add projects by using the `include(String[])` method to this object.

The settings.gradle file also has access to the `gradle.properties` file defined in the settings directory of the build or `<USER_HOME>/.gradle` directory and properties provided on the command line using the `-P` option. The `settings.gradle` file can also execute Gradle tasks, and include plugins and other operations, which can be done in any `.gradle` file.

The Multi-project execution

To determine if the current build process is part of a multi-project build, it searches for the `settings.gradle` file first in the current directory and then in its parent hierarchy. If it finds `settings.gradle` in the same directory, it considers itself as a parent project and then checks for subprojects. In another case, if it finds the `settings.gradle` file in its parent hierarchy, it checks whether or not the current subdirectory is a subproject of the root project that is found. If the current project is part of the root project, then it is executed as a part of the multi-project build, otherwise, as a single project build.

The following is the sample `build.gradle` under the `UserManagement` directory:

```
println "Project name is $name"

project(':login') {
  apply plugin: 'java'
  println "Project name is $name"
```

```
    task loginTask << {
      println "Task name is $name"
    }
  }

  project(':profile') {
    apply plugin: 'java'
    println "Project name is $name"
    task profileTask << {
      println "Task name is $name"
    }
  }
  project(':transactions') {
    apply plugin: 'java'
    println "Project name is $name"
    task transactionTask << {
      println "Task name is $name"
    }
  }
```

Now, try to execute the following command from the `UserManagement` directory:

```
/UserManagement$ gradle
```

```
Project name is UserManagement
Project name is login
Project name is profile
Project name is transactions
:help
```

...

Now, go to the `login` directory and execute the same command; you will find a similar output. The difference is, in the subproject, the help task would be replaced by: `login:help`, because Gradle automatically detects the subproject you are in.

In the first scenario, Gradle found the settings.gradle file in the same directory and found three subprojects. Gradle initialized three subprojects and during configuration phase it executed the configuration statements. We did not mention any tasks, so no task is executed.

In the second scenario, when we executed the Gradle command from the login module, Gradle again started searching for the `settings.gradle` file and found this file in the parent directory, and also found the current project to be a part of the multi-project build, and thus, executed the build script as a multi-project build.

One thing you might have noticed here is that we did not define any `build.gradle` for any of the subprojects. We added all the subprojects to the root project's build file. This is one of the ways you can define the multi-project build. The alternative is to create individual build.gradle files in each of the subprojects. Just remove the project closures from the main build file and copy it to its respective project build file. The new project structure is shown in figure 6.4:

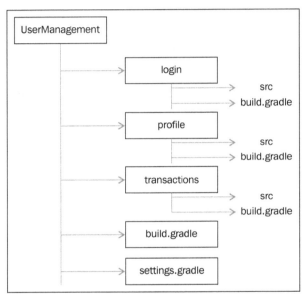

Figure 6.5

Task execution

Before executing a task in the multi-project build, Gradle will search for the task in the root project and in all the subprojects. If the task are found in multiple projects, it will execute all the tasks consecutively. Execute the following command from the `UserManagement` directory:

```
$ gradle loginTask
```

```
Project name is UserManagement
Project name is login
```

```
Project name is profile
Project name is transactions
:login:loginTask
Task name is loginTask
```

```
BUILD SUCCESSFUL
```

Now, copy `loginTask` to the transaction project and try to execute the same command:

```
$ gradle loginTask
....
:login:loginTask
Task name is loginTask
:transactions:loginTask
Task name is loginTask
```

```
BUILD SUCCESSFUL
```

Here, you can see the Gradle-executed `loginTask` in both the `login` and `transactions` projects. To execute a project-specific task, prefix the task name with the project name and use colon (`:`) as a separator—`gradle project:task`. To execute `loginTask` for the `login` module, use the `$ gradle login:loginTask` command.

The multi-project build helps to avoid redundant configurations and allows optimizing and organizing the build file structure appropriately.

In the preceding example, we have three subprojects and all have a dependency on the Java plugin. These subprojects might depend on some common libraries as well. Instead of defining dependencies in each of the subproject build files, we can define a common configuration into the root project. By doing so, the entire subproject will inherit this common configuration. This can be done by using two closures: `allprojects` and `subprojects`. The configuration defined under `allprojects` will be shared by all the subprojects, including the root project, whereas configuration under `subprojects` will be shared by all the subprojects excluding the root project. Add the following `subprojects{}` and `allprojects{}` closures, which are used to build a file and remove the `apply plugin: 'java'` statement from each subproject:

```
println "Project name is $name"
allprojects {
  version = '2.0'
}
subprojects { // for all subprojects
  apply plugin: 'java'
```

```
    repositories {
      mavenCentral()
    }
    dependencies {
      compile 'log4j:log4j:1.2.16'
    }
  }
```

Here, we have added the Java plugin, `repositories` closure, and common dependencies to the `subprojects` closure. So, it will be shared by all the subprojects. We have added a version in `allprojects`, which would be shared by all the subprojects, including the root subproject.

Now, try to execute the following command:

```
$ gradle clean
Project name is UserManagement
Project name is login
Project name is profile
Project name is transactions
:login:clean
:profile:clean
:transactions:clean

BUILD SUCCESSFUL
```

It has executed clean tasks in all the subprojects but not for the root project. Even if you try to execute `UserManagement:clean` task explicitly, it will throw an exception. If you add `apply plugin: 'java'` to the `allprojects` closure, it will add clean task to root project along with the subprojects.

The Flat hierarchy

Apart from the parent/child hierarchy, you can also create the subprojects at the same level, which can be included using the `includeFlat '<projectname>'` syntax.

Let's add one more subproject department at the same level with the `UserManagement` module.

The `department` module can be added as a subproject to the `UserManagement` project by adding the following code in the `settings.gradle` file:

```
includeFlat 'department'
// adding same level project as sub project
```

Interproject dependency

When you execute some common tasks such as `clean` and `compile` (after adding the Java plugin) on a multi-project build, the default execution order is based on their alphabetical order:

```
$ gradle clean

Project name is UserManagement
Project name is department
Project name is login
Project name is profile
Project name is transactions
:department:clean UP-TO-DATE
:login:clean UP-TO-DATE
:profile:clean UP-TO-DATE
:transactions:clean UP-TO-DATE

BUILD SUCCESSFUL
```

The first root project is getting evaluated and then all the subprojects as per their alphabetical order. To override the default behavior, Gradle provides you with a different level of dependency management.

Configuration-level dependency

The configuration-level dependency evaluates or configures a project after the execution of the project on which it depends upon. For example, you want to set some properties in the profile project and you want to use those properties in the login project. You can achieve this using `evaluationDependsOn`. To enable this feature, you should have separate `build.gradle` files for each subproject. Let's create independent `build.gradle` for each subprojects.

You can create each subproject and `build.gradle` in the following pattern.

```
/<project name>/build.gradle
println "Project name is $name"
task <projectName>Task << {
  println "Task name is $name "
}
```

The root project `build.gradle` will look like the following code:

`UserManagement_confDep/build.gradle`

```
println "Project name is $name"
allprojects {
  version = '2.0'
}
subprojects { // for all sub projects
  apply plugin: 'java'
  repositories {
    mavenCentral()
  }
}
```

Now, execute the following Gradle command:

/UserManagement_confDep$ gradle

Project name is UserManagement_confDep

Project name is login

Project name is profile

Project name is transactions

. . .

BUILD SUCCESSFUL

We have executed the Gradle command without any task. It has executed up to the configuration phase and you can see the preceding configuration order in alphabetical order (after root project configuration).

Now, add the following statement in your login project `build.gradle` file:

```
evaluationDependsOn(':profile')
```

Then, execute the Gradle command:

```
/UserManagement_confDep$ gradle
```

```
Project name is UserManagement_confDep
Project name is profile     // Order is changed
Project name is login
Project name is transactions
......

BUILD SUCCESSFUL
```

Now, you can see that the profile configuration is evaluated before the login configuration.

Task-level dependency

There might be a situation when a task of a project may depend on another project task. Gradle allows you to maintain task-level dependencies across subprojects. Here is an example where `loginTask` depends on `profileTask`:

```
project(':login') {
  println "Project name is $name"
  task loginTask (dependsOn: ":profile:profileTask")<< {
    println "Task name is $name"
  }
}
```

Now the output shows the dependency between the tasks:

```
/UserManagement_taskDep$ gradle loginTask
....

:profile:profileTask
Task name is profileTask
:login:loginTask
Task name is loginTask


BUILD SUCCESSFUL
```

If you declare an execution dependency between different projects with `dependsOn`, the default behavior of this method is to also create a configuration dependency between the two projects.

Library dependency

If one of the subprojects needs a class file or JAR file of another subproject to compile, this can be introduced as a compile time dependency. If the login project needs a profile jar in its classpath, you can introduce dependencies at compile level:

```
project(':login') {
  dependencies {
    compile project(':profile')
  }
  task loginTask (dependsOn: ":profile:profileTask") << {
    println "Task name is $name"
  }
}
```

```
/UserManagement_libDep$ gradle clean compileJava
...
:login:clean
:profile:clean
:transactions:clean
:department:compileJava UP-TO-DATE
:profile:compileJava
:profile:processResources UP-TO-DATE
:profile:classes
:profile:jar
:login:compileJava
:transactions:compileJava


BUILD SUCCESSFUL
```

From the output, we can realize that all the dependent modules were compiled before the login compile tasks were executed.

Partial builds

During development, you might need to build the projects again and again. Sometimes you do not make any changes to your dependent subproject, but Gradle by default always builds the dependencies first and then builds the dependent subprojects. This process might affect overall build performance. To overcome this problem, Gradle provides a solution called *partial builds*. Partial builds enable you to build only the required project, not its dependency projects. In the preceding example, we have the compile dependency of the login module on the profile project. To compile the login project without the dependent profile project, command-line option -a can be applied:

```
$ gradle :login:compileJava -a
:login:compileJava


BUILD SUCCESSFUL
```

buildDependents

In an enterprise project, we have project dependencies. When you want to build a project and at the same time you want to build the other dependent projects, the Java plugin provides the buildDependents option.

In the previous example, the login project has compile time dependency on the profile project. We will try to build a profile with the buildDependents option:

```
/UserManagement_libDep$ gradle :profile:buildDependents
. . .
:profile:compileJava UP-TO-DATE
:profile:processResources UP-TO-DATE
:profile:classes UP-TO-DATE
:profile:jar UP-TO-DATE
:login:compileJava UP-TO-DATE
:login:processResources UP-TO-DATE
:login:classes UP-TO-DATE
:login:jar
:login:assemble
:login:compileTestJava UP-TO-DATE
:login:processTestResources UP-TO-DATE
:login:testClasses UP-TO-DATE
:login:test UP-TO-DATE
```

```
:login:check UP-TO-DATE
:login:build
:login:buildDependents
:profile:assemble UP-TO-DATE
:profile:compileTestJava UP-TO-DATE
:profile:processTestResources UP-TO-DATE
:profile:testClasses UP-TO-DATE
:profile:test UP-TO-DATE
:profile:check UP-TO-DATE
:profile:build UP-TO-DATE
:profile:buildDependents
```

```
BUILD SUCCESSFUL
```

Since the login module depends on the profile module, executing the profile project also builds the login project.

buildNeeded

When you build the project, it only compiles the code and prepares the JAR file. If you have compile-time dependencies on the other project, it only compiles the other project and prepares the JAR file. To check the functionality of the complete component, you might want to execute the test cases as well. To execute the test case of the subproject as well as the dependent project, use buildNeeded:

```
/UserManagement_libDep$ gradle :login:buildNeeded
. . .
:login:processTestResources UP-TO-DATE
:login:testClasses UP-TO-DATE
:login:test UP-TO-DATE
:login:check UP-TO-DATE
:login:build UP-TO-DATE
:profile:assemble UP-TO-DATE
:profile:compileTestJava UP-TO-DATE
:profile:processTestResources UP-TO-DATE
:profile:testClasses UP-TO-DATE
:profile:test UP-TO-DATE
```

```
:profile:check UP-TO-DATE

:profile:build UP-TO-DATE

:profile:buildNeeded UP-TO-DATE

:login:buildNeeded UP-TO-DATE


BUILD SUCCESSFUL
```

Here, `buildNeeded` not only executes the login test cases, it also executes the profile test cases.

Testing with Gradle

No piece of software is production ready unless it passes through a proper quality check. It helps to deliver software with minimum defects and saves lots of maintenance effort. However, manual test execution requires lots of time to execute tests and therefore the software release cycle is delayed. Release time and productivity can be improved if tests are automated.

Gradle provides an automated way to execute test code, especially for unit tests. In the following section, we'll explore how to integrate JUnit and TestNG with Gradle.

JUnit

Gradle's Java plugin provides a predefined structure to keep test code and test resources for configuration and execution. As with the source code structure, the default test code location is `src/test/java/<test_package>`. If you follow this convention, you just need to execute the `test` task to run the unit test cases as shown in the following command:

```
$ gradle test
:compileJava

:processResources

:classes

:compileTestJava

:processTestResources

:testClasses

:test
BUILD SUCCESSFUL
```

This test task will perform all the required operations such as the compilation of the source code, compilation of the test code, process resources, and finally, execution of the test cases and creation of reports.

JUnit provides a user-friendly format to understand the result. You will find the following hierarchy after executing the test task:

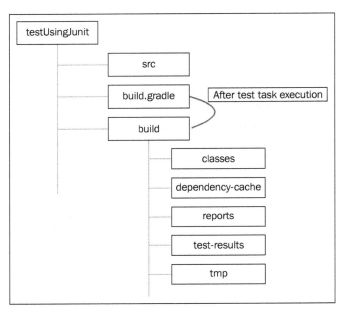

Figure 6.6

The `reports` folder contains a `tests` subdirectory, which has a test summary result in HTML format named `index.html`. If you open the `index.html` file, you will find the following output:

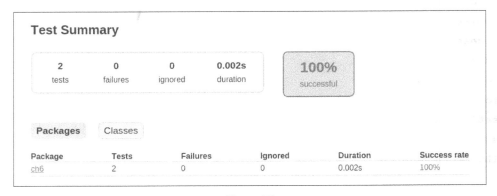

Figure 6.7

It provides a complete analysis of test case scenarios such as number of test cases executed, test cases failed, ignored, and so on. From the report, you can drill down further to the individual test case level by following the hyperlinks on the report page. The report will show a detailed explanation of the error/exception that occurred, if any, and the execution time in a tabular format.

Until now, we have only discussed the execution of the test cases using Gradle. To compile and execute test cases, we need a test framework library. Like any other configuration, you need to mention the JUnit JAR as a dependency for your project. Typically, the dependency is added as a `testCompile` configuration:

```
repositories {
  mavenCentral()
}
dependencies {
  testCompile 'junit:junit:4.12'
}
```

This configuration will download the `junit-4.12.jar` from the Maven repository and the JAR file will be added to the classpath during the compilation and execution phase.

Test configuration

There are different configuration parameters that can be set for test configuration, which help to optimize the resources and customize the behavior based on project requirements.

Sometimes, the test directory structure does not follow the default convention, that is, `src/test/java`. In a similar way to the source code directory configuration, you can configure the new test code location as follows:

```
sourceSets {
  test {
    java {
      srcDir 'testSrc'
    }
  }
}
```

maxParallelForks

Gradle executes the test cases in a separate JVM. By default, Gradle executes all the tests in a single process. You can specify the number of parallel processes by configuring the `maxParallelForks` property in the `test` closure. Its default value is one:

```
test {
maxParallelForks = 3
}
```

To understand how it works exactly, we can modify our previous example. Just create multiple copies of the test class in `src/test/java`. In our example, in the `TestUsingJunitParallel` project, we have created a total of five copies of the same `LoginTest` class as `LoginTest1`, `LoginTest2`, and so on. Now, execute the Gradle command with the `--info` option:

```
TestUsingJunitParallel$ gradle clean --info test | grep 'Test
Executor'
. . . .
. . . .
Successfully started process 'Gradle Test Executor 2'
Successfully started process 'Gradle Test Executor 1'
Successfully started process 'Gradle Test Executor 3'
Gradle Test Executor 2 started executing tests.
Gradle Test Executor 3 started executing tests.
Gradle Test Executor 1 started executing tests.
Gradle Test Executor 3 finished executing tests.
Gradle Test Executor 2 finished executing tests.
Gradle Test Executor 1 finished executing tests.
```

The command-line output shows that three processes were created by Gradle and all the test cases were executed in those processes.

The forkEvery option

This option allows setting the number of test classes per process. The default value is `0`, that is, unlimited. If you set this option to a nonzero value, then a process will be created when this limit is reached.

In the previous example, we have five test classes and we have set the parallel process count to three. Now, we will set the `forkEvery` option to `1`, so every process will execute only one test class:

```
test {
  ignoreFailures = true
  maxParallelForks = 3
  forkEvery = 1
}
```

```
TestUsingJunitParallel$ gradle clean --info test | grep 'Test
Executor'
. . . .
Successfully started process 'Gradle Test Executor 1'
Successfully started process 'Gradle Test Executor 3'
Successfully started process 'Gradle Test Executor 2'
Gradle Test Executor 1 started executing tests.
Gradle Test Executor 2 started executing tests.
Gradle Test Executor 3 started executing tests.
Gradle Test Executor 1 finished executing tests.
Starting process 'Gradle Test Executor 4'. Working directory:
. . . .
Successfully started process 'Gradle Test Executor 4'
Gradle Test Executor 3 finished executing tests.
Gradle Test Executor 2 finished executing tests.
Starting process 'Gradle Test Executor 5'. Working directory:
. . . .
Successfully started process 'Gradle Test Executor 5'
Gradle Test Executor 4 started executing tests.
Gradle Test Executor 5 started executing tests.
Gradle Test Executor 4 finished executing tests.
Gradle Test Executor 5 finished executing tests.
```

From the output, we can observe that Gradle first created three processes, which executed three test classes. Then, other two processes, for example, `'Gradle Test Executor 4'` and `'Gradle Test Executor 5'`, were created to execute another two test files.

ignoreFailures

Whenever any of the test cases fails, the build is marked as FAILED:

```
$ gradle test

. . .

:test


ch6.login.LoginTest > testLogin1 FAILED
   java.lang.AssertionError at LoginTest.java:26


4 tests completed, 1 failed
:test FAILED


FAILURE: Build failed with an exception.

. . .

BUILD FAILED
```

If you want the build to succeed irrespective of the test case outcome, you can add ignoreFailures=true in the build script test closure, as shown in the previous example. Its default value is false. On executing the test task again, the build will be successful as follows:

```
$ gradle test

. . .

ch6.login.LoginTest > testLogin1 FAILED
   java.lang.AssertionError at LoginTest.java:26


4 tests completed, 1 failed

. . .

BUILD SUCCESSFUL
```

filter

Gradle allows you a selective execution of test cases by filtering them based on different patterns. Suppose we have two test packages with four test cases.

`/src/test/java/ch6/login/LoginTest.java` contains 2 test packages as follows:

- `testUserLogin1()`
- `testUserLogin2()`

`/src/test/java/ch6/profile/ProfileTest.java` contains 2 test packages as follows:

- `testUserProfile1()`
- `testUserProfile2()`

The following code snippet shows how to apply a filter based on different patterns:

```
test {
  filter {
    // 1: execute only login test cases
    includeTestsMatching "ch6.login.*"

    //2: include all test cases matching *Test
    includeTestsMatching "*Test"

    //3: include all integration tests having 1 in their name
    includeTestsMatching "*1"

    //4: Other way to include/exclude packages
    include "ch6/profile/**"
  }
}
```

The first filter will identify only two test cases from the `ch6.login` package. The second filter selects all four test cases, as test class names are matching the `*Test` pattern. The third statement finally filters only two test cases: `testUserLogin1()` and `testUserProfile1()`.

Just comment the first two patterns and execute the test with filter pattern *1. Although we have a total of four test cases, you will find that Gradle executes one test case from each package. You can also include or exclude packages by using include or exclude with the package structure mentioned in the preceding example. If you only want to execute a single test class, you can also execute it by appending test classes to the command-line option --tests. Command gradle tests --tests ch6.login.LoginTest will execute only the test case mentioned in the LoginTest class:

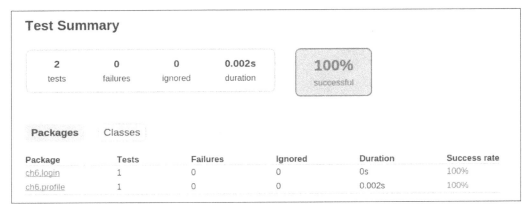

Figure 6.8

TestNG

Gradle also provides integration with the TestNG framework. To write test cases in TestNG, you need to add the dependency in the build.gradle file:

```
dependencies {
  testCompile 'org.testng:testng:6.8.21'
}
```

In our example, we have created a TestNG test class with three test cases. Now, by executing the test task, we get the report file created under build/reports/tests:

```
$ gradle clean test
```

Now, open the `index.html` file and you will see the following output:

Figure 6.9

The look and feel of the report is similar to the JUnit that we saw earlier. Actually, JUnit and TestNG on their own generate completely different report formats, but Gradle reconciles them into a standard look and feel.

As explained in the *JUnit* section, you can also define other properties in the `test` closure such as `ignoreFailures`, `maxParallelForks`, and so on.

```
test{
    useTestNG()
    ignoreFailures = true
    maxParallelForks = 2
    forkEvery = 1
}
```

Execution based on group

In the preceding `test` closure, we have used the `useTestNG` option to enable `TestNG` support. You can also set other options such as groups and listeners in this closure. For example, the following setting only executes test cases with the group name `Smoke` and it creates an additional emailable `TestNG` report in the `reports/tests` folder:

```
useTestNG(){
    includeGroups 'Smoke'
    listeners << 'org.testng.reporters.EmailableReporter'
}
```

In `useTestNG`, you can group test cases based on the group attribute to the `@Test` annotation:

```
@Test(groups = "<group name>")
```

In our example, we have grouped the test cases as Smoke and Integration. On executing the test task, only the verifyArraySize and verifyArrayNotNull test cases will be executed:

```
@Test(groups = "Smoke")
public void verifyArraySize()

@Test(groups = "Smoke")
public void verifyArrayNotNull()

@Test(groups = "Integration")
public void verifyArrayPosition()
```

Execution based on the TestNG suite file

TestNG suite files provide better control to execute tests. In a test suite file, you can define all the test classes and methods that will be included to execute the test case, any filter based on group name, listener information, and so on.

We have created a testng.xml file in the src/test/resource folder. The file has three key pieces of information; the listener configuration to create an emailable report format, included the test group as Smoke and added the ArrayTest file as a test class. Using the test suite file, you can also configure other properties such as thread pool size, whether test classes or test methods will run in parallel, and many more:

```
<!DOCTYPE suite SYSTEM "http://testng.org/testng-1.0.dtd" >
<suite name="Suite1" verbose="1" >
  <listeners>
    <listener class-name="org.testng.reporters.EmailableReporter"
      />
  </listeners>
  <test name="Smoke Test">
    <groups>
      <run>
        <exclude name="Integration" />
        <include name="Smoke" />
      </run>
    </groups>

    <classes>
      <class name="ch6.testng.example.ArrayTest">
      </class>
    </classes>
  </test>
</suite>
```

This suite file can be included in the `test` closure as follows. Then, on executing the test task, reports will be created in the `reports/tests` folder:

```
test {
ignoreFailures = true
  useTestNG(){
    suites("src/test/resources/testng.xml")
  }
}
```

Summary

In this chapter, we have explored different topics of Gradle such as I/O operations, logging, Multi-Project build and testing using Gradle. We also learned how easy it is to generate assets for web applications and Scala projects with Gradle. In the *Testing with Gradle* section, we learned some basics to execute tests with JUnit and TestNG.

In the next chapter, we will learn the code quality aspects of a Java project. We will analyze a few Gradle plugins such as Checkstyle and Sonar. Apart from learning these plugins, we will discuss another topic called Continuous Integration. These two topics will be combined and presented by exploration of two different continuous integration servers, namely Jenkins and TeamCity.

7
Continuous Integration

Continuous Integration is one of the most used terminologies in today's software world. Wherever you go in the software world, everybody talks about continuous integration. So what is continuous integration?

Continuous Integration is the practice of integrating all of the software code in a shared repository; prepare an automated build for every commit, and run the automated tests without any manual effort. It helps developers to detect problems early in fail fast mode. Here, early means as soon as a developer commits the code; within a couple of seconds or minutes (as per the project size), continuous integration process will notify about the success or failure of the build. Since errors are caught in the early stages, it saves a lot of effort while performing integration and functional testing of the application.

In this chapter, we will explore the popular Continuous Integration tools, Jenkins and TeamCity. As this is a Gradle book, we will limit our discussion to basic setup and configuration for these tools. We will also introduce a new topic, code quality management with Gradle. We will learn how **Checkstyle**, **PMD**, and **Sonar Runner** plugins can be integrated with Gradle, and how it can be integrated with Continuous Integration tools.

Jenkins walk-through

Jenkins is one of the most popular open source continuous integration tools which helps to automate software build and the deployment process. It can work with build tools such as Maven, Gradle, and Ant. It supports various source code management systems such as CVS, Git, Subversion, and Perforce. Even simple shell or batch script execution is supported. The main advantage of Jenkins lies in its plugin support. There are more than 1000+ plugins for different functionalities, and if needed, it can be extended to support new requirements.

Some of the main features of Jenkins are:

- Easy to install and configure. Simple web-based UI for managing the server
- Support for a variety of plugins for different builds and deployment related tasks
- A very large community forum
- Support for different repositories like SVN, Git, CVS, and Perforce etc.
- Support for post build hook

Jenkins installation

Jenkins installation is just a two-step process. You need to download `jenkins.war` from `http://jenkins-ci.org/`. You will always get the latest version from this URL. For any previous releases, click on the **past releases** option and decide which version you want.

Once the war file is downloaded, it can be deployed in a container such as Tomcat, or it can be executed using the following command:

```
$ java -jar jenkins.war
Running from: /jenkins/jenkins.war
webroot: $user.home/.jenkins
….
Apr 02, 2015 3:30:32 PM org.eclipse.jetty.util.log.JavaUtilLog info
INFO: Started SelectChannelConnector@0.0.0.0:8080
….
Apr 02, 2015 3:30:37 PM org.jenkinsci.main.modules.sshd.SSHD start
INFO: Started SSHD at port 50566
Apr 02, 2015 3:30:37 PM jenkins.InitReactorRunner$1 onAttained
INFO: Completed initialization
Apr 02, 2015 3:30:37 PM hudson.WebAppMain$3 run
INFO: Jenkins is fully up and running
```

Here, Jenkins started with an inbuilt Jetty container at 8080 port. Default Jenkins home directory will be set to <USER_HOME>/.jenkins. By setting the JENKINS_HOME environment variable, you can set it to any other location. This directory stores all the Jenkins related information such as job information, user account details, plugin information, and Jenkins general settings.

Now open a browser and type the following: `http://localhost:8080` and the Jenkins welcome page will be displayed. That is all. Jenkins is ready for you:

Figure 7.1

Since this is not a Jenkins user guide, we will not be covering Jenkins functionalities in detail. You can go through the tutorials available on Jenkins main website. We will be mostly covering the topics that will be helpful to automate the build process with Gradle.

Jenkins configuration

Only installation is not enough for Jenkins to get started with the Gradle build process. We need to configure some plugins before we start with our first job in Jenkins. Like `task` in Gradle, the unit of execution in Jenkins is job. A build job can perform compilation, run automated tests, package or even deployment related tasks. But before we start working with jobs, we will configure the following plugins for Jenkins.

- Gradle Plugin
- Git Plugin (required if you are using Git as a repository)

Click on the **Manage Jenkins** on the left-hand side vertical menu. You will find a list of different categories available. Click on **Manage Plugins**. You will find the following four tabs:

Figure 7.2

Go to the **Available** tab and filter (top right) for `Gradle Plugin`. You will find Gradle Plugin with the following details:

Gradle Plugin

This plugin makes it possible to invoke Gradle build script as the main build step.

Select the plugin and click on **Download now and Install after restart**. It is better to restart Jenkins after an installation, in order to avoid any issues.

This will add Gradle build execution capability to the Jenkins server. You will be able to see a success message once installation is successful. You might get an error if the system is firewall protected, which can restrict the system when connecting to the internet. In such cases, manually download the plugin (`*.hpi` files) and copy it to `<Jenkins_home>/plugins` directory. Jenkins plugins can be downloaded from `https://updates.jenkins-ci.org/download/plugins/`.

For the examples in this chapter, we are using GitHub as a repository. To work with GitHub, we will add the GitHub plugin to the Jenkins server. We can add it in the same way we added the Gradle plugin. If the plugin is dependent on other plugins, then Jenkins will automatically download the required plugins. You can observe this when we install the GitHub plugin. Jenkins automatically installs the other required plugins such as the Git client plugin, and the Git API Plugin. As mentioned earlier, some plugins might require the Jenkins server to be restarted. In such cases, stop the current process and restart the Jenkins server in order to make the plugin effective.

The next important step is to configure JDK, Gradle, and Git with Jenkins. To configure these settings, open Jenkins URL and click on **Manage Jenkins**, and then **Configure System**.

Enter the correct path to the JDK and save the settings. Jenkins also has an option to install the software automatically from the internet. Take a look at the following screenshot:

Figure 7.3

Figure 7.4 shows how to configure Gradle in Jenkins:

Figure 7.4

Create job

After the Gradle plugin has been successfully installed, we will create the first Gradle build job. Go to Jenkins home page and click on **create new jobs**. There are different categories of jobs that can be created in Jenkins. We will create a **Freestyle project** in this example. For simplicity, we will build the plugin project that we created in *Chapter 4*, *Plugin Management*. A project can be created by simply giving it a name, such as PluginProject, as shown in Figure 7.5. Also, try to avoid spaces in job names, as it is considered as a bad practice.

If you want words to be separated, you can use underscore(_):

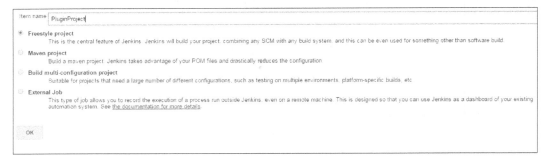

Figure 7.5

Once you click on **OK**, in the next page you will have to configure the job. You will have to configure a few details as follows:

- Source code management location to download the project
- Build step for the project
- Schedule the Build task (daily, hourly, after every commit etc.)
- Put in any post build action to perform

First, we will configure the repository under **Source Code Management**. As we are using the GitHub repository, we need to select the **Git** option.

Figure 7.6

Provide the repository URL and add the authentication (username/password) using the **Credentials** option as configured in Figure 7.6.

Git executable must be set in the Jenkins system configuration, otherwise you will not be able to execute Git commands. If there is any issue with connecting to the URL, Jenkins will show you a proper error message. This helps to debug and resolve the issues. If the URL is validated to be successful, the next step is to choose the build options from one of the options displayed in the following figure:

Figure 7.7

For our project we have selected the option **Build when a change is pushed to GitHub**, which helps to validate every commit by running a build script. You can set any other option as per the build requirement.

The next step is to select a build tool for the project. From the options available, such as shell, Ant, and batch, we will select Gradle as the build tool for this project. This option is highlighted in the next figure:

Figure 7.8

Select the option **Invoke Gradle script** and configure a few basic parameters:

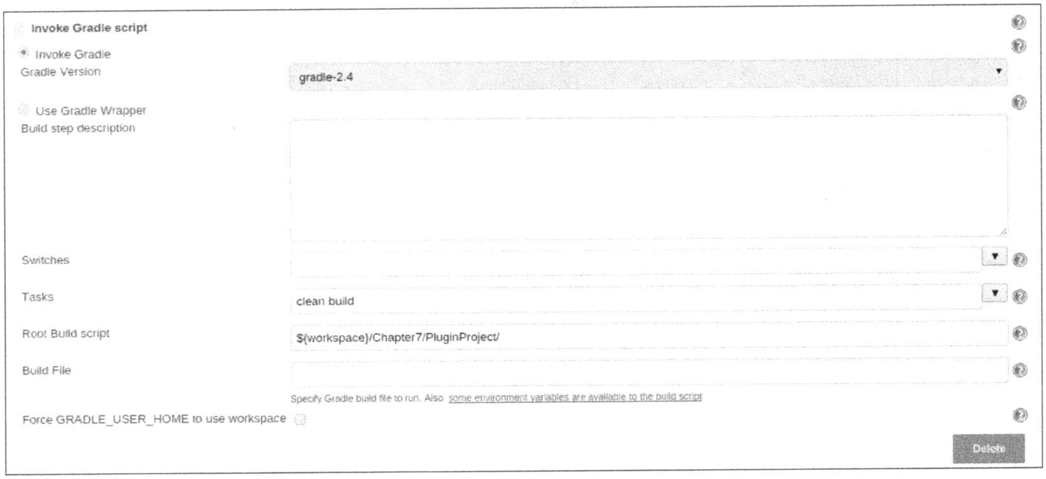

Figure 7.9

We have configured the installed Gradle on the system `gradle-2.4` as the working Gradle version. To build the `PluginProject`, tasks can be set as `clean build` in the **Tasks** text box. If the `build.gradle` file is in the home/root folder of the project, then you can leave the **Root Build Script** textbox empty. However, if it is in another directory, you will have to mention the path relative to the workspace location. Our `build.gradle` file is in the `Chapter7/PluginProject` folder. So we can enter the Root Build script as `${workspace}/Chapter7/PluginProject`. As we are using the build file name as `build.gradle`, which is the default naming convention in Gradle, we do not need to specify the file name in the **Build File** text box. If you are using any other build file name, it has to be mentioned in the **Build file** text box.

You can also add **Post-build Actions** such as publish Java doc, send email notifications, build other projects as per the project requirements.

Now, save the configurations and you will be able to see the project on the dashboard:

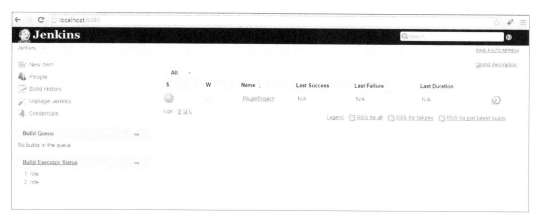

Figure 7.10

Execute job

Although we configured the build to be executed when a change is pushed to the source code management system, build can always be executed manually if you do not want to wait for changes to happen in the repository. Click on the **PluginProject** job on the Jenkins home page, which you had created earlier. You will be navigated to the job console at `http://localhost:8080/job/PluginProject/`.

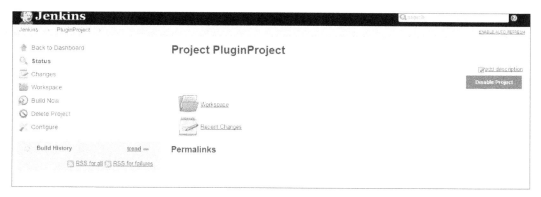

Figure 7.11

On the job console, you will find the **Build Now** option on the left-hand side. Click on the option to execute the job manually. In the console page, you can configure the job at any time by selecting the **Configure** option. Once the job has been executed successfully, you will find similar output as displayed in Figure 7.12 by clicking the **build no** link in the **Build History** section:

Figure 7.12

Build history is displayed in the UI with the latest job execution status on top. Figure 7.13 shows that the 1st and 2nd execution failed with some error, but the 3rd execution was successful. In the **Build History** section, if a job has failed, it will be marked in red. For success, it is blue, and aborted jobs can be identified in gray:

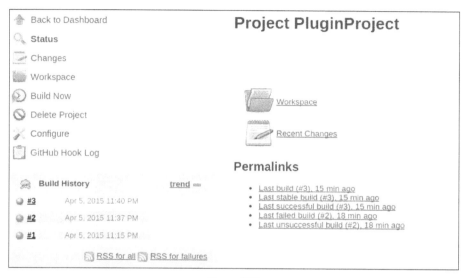

Figure 7.13

The default location for this job is `<USER_HOME>/.jenkins/jobs/<JOB_NAME>/workspace`. If you browse to `<USER_HOME>/.jenkins/jobs` location, you will find a directory created with a job name, that is `PluginProject`, which further contains `config.xml` for job configuration. The job directory has two further sub-directories, builds for executed jobs and workspace where the build actually runs. If you go inside the `builds` directory, you will find the build execution details for each run.

```
mainak@ubuntu:~/.jenkins/jobs/PluginProject/builds$ ls -l
total 20
drwxrwxr-x 2 mainak mainak 4096 Apr  5 23:16 1
drwxrwxr-x 2 mainak mainak 4096 Apr  5 23:38 2
drwxrwxr-x 2 mainak mainak 4096 Apr  5 23:40 3
drwxrwxr-x 2 mainak mainak 4096 Apr  6 00:00 4
drwxrwxr-x 2 mainak mainak 4096 Apr  6 01:07 5
lrwxrwxrwx 1 mainak mainak    1 Apr  5 23:38 lastFailedBuild -> 2
lrwxrwxrwx 1 mainak mainak    1 Apr  6 00:31 lastStableBuild -> 5
lrwxrwxrwx 1 mainak mainak    1 Apr  6 00:31 lastSuccessfulBuild -> 5
lrwxrwxrwx 1 mainak mainak    2 Apr  5 23:12 lastUnstableBuild -> -1
lrwxrwxrwx 1 mainak mainak    1 Apr  5 23:38 lastUnsuccessfulBuild -> 2
-rw-rw-r-- 1 mainak mainak    0 Apr  5 17:24 legacyIds
```

Figure 7.14

The workspace directory contains the project that we have configured for the job. Earlier in the build configuration, we specified the `Build Root` as `${workspace}/Chapter7/PluginProject`. Now if we go to this location, we will find the build folder created for this project:

```
/workspace/Chapter7/PluginProject$ ls -l
total 12
drwxrwxr-x 6 mainak mainak 4096 Apr  6 00:31 build
-rw-rw-r-- 1 mainak mainak  328 Apr  5 23:15 build.gradle
drwxrwxr-x 3 mainak mainak 4096 Apr  5 23:15 src
```

This is just a brief overview of Jenkins configuration. More details can be found at `https://jenkins-ci.org/`. In the next two sections, we will explore Checkstyle, PMD, and Sonar Runner plugins.

Checkstyle and PMD plugins

We have seen how simple it is to create a Gradle build job in Jenkins. We will now add **Checkstyle** and **PMD** plugins to our project for quality checking purposes. There are different approaches that we can follow in order to use these plugins. We can directly add these plugins to Jenkins and run it for our project, or we can use Gradle Checkstyle and PMD plugins and evaluate the project.

We will use the Gradle approach to add Checkstyle and PMD plugins for code quality check, and execute this using Jenkins. Let's create two Gradle files, one for Checkstyle and the other for PMD:

```
build_checkstyle.gradle

    apply plugin: 'groovy'
    apply plugin: 'eclipse'
    apply plugin: 'checkstyle'


    version = '1.0'

    repositories {
      mavenCentral()
    }
    checkstyle {
      toolVersion = 6.5
```

```
      ignoreFailures = true
    }


    dependencies {
      compile gradleApi()
      compile localGroovy()
      compile group: 'commons-collections', name: 'commons-collections',
      version: '3.2'
      testCompile group: 'junit', name: 'junit', version: '4.+'
    }
```

In the build file, we have added additional configuration in the closure `checkstyle` { ... }. If the source code does not pass the CheckStyle rules, it results in build failure. To ignore any build failure due to Checkstyle rule violation; we need to add the `ignoreFailures=true` property in the `checkstyle` closure.

Checkstyle plugin provides the following tasks:

- `checkstyleMain`: This executes Checkstyle against the Java source files
- `checkstyleTest`: This executes Checkstyle against the Java test source files
- `checkstyleSourceSet`: This executes Checkstyle against the given source set's Java source files

For Checkstyle plugin, we need a `checkstyle.xml` file in the `<Project>/config/ checkstyle/` directory. This is the default location. You can find a sample `checkstyle.xml` at: `https://github.com/google/google-api-java-client/ blob/dev/checkstyle.xml`.

It provides a standard quality checks for projects. You can write customized `checkstyle.xml` for your requirements as well.

To use PMD plugin, you can copy the above file and replace `checkstyle` closure with `pmd` closure and remove the `toolVersion` property. If you don't specify a version, Gradle downloads PMD version 5.1.1 by default. You will also need to add apply plugin: `pmd`.

`build_pmd.gradle`

```
    apply plugin: 'groovy'
    apply plugin: 'pmd'


    version = '1.0'
```

```
repositories {
  mavenCentral()
}

pmd{
  ignoreFailures = true
}

dependencies {
  compile gradleApi()
  compile localGroovy()
  compile group: 'commons-collections', name: 'commons-
    collections', version: '3.2'
  testCompile group: 'junit', name: 'junit', version: '4.+'
}
```

PMD plugin provides the following tasks:

- `pmdMain`: This executes PMD against the Java source files.
- `pmdTest`: This executes PMD against the Java test source files.
- `pmdSourceSet`: This executes PMD against the given source set's Java source files

Both the Checkstyle and PMD plugins can be executed using `check` task.

- If you add Checkstyle plugin and execute `check` task, it will call all checkstyle tasks
- If you add PMD plugin and execute `check` tasks, it will execute `pmd` tasks

We will create a new project `QualityCheck` and add the following files to the project:

- `build_checkstyle.gradle`
- `build_pmd.gradle`
- `config/checkstyle/checkstyle.xml`

Checkstyle and PMD plugin are executed in Java code, so we will add some sample Java files under the `src/main/java/` directory. To create a build step in Jenkins, we will create a build step to execute a Checkstyle task (`check` task), as shown in Figure 7.15. You can repeat the same steps for PMD plugin.

For a new configuration, `Root Build script` is set to `${workspace}/Chapter7/QualityCheck`. Also, we added the **Build file** name in the text box as `build_checkstyle.gradle`.

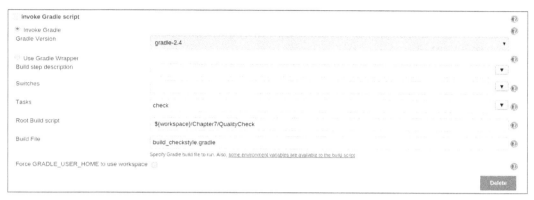

Figure 7.15

Save this configuration and execute the job again. As configured, `build_checkstyle.gradle` file executed on java source code and generated CheckStyle reports for it. You can find the reports under `${workspace}\Chapter7\QualityCheck\build\reports\checkstyle\main.xml`

The Sonar Runner plugin

Sonar is one of the most popular quality management tools which gives complete analysis of a project in terms of lines of code, documentation, test coverage, issues and complexities. Gradle provides seamless integration with Sonar. The only prerequisite is that sonar server should be installed and running. Details on Sonar can be found at `http://www.sonarqube.org/`.

To run sonar runner plugin, we just need to apply plugin `sonar-runner` and configure it to connect to the sonar server.

Create build file `build_sonar.gradle` for your project with the following contents:

```
apply plugin: 'groovy'
apply plugin: 'eclipse'
apply plugin: "sonar-runner"
```

```
repositories {
  mavenCentral()
}

version = '1.0'

sonarRunner {

  sonarProperties {
    property "sonar.host.url", "http://<IP_ADDRESS>:9000"
    property "sonar.jdbc.url",
      "jdbc:h2:tcp://<IP_ADDRESS>:9092/sonar"
    property "sonar.jdbc.driverClassName", "org.h2.Driver"
    property "sonar.jdbc.username", "sonar"
    property "sonar.jdbc.password", "sonar"
  }
}
```

The preceding configuration is self-explanatory. You need to add configurations such as Sonar URL, DB URL, JDBC driver details. Our build file is ready. The next step is to configure a job in the Jenkins server. To configure `sonarRunner` task in Jenkins, we can add a few basic steps as shown in Figure 7.16:

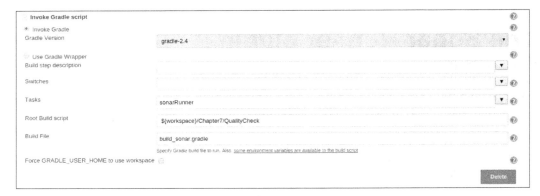

Figure 7.16

Here, the task name is `sonarRunner` and the build file name is `build_sonar.gradle`. Now, execute this job in Jenkins and you will find the output in the console. The output contains a link to the Sonar server. You can follow the link, which will redirect you to the Sonar report, as displayed in Figure 7.17:

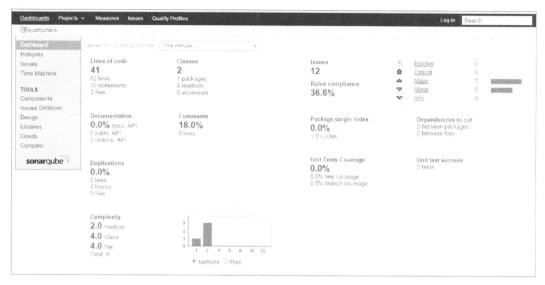

Figure 7.17

As mentioned preceding, Sonar gives an analysis of the project in different areas and you can find the details in the Sonar UI.

TeamCity walk-through

In the previous section, we learned how to configure a Gradle project in Jenkins and how to integrate quality plugins. In this section, we will explore one more popular continuous integration tool, TeamCity. We are assuming that TeamCity is already installed and running on your machine. Therefore, we will skip the TeamCity installation and configuration details. Actually, the installation process is very simple and it can be completed in a few minutes. You can download TeamCity from the following URL: `https://www.jetbrains.com/teamcity/download/` and installation instructions are available at `https://confluence.jetbrains.com/display/TCD9/Installation`.

By default, TeamCity runs on `http://localhost:8111/` and it has one build agent that runs on the server. We will build the same plugin project using TeamCity.

Log in to TeamCtiy and click on Create a project. Provide a project name and description:

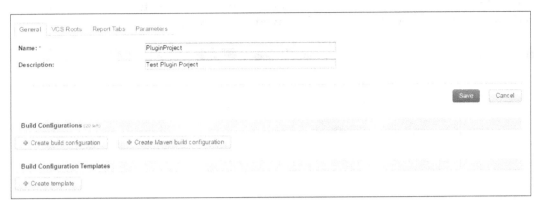

Figure 7.18

Save and then click on the **Create Build Configuration** button. You will need to provide general settings for the project. After general settings, proceed to **Version Control Settings**:

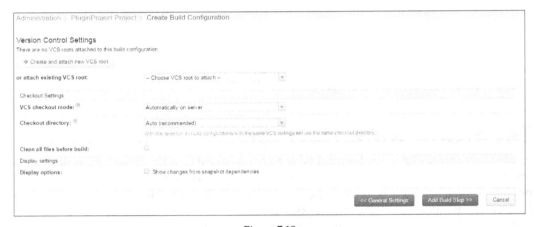

Figure 7.19

The next step is to configure **Create and attach new VCS root**. Choose Git from the drop down, since we are using Git as a repository, as shown in Figure 7.20:

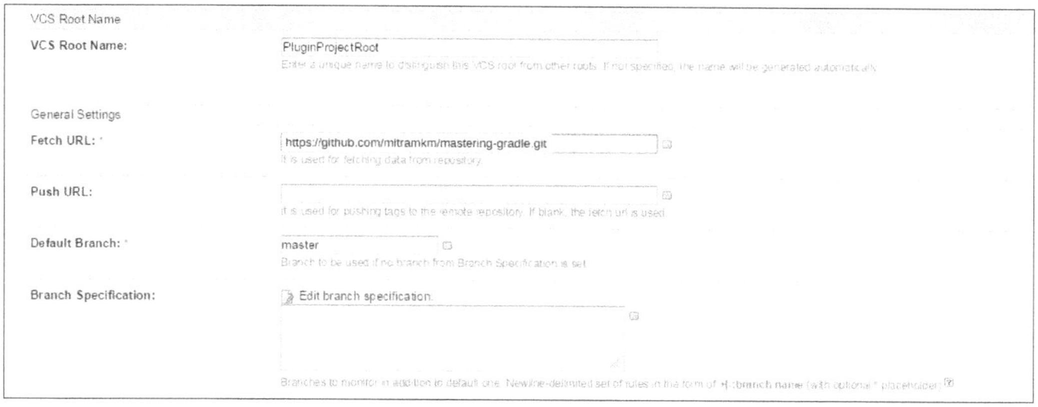

Figure 7.20

Provide **General settings** and the **Fetch URL** of the plugin project, also provide authentication, such as username/password and the Git exe location in **Path To Git**.

At the end of the screen, click on **Test Connection**. If the connection is successful, click on **Save**. The next step is **Add Build Step**.

In the build step, you need to configure the **PluginProject** build file details and build tasks details. For example, we need to provide some basic information such as `clean build` for task, working directory as `Chapter7/PluginProject`, and Gradle and JDK home directory:

New Build Step

Runner type:	Gradle ▼ Runner for Gradle projects
Step name:	 You can specify a build step name to distinguish it from other steps
Execute step:	Only if all previous steps were successful ▼ You can specify step execution policy
Gradle Parameters	
Gradle tasks:	clean build Enter task names separated by spaces; leave blank to use the 'default' task. Example: ':myproject:clean :myproject:build' or 'clean build'.
Incremental building:	☐ Enable incremental building :buildDependents task will be run on projects affected by changes
Working directory:	Chapter7/PluginProject Optional; set if differs from the checkout directory.
Gradle home path:	D:\Soft\gradle-2.4 Path to the Gradle home directory (parent of 'bin' directory). Overrides agent GRADLE_HOME environment variable
Additional Gradle command line parameters:	 Additional parameters will be added to the 'Gradle' command line
Gradle Wrapper:	☐ Use gradle wrapper to build project
Run Parameters	
Debug:	☐ Log debug messages
Stacktrace:	☐ Print stacktrace
Java Parameters	
JDK home path:	C:\Program Files\Java\jdk1.7.0_51 If left blank, the path will be read from JAVA_HOME environment variable or agent's own Java.
JVM command line parameters:	
Code Coverage	

Figure 7.21

Save this configuration and the project will then be ready. The details of the build step can be reviewed in the build configuration screen, as shown in the following screenshot:

Figure 7.22

TeamCity executes the project through TeamCity Agents. TeamCity server installs an agent with the server. You can use this agent to execute the job. Otherwise, you can configure more agents through the **Agents** tab.

Figure 7.23

Once the agent is configured and connected, you can map the project with the build agent and you are ready to run the build job.

Figure 7.24

On clicking on the **Run** button, TeamCity server will execute the build job on mapped agent, and you can see the output of the build job as a success or failure.

In the **Build Log** console, you can also analyze the complete log, as shown in the following screenshot:

Figure 7.25

Summary

In this chapter, we discussed briefly the need for continuous integration in the software development world, and looked into the two most popular continuous integration tools, Jenkins and TeamCity. In this chapter, we learned how easy it is to configure these tools and how we can integrate Gradle with these CI tools. We also learned three different quality plugins of Gradle: Checkstyle, PMD and Sonar Runner. And we executed these quality tasks with the help of Jenkins. There are so many topics to learn in Continuous Integration, Jenkins or TeamCity. Unfortunately, we won't be able to take up those topics in this book. We strongly recommend readers to do further reading in every area left uncovered.

In the next chapter, we will discuss different migration strategies from Ant and Maven to Gradle. This will help to migrate existing Ant or Maven scripts to Gradle.

8
Migration

If you are coming from an Ant or Maven background, the first question that comes to mind is: why Gradle? We have already discussed this topic in the initial chapters. Then, another important question comes up. We already have lots of build code written in Ant or Maven; now, if a new script needs to be written into Gradle, wouldn't it be tough to manage two build tools? In this chapter, we will explain different techniques to migrate existing Ant or Maven script to Gradle build script. In the first section of this chapter, we will discuss different strategies that can be applied to migrate from Ant to Gradle and later sections will cover strategies from Maven to Gradle migration.

Migration from Ant

Ant is one of the initial build tools that became very popular among developers because they can control each and every step of the build process. But writing each and every step means a lot of boilerplate code in the build file. Another feature which was lacking in the initial Ant releases was complexity in dependency management, which was later simplified by introducing an Ivy dependency manager. For Ant users, it is very simple and easy to switch to using Gradle as their build tool. Gradle provides direct integration with Ant using Groovy's `AntBuilder`. Ant tasks are treated as first class citizens in the Gradle world. In the next sections, we will discuss three different strategies: importing Ant file into Gradle, script use of `AntBuilder` class and rewriting to Gradle. These strategies can be followed to migrate from Ant to Gradle.

Importing Ant file

This is one of the simplest ways of integrating the Ant script with Gradle script. It is very useful as the first step of migration where you have lots of build scripts, all written in Ant, and you want to start with Gradle without making any big changes to the current build structure initially. We will start with a sample Ant file. Consider we have the `build.xml` Ant file for a Java project and we perform the following tasks:

1. Build project (compile code and generate a JAR file).

2. Generate checksum of the JAR file.

3. Create a ZIP file that contains the JAR file and checksum file.

The following is the `build.xml` file to perform all three preceding mentioned operations:

```xml
<project name="sampleProject" default="makeJar" basedir=".">

<property name="src" location="src/main/java"/>
<property name="build" location="build"/>
<property name="classes" location="build/classes"/>
<property name="libs" location="build/libs"/>
<property name="distributions" location="build/distributions"/>
<property name="version" value="1.0"/>

<target name="setup" depends="clean">
   <mkdir dir="${classes}"/>
   <mkdir dir="${distributions}"/>
</target>

<target name="compile" depends="setup" description="compile the
source">
   <javac srcdir="${src}" destdir="${build}/classes"
includeantruntime="false"/>
</target>
<target name="makeJar" depends="compile" description="generate the
distributions">
   <jar jarfile="${libs}/sampleproject-${version}.jar"
basedir="${classes}"/>
</target>
<target name="clean" description="clean up">
   <delete dir="${build}"/>
</target>
```

```
<target name="zip" description="zip the jar and checksum"
depends="makeJar,checksum">
    <zip destfile="${distributions}/sampleproject.zip" filesonly="true"
basedir="${libs}" includes="*.checksum,*.jar"  />
</target>

<target name="checksum" description="generate checksum and store
in file" depends="makeJar">
    <checksum file="${libs}/sampleproject-${version}.jar"
property="sampleMD5"/>
    <echo file="${libs}/sampleproject.checksum"
message="checksum=${sampleMD5}"/>
</target>

<target name="GradleProperties">
<echo message="Gradle comments are:: ${comments}"/>
</target>

</project>
```

To build the project, you need to run the following target (in Ant, we execute a target that can be compared to a Gradle task):

```
SampleProject$ ant makeJar
Buildfile: <path>/Chapter8/SampleProject/build.xml

clean:
   [delete] Deleting directory <path>/Chapter8/SampleProject/build

setup:
    [mkdir] Created dir: <path>/Chapter8/SampleProject/build/classes
    [mkdir] Created dir: <path>/Chapter8/SampleProject/build/
distributions

compile:
    [javac] Compiling 2 source files to
<path>/Chapter8/SampleProject/build/classes

makeJar:
      [jar] Building jar:
<path>/Chapter8/SampleProject/build/libs/sampleproject-1.0.jar

BUILD SUCCESSFUL
Total time: 0 seconds
```

The target will execute other required targets such as compile, clean, setup, and so on. This will generate the `sampleproject-1.0.jar` file in the `build/libs` directory. Now, to generate checksum for JAR and to bundle it along with the JAR file, we can run the following target:

```
$ ant zip
```

This target will run the `makeJar` target and all the other dependent targets to create the JAR file and then it will execute the checksum target to generate the `md5` checksum for the JAR file. Finally, ZIP task will bundle the checksum file and the JAR file, and creates a ZIP file inside the `build/distributions` directory.

This is a sample build file for a Java project; you can have additional targets for customized requirements. We can simply import this `Ant` build file in a Gradle build file and will be able to execute Ant targets as Gradle tasks. The content of the build file will look as follows:

```
ant.importBuild 'build.xml'
```

This one line is sufficient to import the Ant build file and go ahead with Gradle. Now try to execute the following:

```
$ gradle -b build_import.gradle zip
::clean
:setup
:compile
:makeJar
:checksum
:zip


BUILD SUCCESSFUL
```

Here we have named the build file as `build_import.gradle`. The preceding command executed all Ant tasks, one after another. You can find the ZIP file created in the `build/distributions` directory.

This is one of the first steps to migrate from Ant to Gradle. This will help initially, if you do not want to play with the existing build script and want to use Gradle. Just importing the Ant file in the Gradle build help you to get started.

Accessing properties

Gradle also enable you to access existing Ant properties and add new properties. To access existing Ant properties, you can use ant.properties, as shown here:

```
ant.importBuild 'build.xml'

def antVersion = ant.properties['version']
def src = ant.properties['src']

task showAntProperties << {
        println "Ant Version is "+ antVersion
        println "Source location is "+ src

}
```

$ gradle -b build_import.gradle sAP

:showAntProperties

Ant Version is 1.0

Source location is D:\Chapter8\SampleProject\src\main\java

BUILD SUCCESSFUL

Here, Gradle script has fetched properties value from the Ant file and we are printing the value in the Gradle task. In a similar fashion, we can set Ant properties in Gradle and access these properties in the Ant build file.

Update the build file with the following statement:

ant.properties['comments'] = "This comment added in Gradle"

This property will be read by the GradleProperties target in the Ant file, as follows:

```
<target name="GradleProperties">
   <echo message="Gradle comments are ${comments}"/>
</target>
```

Now, on executing the `GradleProperties` target, we can find the comments property printed in the console as shown in this code snippet:

```
$ gradle  -b build_import.gradle GradleProperties


Starting Build

...

Executing task ':GradleProperties' (up-to-date check took 0.015 secs) due
to:
  Task has not declared any outputs.
[ant:echo] Gradle comments are:: This comments added in Gradle
:GradleProperties (Thread[main,5,main]) completed. Took 0.047 secs.


BUILD SUCCESSFUL
```

Update Ant tasks

Gradle also enables you to enhance an existing Ant task. In the same way, we enhance any existing Gradle tasks using the `doFirst` or `doLast` closures; Ant tasks can be extended in a similar fashion. Add the following statements in the build file (file: `build_import.gradle`) to add the `doFirst` and `doLast` closures to the `GradleProperties` task:

```
GradleProperties.doFirst {
    println "Adding additional behavior before Ant task operations"
}
GradleProperties.doLast {
    println "Adding additional behavior after Ant Task operations"
}
```

Now, the `GradleProperties` target executes the `doFirst` and `doLast` closures, and the console output is displayed as follows:

```
$ gradle -b build_import.gradle GP


Starting Build

......

:GradleProperties (Thread[main,5,main]) started.

:GradleProperties

Executing task ':GradleProperties' (up-to-date check took 0.003 secs)
due to:
```

```
    Task has not declared any outputs.
Adding additional behavior before Ant task operations
[ant:echo] Gradle comments are:: This comments added in Gradle
Adding additional behavior after Ant Task operations
:GradleProperties (Thread[main,5,main]) completed. Took 0.158 secs.


BUILD SUCCESSFUL
```

Using AntBuilder API

We have seen how easy it is to just import the Ant `build.xml` into Gradle and use Ant targets as Gradle tasks. Another approach is to use the `AntBuilder` class. With `AntBuilder` you can call Ant tasks from the Gradle script. An instance of `AntBuilder` class called 'ant' is available in the Gradle build file. Using this instance, when we call a method, it actually executes an Ant task.

In the following examples, we will use the same `build.xml` file and will explain how to rewrite the tasks to Gradle using `AntBuilder`:

1. Setting the properties:

Ant way	With AntBuilder

`<project`
`name="qualitycheck"`
`default="makeJar"`
`basedir=".">`
 	
`<property name="src"`
`location="src/main/java"/>`
`<property name="build"`
`location="build"/>`
`<property name="lib"`
`location="lib"/>`
`<property name="dist"`
`location="dist"/>`
`<property name="version"`
`value="1.0"/>`
	`defaultTasks "makeJar"`
	
	`def src = "src/main/java"`
	`def build = "build"`
	`def libs = "build/libs"`
	`def classes = "build/classes"`
	`def distributions = "build/`
	`distributions"`
	`def version = 1.0`

2. Cleaning the build directories:

Ant way	With AntBuilder
`<delete dir="${build}"/>`	`ant.delete(dir:"${build}")`

3. Creating new directories:

Ant way	With AntBuilder
```<mkdir dir="${classes}"/>``` ```<mkdir dir="${distributions}"/>```	```ant.mkdir(dir:"${libs}")``` ```ant.mkdir(dir:"${classes}")```

4. Compiling the Java code:

Ant way	With AntBuilder

```<javac srcdir="${src}"```
```destdir="${build}/classes"```
```includeantruntime="false"```
```/>```
	```ant.javac(srcdir:"${src}",```
	```destdir:"${classes}",```
	```includeantruntime:"false")```

5. Create JAR file from the compiled source code:

Ant way	With AntBuilder

```<jar jarfile```
```="${libs}/sampleproject-```
```${version}.jar"```
```basedir="${classes}"```
```/>```
	```ant.jar(```
	```destfile: "${libs}/```
	```sampleproject-${version}.jar",```
	```basedir:"${classes}")```

6. Generate the checksum for JAR:

Ant way	With AntBuilder

```<checksum file="${libs}/```
```sampleproject-${version}.jar"```
```property="sampleMD5"/>```
 	
```<echo file ="${libs}/```
```sampleproject.checksum"```
```message="checksum=${sampleMD5}"```
```/>```
	```ant.checksum(```
	```file:"${libs}/sampleproject-```
	```${version}.jar",```
	```property:"sampleMD5"```
	```)```
	
	```ant.echo(file:"${libs}/```
	```sampleproject.checksum",```
	```message:"checksum=${ant.```
	```sampleMD5}"```
	```)```

7. Bundle the checksum file and JAR file into a ZIP file:

Ant way	With AntBuilder
```<zip destfile ="${distributions}/ sampleproject.zip" filesonly="true" basedir="${libs}" includes="*. checksum,*.jar" />```	```ant.zip(destfile: "${dist}/ sampleproject.zip", basedir:"dist")```

So the complete build file will look as follows:

```
defaultTasks "makeJar"

def src="src/main/java"
def build="build"
def libs="build/libs"
def classes = "build/classes"
def distributions="build/distributions"
def version=1.0

task setup(dependsOn:'clean') << {
   ant.mkdir(dir:"${libs}")
   ant.mkdir(dir:"${classes}")
}

task clean << {
   ant.delete(dir:"${build}")
}

task compileProject(dependsOn:'setup') << {
   ant.javac(srcdir:"${src}",destdir:"${classes}",
includeantruntime:"false")
}

task makeJar << {
   ant.jar(destfile: "${libs}/sampleproject-${version}.jar",
basedir:"${classes}")
}

task zip(dependsOn:'checksum') << {
   ant.zip(destfile: "${distributions}/sampleproject.zip",
basedir:"${libs}")
```

```
    }

    task checksum(dependsOn:'makeJar') << {
        ant.checksum(file:"${libs}/sampleproject-${version}.jar",
property:"sampleMD5")
        ant.echo(file:"${libs}/sampleproject.checksum",
message:"checksum=${ant.sampleMD5}")
    }

    makeJar.dependsOn compileProject
```

Now, execute the ZIP task and check the distributions directory. You will find the `sampleproject.zip` file, created as follows:

```
$ gradle -b build_ant.gradle zip
:clean
:setup
:compileProject
:makeJar
:checksum
:zip


BUILD SUCCESSFUL
```

Note here that `AntBuilder` is most useful for the custom Ant `taskdef` tasks that have not been ported over to Gradle.

Rewriting to Gradle

Until now, we have seen how easy it is to import an Ant file to a Gradle script. We also looked into a different approach, where we used `AntBuilder` instance to replicate the same behavior while migrating from Ant to Gradle. Now, in the third approach, we will rewrite the Ant script in Groovy.

We will continue with the same Ant `build.xml` file and we will convert this to a Gradle build script. In this example, we are building a Java project. As we know, to build a Java project Gradle already provides us with a Java plugin; you just need to apply the Java plugin in the build file and that is all. The Java plugin will take care of all the standard conventions and configurations.

The following are some of the conventions of the Java plugin that we have already discussed in *Chapter 4, Plugin Management*:

Convention used	Description
build	Default build directory name
build/libs	Default jar location
src/main/java; src/test/java	Java source files location
Project name	Archive filename

If the project also follows these conventions, we do not need to write any additional configurations for the project. The only configuration needed is to define the version property; otherwise the JAR will be created without the version information.

So, our new build script will look as follows:

```
apply plugin :'java'
version = 1.0
```

Now, we are done. No need to write any script to create and delete directories, compile files, create JAR tasks, and so on. You can find <projectname>-<version>.jar in the build/libs directory after executing the build command:

$ gradle build

:clean

:compileJava

:processResources UP-TO-DATE

:classes

:jar

:assemble

:compileTestJava UP-TO-DATE

:processTestResources UP-TO-DATE

:testClasses UP-TO-DATE

:test UP-TO-DATE

:check UP-TO-DATE

:build

BUILD SUCCESSFUL

It is so easy to trim around 30 lines of Ant code to two lines of Gradle code. It allowed us to escape all the boilerplate code and concentrate on the main logic. However, all projects can't be simply converted just by applying a plugin or following some convention. You might need to configure sourceSets and other configurations if the project does not follow Gradle or Maven conventions.

Coming back to the example, we have only created the JAR file; two more tasks are pending. We have to generate a file to store the checksum and we need to bundle the checksum file and JAR file in to a ZIP file. We can define two additional tasks to accomplish this, as follows:

```
apply plugin:'java'
version = 1.0

task zip(type: Zip) {
    from "${libsDir}"
    destinationDir project.distsDir
}

task checksum << {
    ant.checksum(file:"${libsDir}/${project.name}-
${version}.jar",property:"sampleMD5")
    ant.echo(file:"${libsDir}/${project.name}.checksum",message:"c
hecksum=${ant.sampleMD5}")
}

zip.dependsOn checksum
checksum.dependsOn build
```

In the preceding build script, checksum task will create the checksum for the jar file. Here we are again using Ant. The checksum task creates checksum, as this is the simplest way in Gradle. We have configured the ZIP task (of type ZIP) to create a ZIP file. Gradle already provides a convention for the build/distributions directory as project.distsDir:

```
$ gradle clean zip

:clean

:compileJava

:processResources UP-TO-DATE

:classes

....

:check UP-TO-DATE
```

```
:build
:checksum
:zip

BUILD SUCCESSFUL
```

Configuration

If you do not want to follow the convention, Gradle provides an easy way to configure projects as per requirement. We will show how to configure previously created Ant tasks in Gradle:

1. Cleaning the build directories:

Ant way	Gradle way

`<target name="clean" description="clean up">`
 	
`<delete dir =   "${build}"/>`
 	
`<delete dir = "${dist}"/>`
`</target>`
	`task cleanDir(type: Delete)`
	`{`
	`    delete "${build}"`
	`}`

2. Creating new directories:

Ant way	Gradle way

`<target name="setup" depends="clean">`
 	
`<mkdir dir = "${build}"/>`
`</target>`
	`task setup(dependsOn:'cleanDir')`
	`<< {`
	`        def classesDir =`
	`file("${classes}")`
	`        def distDir =`
	`file("${distributions}")`
	`        classesDir.mkdirs()`
	`        distDir.mkdirs()`
	`}`

3. Compiling the Java code:

Ant way	Gradle way

``
<target name="compile"
depends="setup"
description="compile the
source">
    <javac srcdir="${src}"
destdir="${build}" />
</target>
``
	``
	compileJava {
	        File classesDir =
	file("${classes}")
	        FileTree srcDir =
	fileTree(dir: "${src}")
	        source srcDir
	        destinationDir classesDir
	
	}
	``

4. JAR the compiled classes:

Ant way	Gradle way

``
<target name="dist"
depends="compile"
description="generate the
distribution">
    <mkdir dir="${dist}"/>
    <jar jarfile="${dist}/
sampleproject-${version}.
jar" basedir="${build}"/>
</target>
``
	``
	task myJar(type: Jar) {
	        manifest {
	        attributes
	'Implementation-Title': 'Sample
	Project',
	                'Implementation-
	Version': version,
	                'Main-Class':
	'com.test.SampleTask'
	        }
	    baseName = project.name +"-"
	+version
	    from "build/classes"
	    into project.libsDir
	
	}
	``

So the final build file (`build_conf.gradle`) with configuration will look as follows:

```
apply plugin:'java'

def src="src/main/java"
def build="$buildDir"
def libs="$buildDir/libs"
def classes = "$buildDir/classes"
def distributions="$buildDir/distributions"
def version=1.0

task setup(dependsOn:'cleanDir') << {
```

```
    def classesDir = file("${classes}")
    def distDir = file("${distributions}")
    classesDir.mkdirs()
    distDir.mkdirs()
}

task cleanDir(type: Delete) {
  delete "${build}"
}

compileJava {
    File classesDir = file("${classes}")
    FileTree srcDir = fileTree(dir: "${src}")
    source srcDir
    destinationDir classesDir
}
task myJar(type: Jar) {
    manifest {
        attributes 'Implementation-Title': 'Sample Project',
            'Implementation-Version': version,
            'Main-Class': 'com.test.SampleTask'
    }
    baseName = project.name +"-" +version
    from "build/classes"
    into project.libsDir
}
task zip(type: Zip) {
    from "${libsDir}"
    destinationDir project.distsDir
}
task checksum << {
    ant.checksum(file:"${libsDir}/${project.name}-${version}.jar",
    property:"sampleMD5")
    ant.echo(file:"${libsDir}/${project.name}.checksum",
    message:"checksum=${ant.sampleMD5}")
}

myJar.dependsOn setup
compileJava.dependsOn myJar
checksum.dependsOn compileJava
zip.dependsOn checksum
```

Now, try to execute the ZIP command. You can find the JAR file and checksum file created in the build/libs directory, and the ZIP file inside the build/distributions directory:

```
$ gradle -b build_conf.gradle zip
:cleanDir
:setup
:myJar
:compileJava
:checksum
:zip

BUILD SUCCESSFUL
```

Migration from Maven

As the size and complexities of Ant files started to increase for enterprise software, developers started searching for better solutions. Maven easily fitted as a solution, as it introduced the concept of conventions over configurations. If you follow certain conventions, it saves a lot of time by skipping boilerplate code. Maven also provided a dependency management solution that was one of the major drawbacks of the Ant tool. Ant didn't provide any dependency management solution whereas Maven came with a built-in dependency manager.

When we discussed migration strategies from Ant to Gradle, you learned that the simplest solution is to import the Ant build.xml file and use it as it is. For Maven migration, we do not have such a feature. Maven users might find it easy to migrate from Maven to Gradle, as both follow these common principles:

- Convention over configurations
- Dependency management solution
- Repositories configuration

To migrate from Maven to Gradle, we will need to write a new Gradle script that mimics the functionality. If you have already worked on Maven, you might have noticed that Gradle uses most of the Maven concepts; thus, it would not be very difficult to migrate from Maven to Gradle. One of the main differences is that Gradle uses Groovy as a build script language, whereas Maven uses XML. In this section, we will discuss some of the most common tasks to convert a Maven script to a Gradle script.

Build filename and project properties

The `GroupId`, `artifactId`, and `version` are the minimum required properties that the user needs to provide in the Maven `pom` file, whereas in Gradle these are not mandatory. Default values are assumed if the user does not configure them. It is always recommended to specify these values to avoid any conflicts:

Maven way	Gradle way
• `<groupId>ch8.example</groupId>` • `<artifactId>SampleMaven</artifactId>` • `<version>1.0</version>` • `<packaging>jar</packaging>`	• `groupid`: Not required. • `artifactId`: Default is the project directory name. • `version`: If not mentioned, artifact will be created without a version. • Packaging depends on the plugin that you apply in the build script.

> If packaging is not mentioned in Maven, by default it will be JAR. The other core packaging are: `pom`, `jar`, `maven-plugin`, `ejb`, `war`, `ear`, `rar`, and `par`.

Properties

The following are the ways in which you can define properties in Maven and Gradle:

Maven way	Gradle way

<pre><properties>
    <src>src/main/java
    </src>
    <build>build</build>
    <classes>
       build/classes
    </classes>
    <libs>
        build/libs
    </libs>
<distributions>
    build/distributions
    </distributions>
    <version>
        1.0
    </version>
</properties></pre>
	<pre>def src="src/main/java"
	def build="build"
	def lib="lib"
	def dist="dist"
	def version=1.0</pre>

Dependency management

Both Maven and Gradle provide a dependency management feature. They manage dependency on their own. You do not need to worry about any second- or third-level dependencies for your project. Similar to the Maven scope (such as compile and runtime), Gradle also provides different configurations such as compile, runtime, testCompile, and so on. The following table lists the scope supported by both Maven and Gradle:

Maven scopes	Gradle scopes
<ul><li>compile</li><li>provided</li><li>runtime</li><li>test</li><li>system</li></ul>	<ul><li>compile</li><li>providedCompile</li><li>runtime</li><li>providedRuntime</li><li>testCompile</li><li>testRutime</li></ul>

As compared to provided scope in Maven, the Gradle war plugin adds two additional scopes, providedCompile and providedRuntime. For test cases also Gradle provides two scopes, testCompile and testRuntime. The following is an example of how you use scope while defining dependencies:

Maven way	Gradle way

`<dependency>`
`<groupId>org.apache.commons</groupId>`
`<artifactId>commons-lang3</artifactId>`
`<version>3.1</version>`
`<scope>compile</scope>`
`</dependency>`
	`dependencies {`
	`    compile group: 'org.apache.commons', name: 'commons-lang3', version:'3.1'`
	`}`

Exclude transitive

In *Chapter 5, Dependency Management*, you learned how to work with dependency management. Maven doesn't differ much in terms of dependency management features. Here is a sample to exclude transitive dependencies in both the build tools:

Maven way	Gradle way

``
<dependencies>
    <dependency>
        <groupId>
            commons-httpclient
        </groupId>
        <artifactId>
            commons-httpclient
        </artifactId>
        <version>3.1</version>
        <exclusions>
            <exclusion>
                <groupId>
                    commons-codec
                </groupId>
                <artifactId>
                    commons-codec
                </artifactId>
            </exclusion>
        </exclusions>
    </dependency>
    ...
</dependencies>
``
	``
	dependencies{
	
	compile('commons-
	httpclient:commons-
	httpclient:3.1') {
	  exclude group:'commons-codec',
	module:'commons-codec'
	}
	
	}
	``

Plugin declaration

A `maven` plugin is a collection of one or more goals that can be applied to a project using the plugins element. A goal in a plugin is executed by the `mvn [plugin-name]:[goal-name]` command. In Maven, generally we have two types of plugins: build plugins and reporting plugins. Build plugin will executed during build process, and should be configured in the `<build/>` element of `pom.xml`. Reporting plugins will be executed during site generation, and are configured using the `<reporting/>` element. Examples of reporting plugins are Checkstyle, PMD, and so on. In Gradle, you just need to apply a plugin statement in the Gradle script or you need to define it in the `buildscript` closure.

The following is a sample code, which describes how to include plugins in Maven and how we define the same in Gradle:

Maven way	Gradle way

``
<build>
<plugins>
<plugin>
<artifactId>maven-compiler-
plugin</artifactId>
<version>2.3.2</version>
<configuration>
<source>1.7</source>
<target>1.7</target>
</configuration>
</plugin>
</plugins>
</build>
``
	• `apply plugin:'<pluginid>'`
	• For custom plugin:
	``
	buildscript {
	ext {
	springBootVersion =
	'1.2.2.RELEASE'
	}
	repositories {
	jcenter()
	maven { url "http://repo.
	spring.io/snapshot" }
	maven { url "http://repo.
	spring.io/milestone" }
	}
	dependencies {
	classpath("org.springframework.
	boot:spring-boot-gradle-
	plugin:1.2.2.RELEASE")
	}
	}
	``

Repository configuration

Repositories are used to download assets and artifacts, and also to publish the artifacts. In Maven, you can define repositories in pom.xml or in settings.xml. In Gradle, you can add repositories in the init script (init.gradle) or in the build.gradle file:

Maven way	Gradle way

``
<repositories>
    <repository>
        <id>rep1</id>
        <name>org repo1</name>
        <url>
          http://company.
repository1
        </url>
    </repository>
</repositories>
``
	``
	repositories {
	maven {
	url "http://company.
	repository1"
	}
	}
	``

Multi-module declaration

Maven and Gradle both provide ways to create multi-module projects, as follows:

Maven way	Gradle way

``
<project>
  <groupId>
    com.test.multiproject
  </groupId>
  <artifactId>
    rootproject
  </artifactId>
  <version>
    1.0
  </version>
  <packaging>
    Pom
  </packaging>
  <modules>
    <module>subproject1</
module>
    <module>subproject2</
module>
  </modules>
</project>
``
	Add `settings.gradle` under root project and include subprojects as follows:
	
	``
	include 'subproject1',
	'subproject2',
	``

Default values

Gradle and Maven both provide default values for certain properties. You can use them as they are, if you want to follow convention and update them if required:

	Maven way	**Gradle way**
Project directory	`${project.basedir}`	`${project.rootDir}`
Build directory	`${project.basedir}/target`	`${project.rootDir}/build`
Classes directory	`${project.build.directory}/classes`	`${project.rootDir}/build/classes`
JAR name	`${project.artifactId}-${project.version}`	`${project.name}`
Test output directory	`${project.build.directory}/test-classes`	`${project.testResultsDir}`
Source directory	`${project.basedir}/src/main/java`	`${project.rootDir}/src/main/java`
Test source directory	`${project.basedir}/src/test/java`	`${project.rootDir}/src/test/java`

Gradle init Plugin

`Build init` plugin can be used to generate the `build.gradle` file from a `pom` file. Command `gradle init --type pom` or `gradle init` creates Gradle build files and other artifacts if executed from a project or directory that has a valid `pom.xml` file.

We created one project, `SampleMaven`, that contains Java files in the `src\main\java\ch8` directory and the `pom.xml` file under the root project directory. The following is the content of the `pom.xml` file:

```
<project xmlns="http://maven.apache.org/POM/4.0.0"
    xmlns:xsi="http://www.w3.org/2001/XMLSchema-instance"
    xsi:schemaLocation="http://maven.apache.org/POM/4.0.0
    http://maven.apache.org/xsd/maven-4.0.0.xsd">
    <modelVersion>4.0.0</modelVersion>

    <groupId>ch8.example</groupId>
    <artifactId>SampleMaven</artifactId>
    <version>1.0</version>
    <packaging>jar</packaging>
```

```
      <dependencies>
        <dependency>
          <groupId>org.apache.commons</groupId>
          <artifactId>commons-lang3</artifactId>
          <version>3.1</version>
          <scope>compile</scope>
        </dependency>
      </dependencies>
    </project>
```

Now, execute the following command:

```
$ gradle init --type pom
:wrapper
:init
Maven to Gradle conversion is an incubating feature.
```

BUILD SUCCESSFUL

Note that Maven to Gradle is an incubating feature. Current DSL and other configurations might change in future. On executing the preceding command, you will find build.gradle, settings.gradle, and Gradle wapper files created in the project directory. The auto-generated build.gradle file has the following content. It automatically adds plugin details, and group and version information.

The content of a system-generated build file is shown in the following code snippet:

```
apply plugin: 'java'
apply plugin: 'maven'

group = 'ch8.example'
version = '1.0'
description = """"""

sourceCompatibility = 1.5
targetCompatibility = 1.5

repositories {
     maven { url "http://repo.maven.apache.org/maven2" }
}

dependencies {
    compile group: 'org.apache.commons', name: 'commons-lang3',
version:'3.1'
}
```

This plugin also supports multiproject build, repository configuration, dependency management, and a lot of other features.

Summary

In this chapter, we discussed migration to Gradle from Ant and Maven. This is a very common scenario in any organization where the existing build script is written in Ant or Maven and it is trying to upgrade to Gradle. This chapter gives some analysis and different approaches, which might help to plan the Gradle migration in a better and more organized way.

In the next chapter, we will discuss the deployment aspect of build automation with Docker.

9
Deployment

A Gradle book will be incomplete, unless we talk about the deployment aspect of a software component. In my opinion, in software engineering the most logical step after build automation is deployment. Deployment itself is a different domain and this has very little to do with Gradle. But still I think it makes sense to discuss build and deployment tools together, so that the reader gets an overview of **Build**, **Deploy**, and **Test** workflow. In this chapter, we will discuss some basics of deployment to give a flavor of the build and deployment process. We will learn how to use tools such as Gradle, Jenkins, and Docker together to create a build, deployment, and test workflow. Before we start, we have to understand, what deployment is. Deployment is as important as the build process in the software life cycle. You can write and build great software, but unless the application is deployed, it does not produce much value. Deployment of software is not just about installing software and starting it. It varies from application to application, operating system to operating system. Some application can be deployed just by copying a JAR file to a particular location; some applications require deployment in a web container, or in external containers and so on. We can generalize the deployment process of software as follows:

1. Prepare the prerequisite hardware and software environment where you want to deploy the application.
2. Copy project assets on the prepared environment.
3. Configure assets based on the environment.
4. Prepare a life cycle of the application such as start, stop, restart, and so on.
5. Do a sanity check of the application to verify its functionality.

So deployment is not just copying the assets and notifying everyone that the application is ready to use. It also involves a lot of other pre and post steps. Deployment process has also been evolved along with the development processes and is still evolving with newer technologies. There was a time when the operation team used to deploy the application manually on specified nodes, configure load balancing mechanism and routing from box to box to effectively handle client requests. Now, with the help of new cloud infrastructures, such as **Infrastructure as a Service (IaaS)** or with various automation tools, with just one click or with some commands, developer can deploy application on one box, cluster environment, cloud-based environment or containerized environment. In this chapter, we will focus on the deployment process with Docker, an application containerization technology. We will have a detailed look into different aspects of Docker such as installation, configuration; benefits of Docker over virtual server node deployment; deploy application inside Docker; and how to make it available to the outside world.

Role of Gradle in deployment

Gradle plays one of the major roles in the build and deployment process. Developer can use a combination of different tools based on the requirement to automate the complete build and deployment process. Tools such as Jenkins, Puppet, Chef, and Docker help to create the build and deployment infrastructure. But for very simple deployments, some of the Gradle features can be useful. Gradle provides a variety of tasks that can automate some of deployment tasks as mentioned previously. Few useful tasks are as follows:

1. Download task to downloading the artifacts (ZIP, WAR, EAR, and so on) and its dependencies.

    You can download artifacts by just adding the list in the dependencies closure. In a similar fashion, you can download all the other dependencies needed to run the software. It is not needed to bundle the software with all the dependencies and make it heavy. It is good to download dependencies at the time of the installing the software to make it lightweight.

2. Unzip or untar tasks to unzip the artifacts.

    Once artifacts and their dependencies are downloaded, next step is to unzip or untar the artifact if required.

3. Configure the application.

    Configuration or localization of the application can be done in Gradle by adding custom tasks.

4. Start/stop the application.

   Start/Stop of the application can be performed using existing Gradle tasks, such as JavaExec or any other custom task.

In my opinion, though these tasks can be automated in Gradle, a better alternative would be a scripting language such as Shell script or Perl. Later in this chapter when we create an example of build and deployment pipeline, the role of Gradle will be a pure build and test tool. We will not explore any task or plugin specific to deployment. Now we will move on to the next topic, Docker, that has become very popular in recent years with the emergence of micro-service architecture.

Docker overview

Docker is an open source container-based virtualization technology that helps to automate the deployment of an application inside a container. Docker uses resource isolation features of the Linux kernel such as cgroups and kernel namespaces and it allows the running of multiple containers independently and isolated from each other on a host machine. The benefit of Docker over virtual machine is that Docker is a light-weight process compared to a virtual machine and it provides resource isolation when sharing the same kernel including drivers of the host machine. Docker is open source technology and supported on different platforms. As Docker is built on top of Linux kernel, it supports Windows and Mac using **Boot2Docker** application.

Some of the main features of Docker are:

- Docker Engine: The light-weight container to create, manage and containerize the application.

- Portability: One of the important features is container-reuse. You can prepare one Tomcat image and use this image as a base image for all other web applications. This image can be deployed in any system like desktop, physical servers, virtual machines, and even in cloud.

- Docker Hub: Docker also has its own SaaS-based public registry shared with developers across the globe. You can fid different kinds of images like MySQL, Tomcat, Java, Redis, and other technologies. Users can create and upload images to this repository.

- Faster delivery: Docker containers are very fast compared to virtual machines. This feature helps in reducing the time for development, testing and deployment.

- API: Docker supports a user friendly API to manage Docker containers.

You might be using virtual machine in an organization infrastructure. Docker is very different from a virtual machine. A virtual machine has its own operating system with device drivers, memory, CPU shares, and son on. On the other hand, a container shares the host operating system and most of these resources with other container on the same host.

Let's look at some differences between Docker and virtual machines:

- Docker uses Linux containers, which share the same operating system, whereas each virtual machine has its own operating system thus increasing the overhead

- Docker uses **Another Union File System (AUFS)** that is a layered file system. It has a read-only part that is shared by all containers and write part that is unique for each container to write its own data

- Docker is a light weight technology that requires minimum resources of its own as it shares the maximum resources, whereas a full VM system shares minimum resources and gets most of resources of its own

- Docker startup time is very less as compared to VM

- Docker is mostly suitable for small applications (Micro Services) that can share the common resources and just isolate itself with some processes, whereas VM is suitable for heavier applications that need full isolation of resources

Now in the next two sections, we will work with Docker installation and then we will learn some of the most used Docker commands.

Installing Docker

To install Docker in Ubuntu Trusty 14.04 LTS, following commands can be used:

```
$ sudo apt-get update
$ sudo apt-get -y install docker.io
```

Alternatively, to get the latest version of Docker you can use this:

```
$ sudo wget -qO- https://get.docker.com/ | sh
```

To know the installed version, you have to run the docker version command, as follows:

```
$ docker version
Client version: 1.6.0
```

```
Client API version: 1.18
Go version (client): go1.4.2
Git commit (client): 4749651
...
```

Docker is also supported on Mac OS X, Windows, or cloud platforms. Docker installation guide for these platforms is available at `https://docs.docker.com/`.

To verify the installation, you can execute the `docker run hello-world` command. This command downloads a test image and runs the command in a container:

```
$ docker run hello-world
Unable to find image 'hello-world' locally
Pulling repository hello-world
91c95931e552: Download complete
a8219747be10: Download complete
Hello from Docker.
```

If the preceding message is displayed on the console, it means the installation is successful. In the next section, we will learn some of the useful Docker commands.

Docker commands

Once Docker is installed on the host machine, it runs as a daemon process. The interface given to users is a Docker client. Communication between Docker daemon and users happens through Docker client. Docker provides a variety of commands for different needs, which helps to automate the deployment process very easily. Now we will learn different Docker commands. As this is not a Docker book, the discussion will be limited to some basic commands. You can refer to the following Docker website for the complete reference guide at `https://docs.docker.com/reference/`.

Help command

Once Docker is installed, to see the list of all the commands supported you can type `docker help`.

This command lists all the available Docker commands. The basic syntax of a Docker command is `docker <options> command <argument>`.

Download image

As we mentioned earlier, Docker provides its own public repository from where you can download the images to get started with Docker. You do not need to reinvent the wheel by creating the image, unless needed. In the repository, you can find lots of images varying from plain vanilla OS to images embedded with Java, Tomcat, MySQL, and so on. To download an image from the repository, you can use the `docker pull <image name>` command, as follows:

```
$ docker pull ubuntu

latest: Pulling from ubuntu

e9e06b06e14c: Pull complete
a82efea989f9: Pull complete
37bea4ee0c81: Pull complete
...
```

By default, this command pulls images from the public Docker registry, but you can configure private registry as well.

The list of images

Once the image is downloaded, you can find the list of images using the `docker images` command, as follows:

```
$ docker images
```

REPOSITORY	TAG	IMAGE ID	CREATED	VIRTUAL SIZE
<none>	<none>	07f8e8c5e660	14 hours ago	188.3 MB
python	2.7	912046e33f03	8 days ago	747.9 MB
ubuntu	latest	d0955f21bf24	6 weeks ago	188.3 MB

It will list all the downloaded images available in the filesystem. You can create one or many containers using images.

Creating a container

Once image is downloaded, you can create a container using the Docker `run` command, as follows:

```
$ docker run -dit --name "testUbuntu1" ubuntu /bin/bash
b25a9d5806a71f411631c4bb5c4c2dd4d059d874a24fee2210110ac9e8c2909a
```

This command creates a container named `testUbuntu1` from the image Ubuntu and the command we have mentioned is `/bin/bash`, to just execute a shell or command-line interface. The output of this command is the container ID. You can access the container by its name `tesUbuntu1` or by the container ID.

Here the `-d` option will start it as a daemon process, the `-i` option is for interactive, and the `-t` option is to allocate a pseudo-`TTY`. Let's create another container as follows:

```
$ docker run -dit --name "testUbuntu2" ubuntu /bin/bash
f9cdd046cbf47f957ef972690592245f27784f5f79ded6ca836afab54b4f9a8f
```

It will create another container with the name `testUbuntu2`. You can create many containers with the same image by giving different names. If you do not specify any name, Docker assigns some default name. The syntax of the run command is `$ docker run <options> <imagename> <command>`.

The container list

To find the list of running containers use the Docker `ps` command, as shown here:

```
$ docker ps
CONTAINER ID        IMAGE              COMMAND           CREATED
STATUS              PORTS              NAMES
b25a9d5806a7        ubuntu:latest      /bin/bash         2 minutes ago
   Up 2 minutes                           testUbuntu1
```

Here, we have created two containers but the output shows only one container `testUbuntu1` that is running. Run the same command now with the `-a` option, as follows:

```
$ docker ps -a
CONTAINER ID        IMAGE                COMMAND           CREATED
STATUS                      PORTS              NAMES
f8148e333eb3        ubuntu:latest        echo hello world  7 seconds ago
   Exited (1) 7 seconds ago                   testUbuntu2
```

```
b25a9d5806a7        ubuntu:latest     /bin/bash           3 minutes ago
  Up 3 minutes                                   testUbuntu1
```

The output lists all the containers with individual status. Notice that the testUbuntu2 container is exited, that is, stopped, whereas testUbuntu1 is still running.

Start/stop container

Once the container is created from the image, it can be started/stopped using the following commands:

```
$ docker start|stop containername|containerid
```

Following is an example of the preceding command:

```
$ docker stop testUbuntu1
$ docker start f8148e333eb3
```

Connecting to a container

If you have started a container and then you want to connect to the running container console, the Docker attach command can be used as shown here:

```
$ docker attach testUbuntu1
[Enter]
root@b25a9d5806a7:/#
```

Use *Ctrl* + *P* + *Q* to exit the container. The exit or ^C command will take you out of the container and additionally, it will stop the running container by killing all the running processes. If you want to just move out of the container without stopping, use *Ctrl* + *P* + *Q*. These commands could be different based on operating systems. Refer to the Docker documentation for more details.

Deleting a container

The Docker rm command deletes or removes a container from the machine, as follows:

```
$ docker rm testUbuntu2
testUbuntu2
```

You can check whether it is deleted properly by running the docker ps -a command:

Removing an image

To remove an image from the system, use the `docker rmi` command. This command will remove the image from the machine. You need to stop any running container before removing the image. This is done as follows:

```
$ docker rmi ubuntu
```

Copying files to the container

With the UNIX `cp` command, a file can be copied from the host to the container. For example, the following command copies the `dir1` folder from the host system to the container's `/home/mycontents` directory. Here we have to provide the absolute path of the container installed in the host machine:

```
$sudo cp -r dir1
/var/lib/docker/aufs/mnt/b25a9d5806a71f411631c4bb5c4c2dd4d059d874a24f
ee2210110ac9e8c2909a/home/mycontents/
```

But this is not a good practice. Alternative solution is to mount the directories when creating the container with the `-v` option:

```
$ docker run -ditP --name testUbuntu -v /home/user1/dir1:/home/dir1
ubuntu
```

The preceding command will create a container named `testUbuntu`. The command also maps the `/home/user1/dir1` directory of host machine to the `/home/dir1` directory of the container.

To copy the contents from the container to host machine, the `docker cp` command can be used, as shown here:

```
$ docker cp testUbuntu1:/home/dir1/readme.txt .
```

Container details

The Docker `inspect` command helps to find the complete details of container run as follows:

```
    $ docker inspect testUbuntu1
    [{
      "Args": [],
      "Config": {
        "AttachStderr": false,
        "AttachStdin": false,
```

```
    "AttachStdout": false,
    "Cmd": [
    "/bin/bash"
    ],
    "CpuShares": 0,
    "Cpuset": "",
    "Domainname": "",
    "Entrypoint": null,
    "Env": [
    "PATH=/usr/local/sbin:/usr/local/bin:
      /usr/sbin:/usr/bin:/sbin:/bin"
    ],
...
...
    "PublishAllPorts": false,
    "VolumesFrom": null
  },
  "HostnamePath": "/var/lib/docker/containers/
b25a9d5806a71f411631c4bb5c4c2dd4d059d8
74a24fee2210110ac9e8c2909a/hostname",
  "HostsPath": "/var/lib/docker/containers/
b25a9d5806a71f411631c4bb5c4c2dd4d059d8
74a24fee2210110ac9e8c2909a/hosts",
"Id":
"b25a9d5806a71f411631c4bb5c4c2dd4d059d874a24fee2210110ac9e8c2909a"
,
"Image":
"d0955f21bf24f5bfffd32d2d0bb669d0564701c271bc3dfc64cfc5adfdec2d07",
  "MountLabel": "",
  "Name": "/testUbuntu1",
  "NetworkSettings": {
      "Bridge": "docker0",
      "Gateway": "172.17.42.1",
      "IPAddress": "172.17.0.22",
      "IPPrefixLen": 16,
      "PortMapping": null,
      "Ports": {}
  },
  "Path": "/bin/bash",
...
...
}
```

It will provide the complete detail of the container such as name, path, network settings, IP address, and so on.

Updating DNS settings

To update DNS settings, you can edit the `/etc/default/docker` file. You can change proxy setting and DNS setting in this file. The content of the file is shown as follows:

```
# Docker Upstart and SysVinit configuration file

# Customize location of Docker binary (especially for development
  testing).
#DOCKER="/usr/local/bin/docker"

# Use DOCKER_OPTS to modify the daemon startup options.
#DOCKER_OPTS="--dns 8.8.8.8 --dns 8.8.4.4"

# If you need Docker to use an HTTP proxy, it can also be
  specified here.
#export http_proxy="http://127.0.0.1:3128/"

# This is also a handy place to tweak where Docker's temporary
files go.
#export TMPDIR="/mnt/bigdrive/docker-tmp"
```

Networking in an important concept and you should spend more time reading about it. More details can be found at `https://docs.docker.com/articles/networking/`.

Creating an image from a container

You might be interested in creating new images from the base container with additional software. Consider an example where you have created the `testUbuntu1` container from the base Ubuntu image. Then you have installed Tomcat server, deployed web application, and maybe you have installed some other required software like Ant, Git, and so on. You might want to save all the changes for future. The following `docker commit` command is useful in this scenario:

```
$ docker commit  -m "Creating new image" testUbuntu1 user1/ubuntu_1
```

This command will create a new image `user1/ubuntu_1` that will comprise a basic Ubuntu image and all the applications installed by you on that container. This command will commit the new image to the local repository. Next time, you can start a container from the new image.

```
$ docker run -dit --name testUbuntu_1  user1/ubuntu_1
```

This command will create the `testUbuntu_1` container using the new image committed earlier. If you have created an account in the Docker repository (`https://registry.hub.docker.com`), you can even push the new images to the public repository.

Running an application in Docker

So far, we have learnt what is Docker and the different commands to work with Docker. In this section, we will develop a web application and we will deploy the web application in a Docker container. For simplicity, we will download a Tomcat image from the Docker repository. Then the Docker container will be started with proper port mapping, so that it can be accessed from the host machine. Finally, a web application will be deployed in the running container.

To create a Tomcat container, we will pull an image from the central repository `https://registry.hub.docker.com/_/tomcat/`. The repository provides support for different versions of Tomcat such as 6, 7, and 8. For this application, we will use Tomcat 7.0.57 version. This version can be downloaded from the registry by running the `docker pull tomcat:7.0.57-jre7` command.

After the image is downloaded, we have to create the container using the downloaded image and then start it. The container is created and started with the `docker run` command with one of the options `-p <host_port>:<container_port>`. This option enables to access the running Tomcat container by routing the host port to the container port. The following command starts the container with the name as `userdetailsservice`. Additionally, the `-rm` option is used to remove the filesystem when the container exits. This is required for the cleanup process:

```
$ docker run -it --rm -p 8181:8080 --name "userdetailsservice"
tomcat:7.0.57-jre7
Using CATALINA_BASE:   /usr/local/tomcat
Using CATALINA_HOME:   /usr/local/tomcat
Using CATALINA_TMPDIR: /usr/local/tomcat/temp
Using JRE_HOME:        /usr
Using CLASSPATH:       /usr/local/tomcat/bin/bootstrap.jar:/usr/local/
tomcat/bin/tomcat-
juli.jar
May 03, 2015 5:03:07 PM org.apache.catalina.startup.VersionLoggerListener
log
INFO: Server version:        Apache Tomcat/7.0.57
...
```

After running the command, the Tomcat server is accessible from the host machine at `http://localhost:8181`:

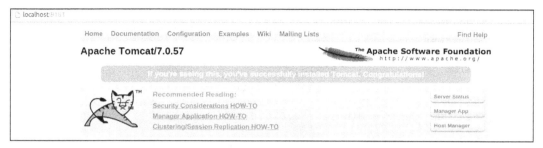

Figure 9.1

Tomcat server is up and running; and the next task is to deploy the web application in the running container. Deploying the web application can be done in multiple ways. Here we will discuss three different approaches to deploy the web application.

- Adding web application as a data volume: Already we have learnt how to mount a data volume with the container using the -v option. This approach can be applied even to deploy a web application. If we have the file structure of the web application on the host machine, it can be mounted to the webapps directory of Tomcat.

  The following command shows an example of deploying an application named `userdetailsservice` in the `/usr/local/tomcat/webapps/` directory of the Tomcat container:

  ```
  $ docker run -it --rm -p 8181:8080 -v
  ~/userdetailsservice:/usr/local/tomcat/webapps/userdetailsserv
  ice --name "userdetailsservice" tomcat:7.0.57-jre7
  ```

- Copying WAR file from host to container: Another approach is to copy the application WAR file directly from the host machine to the container. To achieve this, first we have to start the container with the run command as explained previously:

  ```
  $ docker run -it --rm -p 8181:8080 --name "userdetailsservice"
  tomcat:7.0.57-jre7
  ```

When the container is running, we have to find the long container ID. This can be done as follows using the `docker ps` command with the `--no-trunc` option:

```
$ docker ps --no-trunc
CONTAINER ID
IMAGE               COMMAND           CREATED
STATUS              PORTS             NAMES
1ad08559109a0f5eec535d05d55e76c5ad3646ae7bb6f4fffa92ad47219553
49     tomcat:7.0.57-jre7    "catalina.sh run"    About a minute
ago    Up About a minute    0.0.0.0:8181->8080/
```

Then, we can use the simple UNIX `cp` command to copy the `.war` file to the Docker file system as shown here:

```
$ sudo cp
~/UserDetailsService/build/lib/userdetailsservice.war
/var/lib/docker/aufs/mnt/1ad08559109a0f5eec535d05d55e76c5ad364
6ae7bb6f4fffa92ad4721955349/usr/local/tomcat/webapps
```

However, this approach is not recommended as copying file from host to container is not a good option. Rather we should use the data mount option.

- Tomcat Admin: Tomcat admin tool can be used to deploy web application from a web-based user interface. To deploy a web app from Tomcat admin, you need to have the proper access privilege to the Tomcat manager GUI. The Tomcat image that we downloaded for this example does not allow us to access the Tomcat admin page. So first, we have to enable access for a user by modifying the `tomcat-users.xml` file. We can simply use the `-v` option to bind an existing `tomcat-users.xml` file to the container as follows:

```
$ docker run -it --rm -p 8181:8080 -v ~/Downloads/tomcat-
users.xml:/usr/local/tomcat/conf/tomcat-users.xml --name
"userdetailsservice" tomcat:7.0.57-jre7
```

This approach works well. But if you want to modify the `tomcat-users.xml` file of the container permanently, a different approach can be taken. First, we have to start the Tomcat container with the following command:

```
$ docker run -it --rm -p 8181:8080 --name "userdetailsservice"
tomcat:7.0.57-jre7 command.
```

Then from another terminal, enter the bash of the container using the Docker `exec` command. as shown here:

```
$ docker exec -it userdetailsservice /bin/bash
```

Next step is to modify the `/usr/local/tomcat/conf/tomcat-users.xml` file from a text editor. To do this, we might need to install vim with the `apt-get` install `vim` command. You are free to use any text editor of your choice:

```
root@0ff13ab7f076:/usr/local/tomcat# apt-get update

root@0ff13ab7f076:/usr/local/tomcat# apt-get install vim
```

After vim is installed successfully, we have to add the following lines at the end of the `tomcat-users.xml` file (before `</tomcat-users>`), to enable access to Tomcat-admin GUI for the admin user:

```
    <role rolename="manager-gui"/>
    <user username="admin" password="admin" roles="manager-gui"/>
```

Now, changes have been applied to the container and we have to save the new changes by creating a new image using the `docker commit` command as follows:

```
$ docker commit 0ff13ab7f076 usedetailsimage:v1

1d4cbdbe2b6ba97048431dbe2055f1df4d780cf5564200c5946e0944baf84b8f
```

The new image was saved as `usedetailsimage` with the `v1` tag. This can be verified by listing all the `docker images`:

```
$ docker images
REPOSITORY          TAG             IMAGE ID        CREATED
VIRTUAL SIZE

usedetailsimage     v1              1d4cbdbe2b6b    8 seconds
ago         384.4 MB

hello-world         latest          91c95931e552    3 weeks
ago         910 B

tomcat              7.0.57-jre7     b215f59f9987    3 months
ago         345.9 MB
```

This newly created image can be used to start the Tomcat server as follows:

```
$ docker run -it --rm -p 8181:8080 --name "userdetailsservice"
usedetailsimage:v1
```

After Tomcat is started successfully, we will be able to log in to the Tomcat administrator page at `http://localhost:8181/manager/` with the `admin/admin` credentials. The web application can be deployed by selecting the WAR file to deploy option. Application `userdetailsservice` takes few seconds to start up and it will be visible on the Tomcat admin page as shown in the following screenshot:

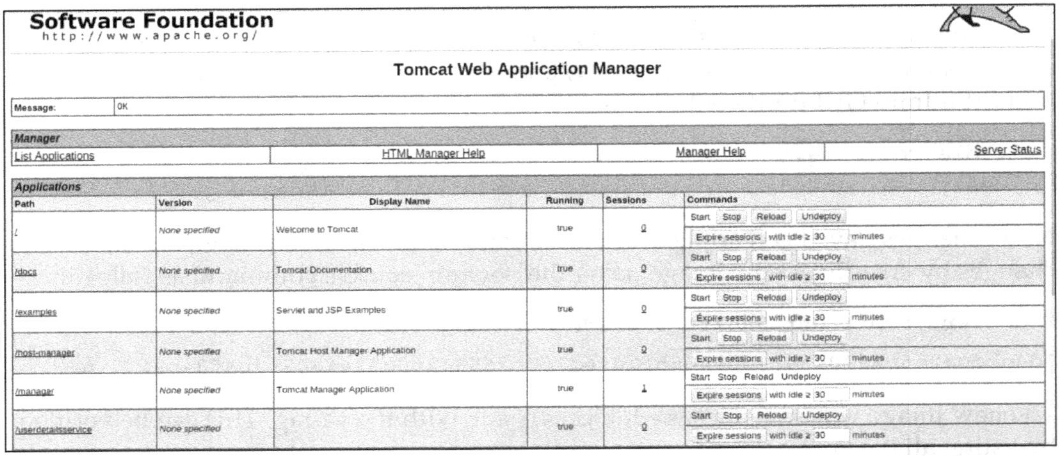

Figure 9.2

Build, Deployment, and Test pipeline

In the last section, we have learned how to create a container like Apache Tomcat with Docker and how to deploy an application in the running container. Once the application is up and running, we can run some automated tests to verify the functionality. That should be easy! What else can be done? Well, throughout this book we have learned how to automate the build process with Gradle; also in *Chapter 7, Continuous Integration,* we discussed continuous integration tools, such as Jenkins. Now we should be able to apply all these knowledge to create a simple build, deploy, and test workflow to automate the complete process from build to deployment. Do not get confused with the continuous delivery pipeline. This is just a simple example to automate the build, deployment, and test together with tools, such as Gradle, Docker, and Jenkins. We can set up the pipeline with three simple steps:

- Automate the process of creating or building the artifacts with Gradle.

- Deploy the newly created libraries in a running container. The container is created and started with Docker.

- Run automated tests to verify the functionalities of the deployed application.

These steps can be sequentially configured and executed with the help of Jenkins. All we need to do is to create a new Freestyle project, say `build_deployment_pipeline`. Then, add the Source Code Management configuration such as Git (Git URL is `https://github.com/mitramkm/mastering-gradle.git`) as shown in the following screenshot. For more details please refer *Chapter 7, Continuous Integration*. After the basic Jenkins job configuration, we have to configure three build steps to automate the build, deployment, and test execution:

Figure 9.3

After the source code management configuration, we have to add a build step in Jenkins to build the web application. In this step, we will execute the `clean war` task on a Gradle project named `UserDetailsService`. This is a simple web application to expose a RESTful service. The Gradle task will create a WAR file in the `build/libs` directory of the project. In the build step configuration, we have specified the `Root Build script` as `${workspace}/Chapter9/UserDetailsService`. So, the WAR file will be created in the `%JENKINS_HOME%/jobs/build_deployment_pipeline/workspace/Chapter9/UserDetailsService/build/libs/` directory:

Figure 9.4

We are done with the first step. Next step is to create a Tomcat container and deploy the WAR file. This can be done by running a shell script that automates the following tasks:

1. Pull Tomcat container from the repository.

2. Check whether any existing container is running. If any container is running, stop and remove that container.

3. Start the container with the required configuration such as port, name, memory, and CPU.

4. Finally, deploy the application.

The following shell script automates all the operations mentioned previously:

```
#!/bin/sh


if [ -z "$1" ]; then
  BUILD_HOME=$(pwd)/UserDetailsService
else
  BUILD_HOME=$1
fi


docker pull tomcat:7.0.57-jre7


runningContainer=`docker ps -l | grep userdetailsservice | awk
  '{print $1}'`


if [ ! -z "$runningContainer" ]
then
  docker stop $runningContainer
  docker rm $runningContainer
fi


docker run -d -v
$BUILD_HOME/build/libs/userdetailsservice.war:/usr/local/tomcat/
webapps/userdetailsservice.war -p 8181:8080 --name
"userdetailsservice" tomcat:7.0.57-jre7
```

The script is ready. We will configure and execute the script as the second build step in the deployment pipeline job. Though we are using shell script to control docker commands, even this can be done using Gradle tasks (such as Exec) or Gradle plugin for Docker. Some Docker plugins are available at `https://plugins.gradle.org/`. You can also explore these plugins, if you want to do everything in Gradle way:

Figure 9.5

After the execution of the second build step, the web application is up and running in the Tomcat container. Finally, we have to verify the functionality of the application by running an automated test suite. The sample web application is a RESTful service, which exposes the `getUsers()` and `createUser()` type functionalities as HTTP GET and POST methods. The following code snippet is an example of `TestNG` cases that can be executed as sanity checks. It makes HTTP GET and HTTP POST calls at `http://localhost:8080/userdetailsservice/userdetails`:

```
@Test
public void createUser() {
  User request = new User("User1", "User user", "user@abc.com");
  User response = resttemplate.postForObject(URL, request,
    User.class);
  Assert.assertEquals(response.getEmail(), "user@abc.com");
}

@Test(dependsOnMethods="createUser")
public void getUsers() {
  User[] response = resttemplate.getForObject(URL, User[].class);
  Assert.assertEquals(response.length, 1);
}
```

To execute the test case, we will create a third build step in the Jenkins pipeline with the task as gradle test. In this example, for simplicity we have created integration test code in the `src/test` folder. Ideally, in the `src/test` directory, we should keep only unit test code. If you are writing any integration or regression test, it should be done in a separate Java project. Another point to remember is that, test task is primarily used to execute unit test code. If you are writing some integration test code, consider creating a new Gradle task (such as `integrationTest`) that runs JUnit, TestNG or any other test suite:

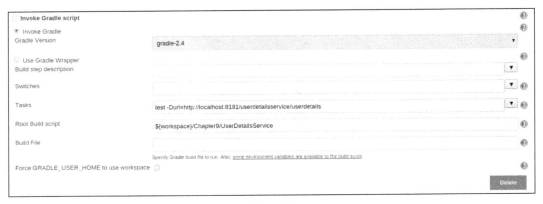

Figure 9.6

Now we are ready to run the job in Jenkins. The job executes three tasks sequentially — building a web application, deploying the application in a newly created container, and finally performing some integration tests. The console output of the complete job is displayed in the following screenshot:

Console Output

```
Started by user anonymous
Building in workspace /home/mainak/.jenkins/jobs/build_deployment_pipeline/workspace
 > git rev-parse --is-inside-work-tree # timeout=10
Fetching changes from the remote Git repository
 > git config remote.origin.url https://github.com/mitramkm/mastering-gradle.git # timeout=10
Fetching upstream changes from https://github.com/mitramkm/mastering-gradle.git
 > git --version # timeout=10
using .gitcredentials to set credentials
 > git config --local credential.helper store --file=/tmp/git3324867988525449137.credentials # timeout=10
 > git -c core.askpass=true fetch --tags --progress https://github.com/mitramkm/mastering-gradle.git +refs/heads/*:refs/remotes/origin/*
 > git config --local --remove-section credential # timeout=10
 > git rev-parse refs/remotes/origin/master^{commit} # timeout=10
 > git rev-parse refs/remotes/origin/origin/master^{commit} # timeout=10
Checking out Revision 07169e64db028c93c210911683a678814266b03d (refs/remotes/origin/master)
 > git config core.sparsecheckout # timeout=10
 > git checkout -f 07169e64db028c93c210911683a678814266b03d
 > git rev-list c29ff3dc3a522cb522dd658648be49a5831eaf66 # timeout=10
[Gradle] - Launching build.
[UserDetailsService] $ gradle clean war
:clean
:compileJava
:processResources UP-TO-DATE
:classes
:war

BUILD SUCCESSFUL

Total time: 2 mins 51.134 secs

This build could be faster, please consider using the Gradle Daemon: http://gradle.org/docs/2.4/userguide/gradle_daemon.html
Build step 'Invoke Gradle script' changed build result to SUCCESS
[workspace] $ /bin/sh -xe /tmp/hudson6916351860654902258.sh
+ pwd
+ sudo Chapter9/dockerscript.sh /home/mainak/.jenkins/jobs/build_deployment_pipeline/workspace/Chapter9/UserDetailsService
Pulling repository tomcat
b215f59f9987: Pulling image (7.0.57-jre7) from tomcat
b215f59f9987: Pulling image (7.0.57-jre7) from tomcat, endpoint: https://registry-1.docker.io/v1/
b215f59f9987: Pulling dependent layers
511136ea3c5a: Download complete
8771fbfe935c: Download complete
0e30e84e9513: Download complete
c90a56bfe7dd: Download complete
4b976fb59d87: Download complete
e43216666b96: Download complete
1d1873aa2b8d: Download complete
834592b9ae6e: Download complete
518febcc1732: Download complete
0ada0f19a068: Download complete
dd68d8361188: Download complete
63eb73f7c69c: Download complete
73fe97cd4fa4: Download complete
5162fa7b1444: Download complete
c0ab07417d5d: Download complete
2a1fe0d9edc6: Download complete
f79bbdd6e5ad: Download complete
6ebe0b2feb63: Download complete
b215f59f9987: Download complete
b215f59f9987: Download complete
Status: Image is up to date for tomcat:7.0.57-jre7
1c26e8da3cb9
1c26e8da3cb9
2dd1d51069bdc2d0a65fe5a601c3996090399fa6e37ca31aa06575ea1654018a
[Gradle] - Launching build.
[UserDetailsService] $ /home/mainak/GradleProject/gradle-2.4/bin/gradle test -Durl=http://localhost:8181/userdetailsservice/userdetails
:compileJava UP-TO-DATE
:processResources UP-TO-DATE
:classes UP-TO-DATE
:compileTestJava
:processTestResources UP-TO-DATE
:testClasses
:test

BUILD SUCCESSFUL

Total time: 44.539 secs
```

Figure 9.7

Summary

In this chapter, we discussed about application deployment and how to containerize an application with the help of Docker. We learned how to automate build, deploy, and test workflow with Gradle, Docker, and Jenkins.

In the next chapter, we will cover Android application development and its build process using Gradle.

10
Building Android Applications with Gradle

With an increasing number of smartphone users in recent years, mobile application development has become one of the major areas to focus on other than big data and Cloud computing. Most of the companies are coming up with mobile apps for their products such as games, social networking, e-commerce, and so on. And this trend is surely going to increase in next few years. So, in the last chapter, we will cover the topic related to mobile technology.

In this chapter, we will discuss how to create a basic Android application with Android Studio as IDE and how to build the application with Gradle. We already know that the Gradle philosophy is based on conventions rather than configurations, and it is much easier to write a build automation infrastructure with Gradle in comparison to other build tools available in the market. This is one of the reasons why Gradle is the official build tool for Android. You just write few lines of code in the build file and the application is ready for different platforms and versions, such as free or paid. It also provides support to sign application before release. With Gradle, you can run the application on an emulator or physical devices to run unit and function tests.

In this chapter, we will primarily focus on two areas: a quick overview of Android application development with Android Studio and various aspects of Gradle as a build tool for Android. As this is a Gradle book, our discussion will be focused on understanding the Gradle features.

Creating Android project using Android Studio

We will start by creating a sample Android application, which will display Hello World when you open it on a mobile device. You can use Eclipse with the **Android Development Tool (ADT)** plugin or Android Studio, which has been released by Google. Android Studio is based on IntelliJ IDEA and it is now the most preferred IDE for building Android applications. Both Eclipse with ADT and Android studio setup instructions can be found at http://developer.android.com/sdk/index.html.

In this chapter, we will use Android Studio for application development. Once you have downloaded and installed Android Studio on your system, start Android Studio. Android Studio also installs Android SDK, which is required to compile and execute Android applications. To create an application, navigate to **File | New Project**. You will see the following screen:

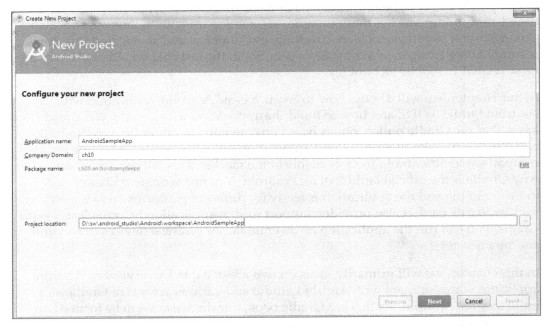

Figure 10.1

Click on the **Next** button and follow the steps. On the activity screen, select
Blank Activity:

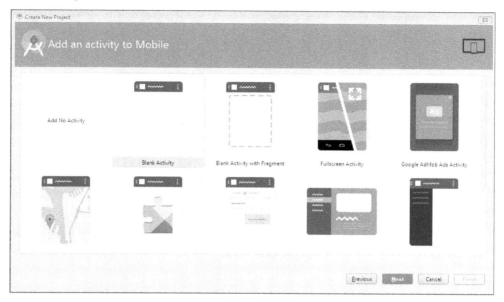

Figure 10.2

For this chapter, our main purpose is to create a sample application and emphasize
on the build process of the Android application with Gradle. So it is not required to
create a full-fledged Android application. Therefore, the sample application will do
just one job, which is to display Hello World when you launch the application.

To complete the project setup, in the **Customize the Activity** screen, provide the details such as **Activity Name**, **Title**, and so on:

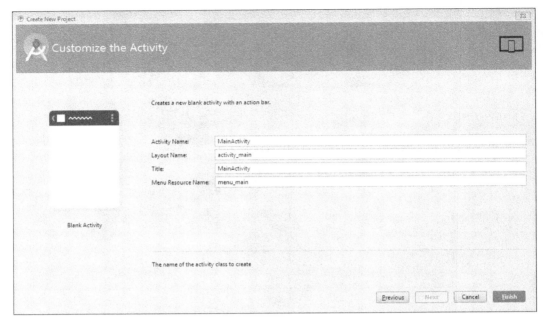

Figure 10.3

Once you click on **Finish**, Android studio will create the project and the directory structure will be as follows:

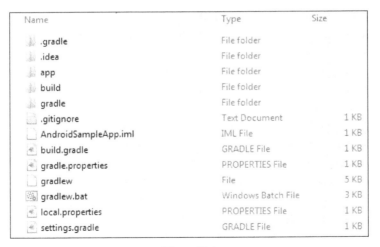

Figure 10.4

In the project home directory, you will find the `build.gradle` and `settings.gradle` files. This means that Android Studio has created a multi-project build structure. In *Chapter 6, Working with Gradle*, we have already covered the multi-project structure, in which a parent project contains one or more subprojects. The parent project contains all the common configurations and other related details that are shared among the subprojects.

Android Studio creates one `build.gradle` for the parent project and individual `build.gradle` files for the subprojects. It also creates `settings.gradle` file that includes all the subprojects that are part of this parent project. You will also find the `local.properties` file. This file has information about the location of the Android SDK. The content of this file will be as follows:

```
sdk.dir=<Location of Android sdk>
```

Android Studio also adds Gradle Wrapper, which means the Android project can be built on a machine where Gradle is not installed. Gradle Wrapper automatically installs Gradle and executes the build.

The actual Android application is in the `app` directory that has the source code, resource, and so on. The content of app directory is as shown here:

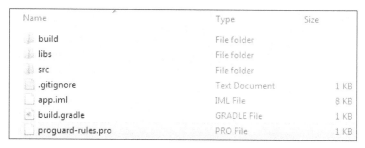

Name	Type	Size
build	File folder	
libs	File folder	
src	File folder	
.gitignore	Text Document	1 KB
app.iml	IML File	8 KB
build.gradle	GRADLE File	1 KB
proguard-rules.pro	PRO File	1 KB

Figure 10.5

It contains the `src` directory for the Java source code and test code.

Source and test directories are `src/main/java` and `src/androidTest/java`, respectively, as shown in the following screenshot:

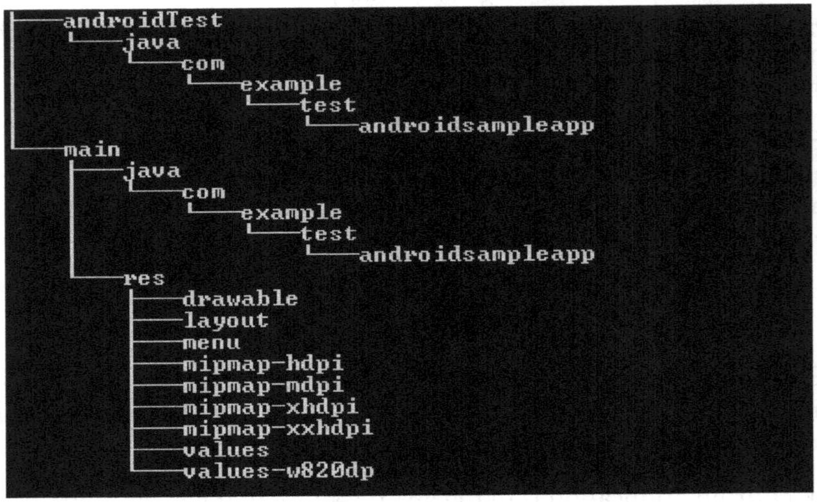

Figure 10.6

Already you are aware of Java plugin and its default conventions. If we include Java plugin in a project, the source structure is `src/main/java` and `src/main/resources`. For Android plugin apart from these two directories, you can also add extra files and folders specific to Android conventions, as mentioned here:

- `AndroidManifest.xml`
- `res/`
- `assets/`
- `jni/`
- `proguard-rules.pro`

This can be configured in the `android` closure as `sourceSets` properties, as follows:

```
android {
sourceSets {
  main {
    java {
      manifest.srcFile 'Manifest.xml'
      res.srcDirs = ['src/res']
      assets.srcDirs = ['src/assets']
    }
  }
}
}
```

We will discuss some of the important concepts here. You can find more details at `https://developer.android.com/sdk/index.html`.

The `AndroidManifest.xml` file is one of the important files that must be present in the application directory. It contains some important information related to the application, such as activities, content providers, permissions, and so on. Manifest file contains only predefined elements. Some values are populated from the Gradle properties. You cannot add any custom element in the manifest file. Elements such as `<manifest>` and `<application>` are mandatory and they appear only once. Other elements are optional and can be applied once or multiple times.

The `res` directory is used to place resources. You can place all the application resources, such as layout files, drawable files, and string values under the `res` directory. You can find more details about resources at `http://developer.android.com/guide/topics/resources/providing-resources.html`.

The directories supported inside the `res` directory are:

- `animator`
- `anim`
- `color`
- `drawable`
- `mipmap`
- `layout`
- `menu`
- `raw`
- `values`
- `xml`

The `assets` directory may contain all the basic files. Files under this directory will be part of the `.apk` file without any modification and the original file name is preserved.

`jni` contains native code using the Java Native Interface.

`proguard-rules.pro` contains the ProGuard-related settings. We will discuss ProGuard settings later in this chapter.

Building the Android project with Gradle

We created the application with one simple activity and now we will try to build the application with Gradle. Android Studio has automatically generated two build files for the project; one `build.gradle` file in the root folder of the project and other build file in the `app` directory. We will use the `build.gradle` file of the subproject (app folder) to build the Android application. This `build.gradle` file has the following content:

```
apply plugin: 'com.android.application'

android {
  compileSdkVersion 22
  buildToolsVersion "22.0.1"

  defaultConfig {
    applicationId "ch10.androidsampleapp"
    minSdkVersion 15
    targetSdkVersion 22
    versionCode 1
    versionName "1.0"
  }
  buildTypes {
    release {
      minifyEnabled false
      proguardFiles getDefaultProguardFile('proguard-
        android.txt'), 'proguard-rules.pro'
    }
  }
}

dependencies {
  compile fileTree(dir: 'libs', include: ['*.jar'])
  compile 'com.android.support:appcompat-v7:22.1.1'
}
```

In the very first line, we applied a plugin with the `apply plugin: 'com.android.application'` statement. This is similar to applying any other standard Gradle plugin. But from where will this plugin jar be downloaded? If you check the `build.gradle` file in the parent project, you will find the following entry:

```
buildscript {
  repositories {
    jcenter()
  }
```

```
    dependencies {
        classpath 'com.android.tools.build:gradle:1.2.3'
    }
}
```

In the `buildscript` closure, we have defined dependencies as `com.android.tools.build:gradle:1.2.3`. This JAR file will be downloaded from the `jcenter` repository and it will be added to the classpath of the `build.gradle`.

Next part of the build file is the android closure definition where we define all the basic configurations related to the application such as SDK version, minimum SDK version supported, target SDK version, application ID, and versioning.

Next, we have the standard `dependencies` closure to define compile and runtime dependencies for the application. Here, we have included the `lib` directory and `appcompat-v7 jar` as dependencies.

With these simple configurations, we are ready to build the application with Gradle. We have applied Android plugin in the build file. Now, we will explore different tasks available to build the project. Type `gradle tasks` on the command prompt to get the list of tasks, as shown here:

```
> gradle tasks


Android tasks
-------------

androidDependencies - Displays the Android dependencies of the project.
signingReport - Displays the signing info for each variant.


Build tasks
-----------

assemble - Assembles all variants of all applications and secondary
packages.
assembleAndroidTest - Assembles all the Test applications.
assembleDebug - Assembles all Debug builds.
.................. .  .
compileDebugSources
compileDebugUnitTestSources
compileReleaseSources
compileReleaseUnitTestSources
```

```
mockableAndroidJar - Creates a version of android.jar that's suitable for
unit tests.
```

....

```
Install tasks
- - - - - - - - - - - - -
installDebug - Installs the Debug build.
installDebugAndroidTest - Installs the android (on device) tests for the
Debug build.
uninstallAll - Uninstall all applications.
uninstallDebug - Uninstalls the Debug build.
uninstallDebugAndroidTest - Uninstalls the android (on device) tests for
the Debug build.
uninstallRelease - Uninstalls the Release build.
```

....

 Note that to build Android project, you need Gradle 2.2.1 and above.

Following are the some of the important tasks that you might need to build an Android application:

- `assemble`: This task is same as the assemble task in the Java plugin that is used to assemble the output of the application.

- `check`: This is similar to the Java plugin check task, it runs all the checks.

- `clean`: This task removes all the artifacts created during build process.

- `build`: This task executes the assemble and check task and builds the application artifacts.

- `androidDependencies`: This task will display all the Android dependencies of the project.

- `connectedCheck`: It will execute the check task on all the connected devices in parallel

- `install<buildVariant>`: You can find various install tasks (such as `installDebug`, `installRelease`) that are used to install specific `buildVariant` on a device. We will discuss more on the `buildVariant` in a later section of the book.

buildTypes

The `buildTypes` configuration is used to define types or environments of build, such as debug, release, QA, and staging to build and package the app. By default, when you build the Android project, you can find both the debug and release versions that were created in the `build/outputs/apk` directory. By default, the debug version is signed with a key/certificate that is created automatically with a known username/password. The release build type is not signed during the build process; therefore, you can find the `app-release-unsigned.apk` file created for the release build type. Release build type needs to be signed before deploying it in any device.

You can customize both build and release build types and also extend the build types by adding your own build types, as follows:

```
buildTypes {
  release {
    minifyEnabled false
    proguardFiles getDefaultProguardFile('proguard-android.txt'),
      'proguard-rules.pro'
  }
  staging.initWith(buildTypes.release)
  staging {
    debuggable true
  }
}
```

Here we have added one more build type `staging` (for staging environment), and configured it to be a copy of the release build type and added `debuggable true`. You can modify the following properties for any build types:

Property name	Default values for debug type	Default values for release and other types
`debuggable`	`true`	`false`
`jniDebuggable`	`false`	`false`
`renderscriptDebuggable`	`false`	`false`
`renderscriptOptimLevel`	3	3
`applicationIdSuffix`	`null`	`null`
`versionNameSuffix`	`null`	`null`
`signingConfig` (discussed later)	`android.signingConfigs.debug`	`null`
`zipAlignEnabled`	`false`	`true`
`minifyEnabled` (discussed later)	`false`	`false`

Table 10.1

Also, for each build type, you can define their build type-specific SourceSet such as `src/<build type>`. As mentioned in the preceding example, you can define a new directory `src/staging` and put the staging-related source code and resources in this directory.

Also for each build type, new tasks will be added by the Android plugin in the following format: `assemble<buildtype>`, `install<buildtype>`, `compile<buildtype>`, `jar<buildtype>`. This can be observed by executing the `gradle task` command, as shown here:

```
> gradle  tasks | grep -i staging
assembleStaging - Assembles all Staging builds.
compileStagingSources
compileStagingUnitTestSources
installStaging - Installs the Staging build.
uninstallStaging - Uninstalls the Staging build.
lintStaging - Runs lint on the Staging build.
testStaging - Run unit tests for the staging build.
jarStagingClasses
```

As mentioned previously, these task are only associated with the staging build types.

ProGuard settings

For `release` build type, Gradle provides access to the Proguard tool that is used to optimize and obfuscate the code. It shrinks the source code and makes the `.apk` file smaller in size. You can enable/disable this feature by setting `minifyEnabled` in the `buildTypes/release` closure. As mentioned in *Table 10.1*, the default value is set to `false`; so set it to `true` if you want to enable it.

The default setting can be obtained using the `getDefaultProguardFile('proguard-android.txt')` method. You can find the location of the ProGuard tool at `<Android sdk dir>/tools/proguard`. If you want to provide custom rules for the project, you can add it to the `proguard-rules.pro` file provided by Android studio. You can even add your own files with different names:

```
buildTypes {
  release {
    minifyEnabled true
    proguardFiles getDefaultProguardFile('proguard-android.txt'),
      'proguard-rules.pro'
  }
}
```

Build flavors

Build flavors or product flavors are different from build type. It is another level of separation, which allows building multiple flavors of the application, such as paid version, free version, phone version, and tab version. Each version of the application can have its own separate features and different hardware requirements. The combination of `productFlavors` and `buildTypes` forms a build variant and a different APK is generated for each build variant. Product flavors are defined under the `productFlavors` closure:

```
productFlavors {
  phone{
    applicationId "ch10.androidsampleapp"
    minSdkVersion 14
    targetSdkVersion 20

    versionName "1.0-phone"
  }
  tab {
    applicationId "ch10.androidsampleapp"
    minSdkVersion 15
    targetSdkVersion 22
    versionName "1.0-tab"
  }
}
```

Now, if we build the project with the `gradle clean build` command, we will find different APK files created in the `build/outputs/apk/` directory. We have two flavors (`phone` and `tab`) with four build types (`debug signed`, `debug unaligned`, `staging`, and `release`). Therefore, total $2*4 = 8$ APK files will be created in the build process.

app-phone-debug.apk	APK File	1,008 KB
app-phone-debug-unaligned.apk	APK File	1,008 KB
app-phone-release-unsigned.apk	APK File	990 KB
app-phone-staging-unsigned.apk	APK File	990 KB
app-tab-debug.apk	APK File	1,008 KB
app-tab-debug-unaligned.apk	APK File	1,008 KB
app-tab-release-unsigned.apk	APK File	990 KB
app-tab-staging-unsigned.apk	APK File	990 KB

Figure 10.7

When we added `staging` as the build type in the previous section, we observed that Gradle had automatically created some tasks. Similarly, for each flavor configuration, Gradle will add different tasks such as `assemblePhoneDebug` and `assembleTabDebug`:

```
> gradle tasks | grep -i phone
assemblePhone - Assembles all Phone builds.
assemblePhoneDebug - Assembles the DebugPhone build.
assemblePhoneDebugAndroidTest - Assembles the android (on device) tests
for the PhoneDebug build.
assemblePhoneRelease - Assembles the ReleasePhone build.
assemblePhoneStaging - Assembles the StagingPhone build.
compilePhoneDebugAndroidTestSources
compilePhoneDebugSources
compilePhoneDebugUnitTestSources
compilePhoneReleaseSources
compilePhoneReleaseUnitTestSources
compilePhoneStagingSources
compilePhoneStagingUnitTestSources
installPhoneDebug - Installs the DebugPhone build.
installPhoneDebugAndroidTest - Installs the android (on device) tests for
the PhoneDebug build.
uninstallPhoneDebug - Uninstalls the DebugPhone build.
uninstallPhoneDebugAndroidTest - Uninstalls the android (on device) tests
for the PhoneDebug build.
uninstallPhoneRelease - Uninstalls the ReleasePhone build.
uninstallPhoneStaging - Uninstalls the StagingPhone build.
connectedAndroidTestPhoneDebug - Installs and runs the tests for
DebugPhone build on connected devices.
lintPhoneDebug - Runs lint on the PhoneDebug build.
lintPhoneRelease - Runs lint on the PhoneRelease build.
lintPhoneStaging - Runs lint on the PhoneStaging build.
testPhoneDebug - Run unit tests for the phoneDebug build.
testPhoneRelease - Run unit tests for the phoneRelease build.
testPhoneStaging - Run unit tests for the phoneStaging build.
jarPhoneDebugClasses
jarPhoneReleaseClasses
jarPhoneStagingClasses
```

Product flavors extend the configuration from the `defaultConfig` closure. You can overwrite the default configurations inside each product flavor. For each flavor, you can also have a separate source code and the required files as `src/<flavor>/java`, `src/<flavor>/resources`, and so on.

Running the application on a device/emulator

Once an application is built, you will want to install or run the application, either on an emulator or a physical mobile device. For simplicity, we will run the application on an emulator. During the development phase, with the help of an emulator you can test the application on different platforms without using devices. Some of the advantages of using an emulator are as follows:

- You can test the application on multiple emulator devices

- You can test with different hardware features such as sound, webcam, or sensors

- You control battery power, phone location, network settings, such as 2G or 3G, and so on

Emulators are very flexible, but using too many emulators can bring down your system performance. Based on your system configuration, you should carefully configure the emulators. You can add new emulator devices using AVD Manager as shown in the following screenshot:

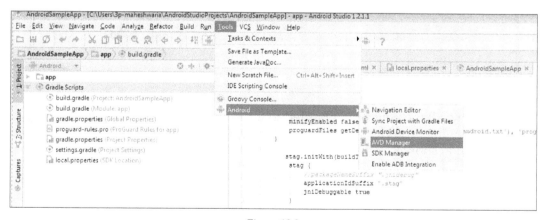

Figure 10.8

It will show the existing emulator devices. You can create a new device as per application requirement. For more information, refer to this link `http://developer.android.com/tools/help/emulator.html`.

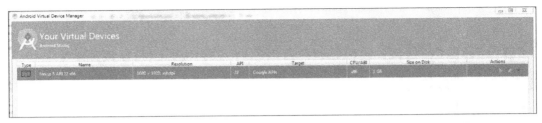

Figure 10.9

You can start the emulator by clicking on the start symbol in the **Actions** column. For our example, we created a **Nexus 5 API 22x86** emulator to test the application. Alternatively, you can also start the emulator device by executing the following command on the command prompt:

```
>%ANDROID_SDK%\tools\emulator.exe -netdelay none -netspeed full -avd
Nexus_5_API_22_x86
```

It takes a while to initialize the emulator. Once the emulator is up and running, we should be able to run the application from Android Studio. Go to the **Run** menu and choose **Run app**.

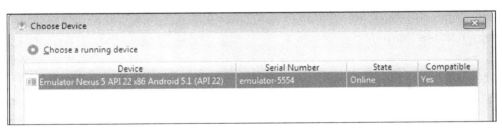

Figure 10.10

This will show all the devices (connected to the system) and the emulator that is up and running. You can select any of the running devices and click **OK**. The application should be visible in the emulator after few seconds.

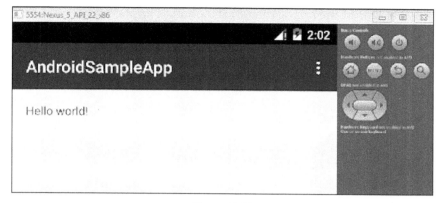

Figure 10.11

Alternatively, you can also install the application using the `gradle` `install<buildVariant>` command. We have already created different build variants and flavors in the previous section. Let's try to install the `PhoneDebug` variant on the emulator. This is done as follows:

```
> gradle installPhoneDebug
:app:preBuild UP-TO-DATE
:app:prePhoneDebugBuild UP-TO-DATE
:............
............
:app:mergePhoneDebugAssets UP-TO-DATE
:app:compilePhoneDebugJava UP-TO-DATE
:app:compilePhoneDebugNdk UP-TO-DATE
:app:compilePhoneDebugSources UP-TO-DATE
:app:preDexPhoneDebug UP-TO-DATE
:app:dexPhoneDebug UP-TO-DATE
:app:validateDebugSigning
:app:packagePhoneDebug UP-TO-DATE
:app:zipalignPhoneDebug UP-TO-DATE
:app:assemblePhoneDebug UP-TO-DATE
:app:installPhoneDebug
Installing APK 'app-phone-debug.apk' on 'Nexus_5_API_22_x86(AVD) - 5.1'
Installed on 1 device.

BUILD SUCCESSFUL

Total time: 24.543 secs
```

You will be able to find the application in the phone's application list. AndroidSampleApp is the application that we installed using Gradle task. You can launch the application and check the output. It will display Hello World.

To uninstall the application using Gradle, use the gradle uninstall command as follows:

```
> gradle uninstallPhoneDebug
```

Signing the release version

You might have observed while running gradle tasks that the release related install tasks are not created; for example, installPhoneRelease, installTabRelease, and so on. Release build type-related tasks will be available, if you sign the application using keystore. Now, we will try to sign an application using a keystore. If you already have a valid keystore, you can use that file to sign the application; otherwise you will need to generate a new keystore by using the following command:

```
> keytool -genkey -v -keystore myCustomkey.keystore -alias customKey
-keyalg RSA -keysize 2048 -validity 10000
```

To create the keystore, we need to provide some basic details. On entering all the details, the preceding command will generate the myCustomkey.keystore file. Now, we have to update build.gradle with the following configurations to enable the signing of the application:

```
android {

......
signingConfigs {
  release {
    storeFile file("myCustomkey.keystore")
    storePassword "welcome"
    keyAlias "customKey"
    keyPassword "welcome"
  }
}
      ...............
buildTypes {
  release {
    minifyEnabled false
    signingConfig signingConfigs.release
```

```
        proguardFiles getDefaultProguardFile('proguard-android.txt'),
          'proguard-rules.pro'
    }
      ...............
  }
```

Now, if we execute the `gradle tasks` command, we will find new tasks have been added for the release builds. Similarly, new APK files will be created in the `apk` folder:

```
> gradle tasks | grep -i install

Install tasks

installPhoneDebug - Installs the DebugPhone build.

installPhoneDebugAndroidTest - Installs the android (on device) tests for
the PhoneDebug build.

installPhoneRelease - Installs the ReleasePhone build.

installPhoneStaging - Installs the StagingPhone build.

installTabDebug - Installs the DebugTab build.

installTabDebugAndroidTest - Installs the android (on device) tests for
the TabDebug build.

installTabRelease - Installs the ReleaseTab build.

installTabStaging - Installs the StagingTab build.

uninstallAll - Uninstall all applications.

. . . .
```

Summary

In this chapter, we briefly discussed Android development with Gradle as a build tool. We also discussed different closures provided by the Android plugin and how to build an Android project by following the default conventions. We also explained how to customize the build file to fulfill the new project requirements. Of course, there are a lot of things to discuss, such as Android development and Android with Gradle, and we were not able to cover everything in a single chapter. It would require a separate book to detail out all the features of the Android plugin. But we think that we covered most of the basic and important steps required to build an Android project, which will help you to get started with Gradle as an Android build system.

Index

A

B

C

I

IDE
  about 21
  Gradle project, working with 22-26
  using, with Gradle 20
imperative build tools 4
in-built plugin, Gradle
  about 77
  build and test plugins 78
  code analysis plugins 78
  IDEs plugins 78
in-built tasks, Gradle
  about 68
  Copy Task 68
  Rename Task 68
  Zip task 68
incremental build 64
Infrastructure as a Service (IaaS) 214
initialization script
  defining 16
  uses 16
init plugin 210, 211
installation
  Jenkins 168, 169
Integrated Development Environment. *See*
    IDE
Ivy repository 101

J

jar task 114
Java
  Groovy, integrating with 30
Java Collection Framework (JCF) 40
Java plugin
  about 79
  configuration 84-86
  conventions 79-84
Jenkins
  about 167, 168
  configuration 169, 170
  installation 168, 169
  installation, URL 168
  job, creating 171-174
  job, executing 175-178
  URL 178

Jetty plugin
  about 126
  jettyRun task 126
  jettyRunWar task 126
  jettyStop task 126
JUnit
  integrating, with Gradle 155-157
  integrating, with TestNG 162, 163
  test configuration 157

L

List 41
logging
  about 131
  level, controlling 132, 133
  levels 131

M

Mac/Linux
  Gradle, installing on 7
Map 42, 43
Maven
  default values 210
  dependency management 206
  filename, building 205
  Gradle init plugin 210
  migrating from 204-211
  multi-module declaration 209
  plugin declaration 207
  project properties 205
  properties, defining 205
  repository configuration 208
  transitive dependencies, excluding 207
maven-publish plugins
  about 117-120
  custom POM 121
  local-hosted repository, publishing
    to 120, 121
methods 36, 37
Multi-project build
  about 142
  buildDependents option 153, 154
  build.gradle file 143
  buildNeeded option 154, 155

Tomcat administrator page
  URL 228
Tomcat container
  creating, URL 224
transitive dependencies
  about 109
  excluding 207

V

version conflicts scenarios
  fail on conflict 106
  force specific version 106
  latest version 105

W

War plugin
  about 123-126
  URL 126
webAppDirName property 125
Windows
  Gradle, installing on 6

Thank you for buying
Mastering Gradle

About Packt Publishing

Packt, pronounced 'packed', published its first book, *Mastering phpMyAdmin for Effective MySQL Management*, in April 2004, and subsequently continued to specialize in publishing highly focused books on specific technologies and solutions.

Our books and publications share the experiences of your fellow IT professionals in adapting and customizing today's systems, applications, and frameworks. Our solution-based books give you the knowledge and power to customize the software and technologies you're using to get the job done. Packt books are more specific and less general than the IT books you have seen in the past. Our unique business model allows us to bring you more focused information, giving you more of what you need to know, and less of what you don't.

Packt is a modern yet unique publishing company that focuses on producing quality, cutting-edge books for communities of developers, administrators, and newbies alike. For more information, please visit our website at www.packtpub.com.

About Packt Open Source

In 2010, Packt launched two new brands, Packt Open Source and Packt Enterprise, in order to continue its focus on specialization. This book is part of the Packt Open Source brand, home to books published on software built around open source licenses, and offering information to anybody from advanced developers to budding web designers. The Open Source brand also runs Packt's Open Source Royalty Scheme, by which Packt gives a royalty to each open source project about whose software a book is sold.

Writing for Packt

We welcome all inquiries from people who are interested in authoring. Book proposals should be sent to author@packtpub.com. If your book idea is still at an early stage and you would like to discuss it first before writing a formal book proposal, then please contact us; one of our commissioning editors will get in touch with you.

We're not just looking for published authors; if you have strong technical skills but no writing experience, our experienced editors can help you develop a writing career, or simply get some additional reward for your expertise.

Android Application Development with Maven

ISBN: 978-1-78398-610-1   Paperback: 192 pages

Learn how to use and configure Maven to support all phases of the development of an Android application

1. Learn how to effectively use Maven to create, test, and release Android applications.

2. Customize Maven using a variety of suggested plugins for the most popular Android tools.

3. Discover new ways of accelerating the implementation, testing, and maintenance using this step-by-step simple tutorial approach.

Learning Android Application Testing

ISBN: 978-1-78439-533-9   Paperback: 274 pages

Improve your Android applications through intensive testing and debugging

1. Focus on Android instrumentation testing to ensure full application coverage.

2. Apply testing techniques and utilize tools to improve Android application development.

3. Build intensively tested and bug free Android applications.

Maven Build Customization

ISBN: 978-1-78398-722-1   Paperback: 270 pages

Discover the real power of Maven 3 to manage your Java projects more effectively than ever

1. Administer complex projects customizing the Maven framework and improving the software lifecycle of your organization with "Maven friend technologies".

2. Automate your delivery process and make it fast and easy.

3. An easy-to-follow tutorial on Maven customization and integration with a real project and practical examples.

Effective Gradle Implementation [Video]

ISBN: 978-1-78216-766-2   Duration: 03:07 hours

Build, automate, and deploy your application using Gradle

1. Setting up basic and multi-module Java projects.

2. Learn more about the Gradle JavaScript plugin to build your own JavaScript projects.

3. Familiarize yourself with Scala plugin support with available tasks, layout, setup, and dependencies.

Please check **www.PacktPub.com** for information on our titles

www.ingramcontent.com/pod-product-compliance
Lightning Source LLC
Chambersburg PA
CBHW060525060326
40690CB00017B/3385